Social Work Malpractice and Liability

Social Work Malpractice and Liability

Strategies for Prevention

Frederic G. Reamer

with a foreword by Robert H. Cohen, J.D.
A.C.S.W., General Counsel, National
Association of Social Workers

Columbia University Press
New York

Columbia University Press
New York   Chichester, West Sussex

Copyright © 1994 Columbia University Press
All rights reserved

Library of Congress Cataloging-in-Publication Data

Reamer, Frederic G., 1953–
    Social work malpractice and liability : strategies for prevention
/ Frederic G. Reamer ; with a foreword by Robert H. Cohen.
       p.   cm.
    Includes bibliographical references and index.
    ISBN 0–231–08262–2
    ISBN 0–231–08263–0 (pbk.)
       1. Social workers—Malpractice—United States.   2. Social workers—
    Legal status, laws, etc.—United States.   I. Title.
    KF3721.R43   1994
    346.7303'3—dc20
    [347.306633]   94–7628
                                                                      CIP

∞

Casebound editions of Columbia University Press books are printed on
permanent and durable acid-free paper.

Printed United States of America

c 10 9 8 7 6 5 4 3 2 1
p 10 9 8 7 6 5 4 3 2 1

For Deborah, Emma, and Leah

Contents

Salus populi suprema est lex [The good of the people is the greatest law].
—Cicero

Foreword

Social work is among the most demanding professions. Every social worker in direct practice must make critical decisions affecting the well being and at times even the survival of others. Should an abused child be returned home? Must the pregnant teenager's wish to conceal her condition from her family be honored? What measures should be taken when a client poses a threat of harm to self or others? Are there circumstances that might warrant overriding the autonomy of an impaired colleague or client? How should one respond to information requests from clients, family, attorneys and others? When should a social worker disclose, intervene, refer, consult, commit, withdraw, go forward, warn? Now in his excellent new work Frederic Reamer addresses a host of such issues in straightforward, informative fashion. He explains legal concepts—malpractice, privileged communications, informed consent—clearly and accurately. Citations to case law abound, and summaries of court decisions are used throughout the text to elucidate, to dramatize, and to illustrate the variety and the parameters of judicial rulings that have implications for social work practice.

Dr. Reamer's legal research and his ability to relate the law to the dilemmas and challenges that confront social workers on the job, in their agencies, and in their private offices is impressive. He has set for himself the goal of providing social workers with "an in-depth and practical guide to help practitioners recognize, prevent, and cope with risks they encounter in their work." *Social Work Malpractice and Liability: Strategies for Prevention* more than meets that objective. It prods the reader to think and to question, to look within and observe without. For some this will stir anxiety. To learn that there may be no definitive answer to certain "simple" questions, that risks may lurk where one has always felt secure, can be profoundly disturbing.

Yet the careful reader will gratefully welcome this book. The social worker engaged in direct practice will find much concrete advice, useful guidance in making defensible decisions in those critical instances in which competent professionals may differ on the preferred course of action, and valuable strategies for reducing exposure to legal liability. That social work practice, especially private clinical practice, cannot be rendered risk free is not the fault of the author. The complexities of present day practice, the heightened expectations of clients, the increased resort to legal redress by disaffected consumers, and the creativity of lawyers present a playing field quite different from that which existed less than a generation ago. The relatively exclusive relationship between social worker and client and upon which trust has been predicated must accommodate to the emergence of managed care arrangements and the prospect of more extensive restructuring of the nation's health and mental health-care delivery systems in coming years. Access by third parties to client information, including diagnoses and other personal data, poses new ethical problems and perhaps legal questions yet to be explored.

What Dr. Reamer has given us is an overview of the new rules, the expanded boundaries, and higher stakes with which participants are now confronted. If the author did no more than raise our awareness and heighten our understanding of the legal context that defines and determines much of social work practice, his contribution would be substantial. But he has done far more. He has drawn broadly from the literature of risk management and from his own rich background as an ethicist, researcher, writer, teacher, and expert witness to inform and instruct social workers who seek guidance in minimizing the legal risks inherent in their practice.

In my experience as the National Association of Social Workers' general counsel, I have found that social workers' awareness of potential liability has risen dramatically in recent years. I frequently receive calls concerning client abandonment, reporting requirements, record requests, clients at risk, testifying in court, being deposed, responding to subpoenas, or dealing with angry clients and former clients disposed to litigation. Although their sensitivity to the legal ramifications of such situations is commendable, callers often overlook the clinical dimension. Repeatedly, I have found that the need for a clinical perspective, the exercise of professional judgment or ethical choice, is central to the matter at hand. Not infrequently, for example, an understandingly anxious social worker, alarmed by a client who appears to be suicidal, becomes preoccupied with the potential for personal liability in the event the client does commit suicide. But this is first and foremost a treatment issue. By addressing the clinical aspects of the crisis promptly, aggressively, responsibly—by practicing within accepted professional norms—the therapist will thereby lessen the risk of liability if indeed the client acts out. Whether, for example, the social worker should seek immediate (involuntary) hospitalization or alert a third party is a clinical decision, not a matter of law. If the decision is well founded and appropriate and normative steps have been taken, the action—to hospitalize, to notify third persons, or to do neither—is likely to prove legally defensible.

Among the questions most frequently raised by social workers are those concerning confidentiality and information disclosure. Here also the decision often involves a careful weighing of clinical, ethical, and legal considerations. Chapter 2, "Confidentiality and Privacy," treats this subject in depth with particular attention to the landmark *Tarasoff* case and its progeny. The discussion of the *Tarasoff* decision, its ramifications, and its relevance to current dilemmas involving duty to warn in conjunction with AIDS cases bears careful study.

The subject of supervisory liability—a growing concern for

both agency-based and nonagency-affiliated supervisors—which is addressed in chapter 5, is required reading for anyone engaged in supervision or administration or who anticipates such a role in the course of their professional career. There is a dearth of literature on the topic of legal risks and malpractice issues associated with social work supervision. The sparse case law primarily reflects lawsuits brought against nonsocial work supervisors in medical, health, and mental health settings, and guidance from these cases must be inferred. In addition, the doctrine of *respondeat superior* (which Dr. Reamer clearly and simply explains) is applicable to potential supervisory liability in the context of social work practice. Dr. Reamer's treatment of this important dimension of professional risk and his cautionary discussion of preventing supervisory liability go far toward filling this gap and providing an outline of measures that supervisors and administrators need to consider as part of their risk-management strategy.

In his concluding chapter Dr. Reamer discusses the interrelationships of good practice, good ethics, and liability. His observations regarding ethical practice, which comport with my own experience, are worth noting. "Familiarity with the general subject of professional ethics, ethical dilemmas, and ethical decision making can, by itself, enhance the likelihood that social workers will make sound judgments that may, after all, be the most powerful preventive of malpractice and liability claims." The author goes on to state, "In the final analysis, however, skillful and ethical practice is the most effective way to prevent malpractice and liability in social work." Such advice is both sound and reassuring for all who deem themselves competent and ethical practitioners. However, as Dr. Reamer has illustrated throughout his book, goodwill, professional skill, and ethical practice cannot guarantee social workers that they will not be named as defendants in malpractice suits. Of course there can be no guarantees. But ethical and skillful practice, coupled with knowledge of the risks that abound and of the strategies to mitigate these, will go far toward reducing the possibility of being sued.

Dr. Reamer's book should prove immensely valuable to social workers at all levels of training and experience. Practice risks are confined to neither the line worker nor the administrator, neither the novice nor the seasoned clinician. There are lessons to be learned by each. Certainly, the earlier in a career—preferably commencing at the undergraduate or graduate level—a social worker begins to think about practicing within accepted norms, abiding by the spirit as well as the letter of ethical precepts and becoming cognizant of the legal environment within which practice occurs, the greater the likelihood of a professional career unencumbered by malpractice litigation. But it is never too late to study and to apply strategies for prevention. *Social Work Malpractice and Liability: Strategies for Prevention* is a book destined to be widely read and often quoted for many years to come.

> Robert H. Cohen, J.D., A.C.S.W.
> General Counsel
> National Association of Social Workers

Preface

That there is a need for this book is unfortunate. After all, what social worker wants to spend time reading and thinking about being sued?

Lawsuits alleging professional malpractice and liability are, however, a fact of modern life. The frequency of social work malpractice and liability claims is increasing, as is the cost to social workers. I am not just referring to the financial cost, mind you. I am also referring to the emotional cost exacted when one is sued. Even in those instances when a social worker has done nothing wrong, being named in a lawsuit is psychologically taxing. Moreover, lawyers need to be consulted (and paid), depositions must be conducted, and reputations need to be repaired or preserved. Under the best of circumstances being involved in a lawsuit is a miserable experience. Under the worst of circumstances it can be devastating.

Unfortunately, social workers get little training to help them prevent malpractice and liability claims. Professional education typically includes little on the subject of what has come to be known in the trade as "risk management." Although more and more social workers are learning about professional ethics, professional and continuing education rarely includes a systematic introduction to malpractice and liability risks and ways to prevent them. My hope is that this book will help remedy the situation.

Since the early 1980s I have had the privilege of speaking to thousands of social workers throughout the United States and abroad about the subject of professional ethics. When I started to receive invitations to deliver lectures and workshops on the topic, my focus was primarily on ethical issues in social work and the nature of ethical decision making when confronted with difficult dilemmas.

Over time, however, I noticed a distinct trend. During breaks and after my presentations I began to get more and more questions that started along the lines of "I was wondering if I can get sued for _____?" (Fill in the blank.) It did not take me long to figure out that while I was preoccupied with perplexing philosophical issues related to social work ethics, many in my audiences were consumed with concern about lawsuits. This should not have been much of a surprise because many ethical issues I was presenting broached complicated legal questions as well.

What this meant, of course, was that I found myself learning more and more about the malpractice and liability risks associated with social work practice. Over the years I have collected scores of case examples from conference participants, colleagues, and court cases in which I have served as an expert witness.

It is sad, in a way, that the profession has generated so much concern about the topics of malpractice and liability. It really is an unfortunate distraction from social work's principal mission. From my point of view, however, this also represents an important opportunity to convert this concern into education about good practice and good ethics—the ultimate prevention for malpractice and liability claims.

To date the social work literature has not included a comprehensive, systematic discussion of malpractice and liability risks in the profession. Although several important publications on malpractice and liability exist, these tend to be brief (e.g., Levine 1976; Green and Cox 1978; Bernstein 1981; Antler 1987; Saltzman and Proch 1990) or focused on one aspect of social work practice (e.g., Besharov 1985, which focuses on child welfare). My hope is that *Social Work Malpractice and Liability* will provide social workers with an in-depth and practical guide to help practitioners recognize, prevent, and cope with risks they encounter in their work.

The book is designed to assist social workers involved in direct practice and in social work supervision and administration. After I introduce the concepts of negligence, malpractice, and liability, and a brief discussion of the incidence of liability claims in social work (chapter 1), I turn to a series of discrete topics related to risk management. These include problems related to privacy and confidentiality (chapter 2), improper treatment and delivery of services (chapter 3), impaired practitioners (chapter 4), supervision (chapter 5), consultation and referral (chapter 6), fraud and deception (chapter 7), and termination of service (chapter 8). I conclude the book with a series of practical suggestions for social workers who are named as defendants in lawsuits and some observations about the role of good practice and good ethics as ways to prevent malpractice and liability claims (chapter 9).

This book contains considerable case material. The cases have been drawn from several sources, including legal texts, law reporters (published summaries of legal cases), court documents, newspaper accounts, and my own personal involvement in a wide variety of malpractice and liability cases. Some case illustrations are drawn from publications such as *Mental Health Law News*, which provides periodic updates of recently litigated cases. Other case examples are drawn from textbooks and original court opinions published in various state, federal, and regional reporters. Most cases cited are a matter of public record; in some instances, it was not possible to provide dates for the decisions because these cases were described only in secondary sources and were not published. In several instances I report case-related details in disguised form to protect the privacy of the parties involved.

It is important to note that I am not an attorney, and I am not offering legal advice in this book. Although this book includes information and commentary about legal concepts and cases, readers who believe they need or want legal advice should consult an attorney with expertise in professional malpractice and liability.

One of the things I have noticed when I speak to social workers about this subject is that their anxiety tends to increase. Contemplating being named in a lawsuit is not exactly fun. What I have found, however, is that whatever anxiety this topic produces can stimulate determined efforts to enhance the quality of social work practice. Perhaps the most effective way for social workers to protect themselves from lawsuits is to offer competent and ethical service to clients. Sometimes, anxiety can serve a useful purpose by inspiring constructive action. As the nineteenth-century Scottish writer Thomas Carlyle said, "Talk that does not end in any kind of action is better suppressed altogether."

Social Work Malpractice and Liability

1 | Professional Malpractice and Liability: An Overview

Imagine that you are a social worker employed at a family service agency. For three months you have been counseling a twenty-six-year-old man who was referred to you by the staff of a local psychiatric hospital, following the young man's inpatient treatment for depression.

Your client has made considerable progress. He is holding down a job for the first time in five years, living independently in his own apartment, and is romantically involved with a young woman. Your client reports that he is happier than he has ever been.

Your telephone rings one afternoon, and your client says, in a fearful voice, that he needs to see you as quickly as possible. He explains that he does not want to discuss the matter over the telephone, and you agree to meet him early the following morning.

Your client arrives on time. His affect is flat, and he seems unusually distressed. After ushering him into your office, your client explains that he was just informed by his physician that he has tested positive for HIV, the virus that causes AIDS. He

...lains that he is shocked by the diagnosis and needs help dealing with the terrible news.

You and your client spend the next hour talking about the implications of the diagnosis, the client's prognosis, and ways he might cope with the sudden change in his life circumstances. The session is poignant, filled with tears and anguish.

Toward the end of the session you realize that you have not talked about your client's girlfriend, with whom, your client has told you in previous sessions, he has been sexually active. You ask your client whether he has yet shared this news with his lover. He hesitates and says that he has not been able to share the news with her, that he is afraid she will leave him if she knows that he is HIV positive. You explore this with your client and try to persuade him that his lover must know about his infection so that she can support him and protect herself.

At this point your client begins to cry and says that he simply cannot share this news with his lover, especially because such disclosure could mean that she will learn that he was involved, some four years earlier, in a sexual relationship with a man. Your client tries to assure you that he will protect his lover by engaging in "safer" sex and that he would never do anything to harm her.

All your efforts to persuade your client to share this information with his lover fail. You tried various clinical techniques to get him to a point where he is willing to disclose this information to his lover on his own. You offered to role-play the disclosure and to sit in on the actual conversation to offer support. Nothing worked. You consult your supervisor, who convinces you that you have an obligation to take steps to disclose your client's diagnosis to his lover. Given the health risk involved, your supervisor argues, you would be remiss if you did not disclose the confidential information.

You inform your client of your obligation to disclose; understandably, he is quite upset with you. You then make an appointment to see his lover and explain to her what you have learned. Your client feels betrayed and angry. He is so angry that he is considering filing suit against you and your agency, alleging violation of his right to confidentiality.

What is the likelihood that you would be found liable for violating your client's right to confidentiality? What steps might you have taken to avoid this predicament?

Such questions are being posed with increasing frequency in social work. Malpractice and liability claims are being filed against social workers more often than ever before. In a distressing number of cases social workers are being charged with incompetent practice and ethical misconduct. Although many claims are not successful—they may not be meritorious or substantiated—many are.

As a result every contemporary social worker needs to be acquainted with the nature of professional malpractice and liability. What kinds of claims are being filed against social workers? with what frequency? What constitutes negligence and malpractice? How can social workers avoid liability? These are the principal questions that will concern us.

The Nature of Negligence, Malpractice, and Liability

Professional malpractice is generally considered a form of negligence. The concept applies to professionals who are required to perform in a manner consistent with the legal concept of the *standard of care* in the profession, that is, the way an ordinary, reasonable, and prudent professional would act under the same or similar circumstances (Austin, Moline, and Williams 1990; Cohen and Mariano 1982; Hogan 1979; Meyer, Landis, and Hays 1988; Schutz 1982). Malpractice in social work usually is the result of a practitioner's active violation of a client's rights (in legal terms, *acts of commission, misfeasance,* or *malfeasance*) or a practitioner's failure to perform certain duties (*acts of omission* or *nonfeasance*).

Some malpractice and liability claims result from genuine mistakes or inadvertent oversight on the part of social workers (a passenger in an elevator overhears a social worker talking about confidential aspects of a case with a colleague); others ensue from a deliberate decision to risk a claim (a social worker decides to divulge confidential information about a client in order to protect a third party from harm). Claims also are triggered by a social worker's unethical behavior or misconduct (sexual contact with a client or embezzling a client's funds).

In general, malpractice occurs when there is evidence that

1. at the time of the alleged malpractice, a legal duty existed between the practitioner and the client (as in the opening example concerning the obligation to keep information about the client's diagnosis confidential);

2. the practitioner was derelict in that duty, either through an action that occurred or through an omission (confidential information was divulged to the client's lover without the client's consent);

3. the client suffered some harm or injury (the client alleges that he suffered emotional distress and required additional psychiatric care after the unauthorized disclosure, that he lost time and wages at work, and that he was deprived of his lover's affection and companionship); and

4. the harm or injury was directly and proximately caused by the professional's dereliction of duty (the client's injuries were the result of the social worker's unauthorized disclosure of confidential information).

The Incidence of Social Work Malpractice and Liability

The number of liability and malpractice claims filed against professionals in general has increased at a disturbing pace. Malpractice suits have increased exponentially since the mid-1960s. Many scholars believe, in fact, that 90 percent of all malpractice suits ever filed in the United States have been filed in the last twenty to twenty-five years (Austin, Moline, and Williams 1990; also see Litan, Swire, and Winston 1988; Meyer, Landis, and Hays 1988; Trent 1978). As Cohen and Mariano (1982) assert,

> In the past, a lawsuit against a mental health professional was a relatively rare occurrence. Whereas the average neurosurgeon could expect to be sued approximately once for every two years of practice, the average psychiatrist could expect to be sued once for every 50 to 100 years of practice (Trent and Muhl 1975). For psychologists, social workers, and other mental health professionals who do not administer medication, the risk of incurring professional liability was even lower than that of the psychiatrist. In recent years, however, the rel-

ative immunity from litigation enjoyed by mental health professionals has begun to erode. (p. xiii)

Not surprisingly, physicians in medical specialties have been
sued more than other helping professionals. Psychotherapists in
general are sued much less frequently, although the numbers
have been increasing (Austin, Moline, and Williams 1990;
Meyer, Landis, and Hays 1988).

Unfortunately, no central repository of information about
malpractice and liability claims filed against social workers
exists. Social workers are insured by several private companies,
which do not pool their claims data and for proprietary reasons
do not generally make claims data available to the public.

Fortunately, however, the largest insurer of social workers, the
National Association of Social Workers (NASW) Insurance
Trust, has made some claims data available (Reamer, in press).
These data provide a valuable snapshot of the incidence and
nature of claims filed against social workers.

The NASW Insurance Trust, a subsidiary of the National
Association of Social Workers, sponsors malpractice and liability coverage for NASW members. The trust began offering liability coverage to NASW members in 1969.

Claims filed against NASW members insured through this
program are increasing. According to data compiled by the
administrator of the NASW insurance program, American Professional Agency, Inc., only 1 claim was filed in 1970; however,
40 claims were filed in 1980, and 126 claims were filed in 1990.
Between 1969 (the first full year in which claims were filed) and
1990, 634 claims were filed against NASW members insured
through the Trust, although not all were substantiated.

Claims have been made in twenty-seven categories, which
can be divided into two broad groups (claims that cannot be classified in one of these categories are placed in a miscellaneous category). The first includes claims that allege that social workers
carried out their duties improperly or in a fashion inconsistent
with the profession's standard of care (so-called acts of commission or misfeasance/malfeasance). Examples include flawed
treatment of a client (*incorrect treatment*), sexual impropriety,
breach of confidentiality or privacy, improper referral to another

service provider, defamation of a client's character (as a result of slander or libel), breach of contract for services, violation of a client's civil rights, improper civil commitment of a client (*false imprisonment/arrest*), wrongful removal of a child from a home (*loss of child custody*), assault and battery, improper termination of service (*abandonment*), improper licensing of staff, and improper peer review.

The distinction between *misfeasance* and *malfeasance* is an important one. Misfeasance is ordinarily defined as the commission of a proper act in a wrongful or injurious manner or the improper performance of an act that might have been performed lawfully. Examples include flawed informed-consent procedures or inadvertent disclosure of confidential information. Malfeasance is ordinarily defined as the commission of a wrongful or unlawful act. Examples include embezzlement of a client's funds, sexual contact with a minor, and violation of a client's civil rights (Gifis 1991).

The second broad category includes claims that allege that social workers failed to carry out a duty that they are ordinarily expected to carry out, according to the profession's standard of care (so-called acts of omission or nonfeasance). Examples include failure to diagnose properly, failure to prevent a client's suicide, failure to supervise a client properly, failure to protect third parties from harm, failure to treat a client successfully or at all (*failure to cure—poor results*), and failure to refer a client for consultation or treatment. In subsequent chapters I shall explain more fully the specific allegations contained under these broad headings.

As displayed in table 1, the claims categories involving the most individual practitioners (as opposed to agencies) during this twenty-one year period were *incorrect treatment* (18.6 percent of total claims) and *sexual impropriety* (18.5 percent of claims). Thus, just two of the twenty-eight categories account for nearly two-fifths of all claims filed in the history of the program. *Incorrect treatment* encompasses a wide variety of allegations, including failure to introduce appropriate therapeutic intervention or failure to implement intervention techniques properly. *Sexual impropriety* may include fondling of, harassment of, or intercourse with a client.

Table 1

Frequency and Relative Cost of Malpractice Claims
Filed Against Individual Social Workers: 1969–1990

Malpractice Category	Total Number	(%)	Dollar Percent
Incorrect treatment	118	(18.61)	19.22
Sexual impropriety	117	(18.45)	41.34
Breach of confidence/privacy	55	(8.68)	4.21
Diagnosis-failure to or incorrect	36	(5.68)	5.18
Miscellaneous	33	(5.21)	4.42
Suicide of patient	32	(5.05)	10.77
Improper referral/placement	28	(4.42)	2.05
Improper death: patient or others	23	(3.63)	2.57
Defamation-libel/slander	21	(3.31)	0.66
Breach of contract	19	(3.00)	1.20
Loss from evaluation	16	(2.52)	1.22
Violation of civil rights	16	(2.52)	0.20
Countersuit for fee collection	16	(2.52)	0.10
False imprisonment/arrest	14	(2.21)	0.96
Violation of legal regulations	14	(2.21)	0.43
Loss of child custody/visitation	13	(2.05)	0.57
Failure to supervise properly	12	(1.89)	0.21
Assault and battery	11	(1.74)	0.57
Failure to warn	8	(1.26)	2.58
Premises liability	8	(1.26)	0.01
Child placement removal	6	(0.95)	0.10
Bodily injury	5	(0.79)	0.76
Failure to treat	4	(0.63)	0.11
Undue influence	3	(0.47)	0.42
Abandonment	3	(0.47)	0.13
Licensing or peer review	2	(0.32)	0.00
Failure to cure-poor results	1	(0.16)	0.00
Failure to refer	0	(0.00)	0.00
TOTALS	634	(100%)	(100%)

NOTE: The data reported in this table are provided with permission from the NASW Insurance Trust.
Because decimals were rounded to two places, the totals for two columns do not equal 100 percent.

Categories with the next greater frequency of claims include *breach of confidence/privacy* (8.7 percent), *diagnosis—failure to or incorrect* (5.7 percent), *miscellaneous* (5.2 percent), and *suicide of patient* (5.1 percent). Each remaining claims category encompassed less than 5 percent of the total.

Of course, not all claims have merit. Some are frivolous or lack evidence of professional malpractice or misconduct. However, many claims do have merit or are settled out of court in order to minimize loss and legal expenses. In either case the result may be costly.

Table 1 also contains data on the insurance payments for each of the twenty-eight claims categories. More than two-fifths (41.34 percent) of insurance payments were the result of claims concerning sexual impropriety, and nearly one-fifth (19.22 percent) of insurance payments were for claims concerning incorrect treatment. Thus, these two claims categories alone account for nearly three-fifths of expended dollars. Approximately 11 percent of total dollars spent was for cases involving clients' suicides. No other claims category constituted more than 6 percent of total dollars expended.

The similarity between these claims data for social workers and claims data for psychologists is remarkable (Austin, Moline, and Williams 1990:16–17; Meyer, Landis, Hayes 1988:21). Pope (1986) reports on the frequency of successful claims filed against psychologists between 1976 and 1986 (Austin, Moline, and Williams 1990:16–17). Although the time period covered by Pope is shorter than that in table 1 for social workers, the similarities are striking. As with social workers the most frequent claims categories for psychologists during this ten-year period were *sexual contact* (psychologists, 18.5 percent of claims; social workers, 18.5 percent of claims) and *treatment error* (psychologists, 15.2 percent of claims; social workers, 18.6 percent of claims). Further, these two claims categories were the most expensive for both psychologists and social workers. Approximately 45 percent of dollars spent in response to claims against psychologists resulted from claims of sexual contact (versus 41 percent for claims alleging sexual impropriety by social workers). Approximately 14 percent of dollars spent in response to claims against psychologists resulted from claims of treatment error (versus 19 percent of dollars spent for claims alleging incorrect treatment by social workers).

The impressive similarity of the claims pattern for social workers and psychologists suggests of course that the determinants of these problems are not entirely specific to each profession. Perhaps we must look at the helping professions more generally in order to shed light on the causes of malpractice and negligence.

Key Concepts in Malpractice and Negligence

As noted earlier, malpractice is a form of negligence that occurs when a practitioner acts in a manner inconsistent with the profession's standard of care—the way an ordinary, reasonable, and prudent professional would act under the same or similar circumstances.

Suits that allege malpractice are civil suits (in contrast to criminal proceedings). Ordinarily, civil suits are based on tort or contract law, with plaintiffs (the individuals bringing the suit) seeking some form of redress for injuries they claim to have incurred (Hogan 1979). These injuries may be economic (lost wages or the cost involved in seeking psychiatric care), physical (resulting from a suicide attempt or an attempt to restrain an impaired client), or emotional (depression or anxiety brought about by the inappropriate disclosure of confidential information). Although much less common, a plaintiff may also allege denial of constitutional rights (individuals hospitalized against their wishes may allege that their rights to liberty and due process have been abridged).

As in criminal trials, defendants in civil suits are presumed blameless until proved otherwise. In ordinary civil suits defendants will be found liable for their actions based on the standard of *preponderance of the evidence*. This is in contrast to the stricter standard of *beyond a reasonable doubt* used in criminal proceedings. In the exceptional civil case (such as a contract between family members to pay for services) the court may expect *clear and convincing evidence*, a standard of proof that is greater than preponderance of the evidence but less than for beyond a reasonable doubt (Gifis 1991).

In principle, tort law—which entails rules allowing injured parties to seek compensation through the courts from those responsible for the harm—performs three important functions in society. First, it deters behavior that causes injuries, in that a price must be paid for injuring another party. Second, tort law provides opportunity for retribution against those responsible for the injury. Finally, tort law provides a mechanism for compensating the injured party (Litan, Swire, and Winston 1988).

Most legal actions brought against social workers involve tort law, or law involving private or civil wrongs or injuries resulting from a breach of a legal duty (as opposed to contract or criminal law). Torts may be unintentional (negligent) or intentional. *Unintentional torts*, which include the various forms of negligence and malpractice discussed elsewhere in this book, concern instances in which the social worker's performance is alleged to have fallen below the standard of care for the profession. *Intentional torts*—such as defamation of character or assault and battery—do not require evidence of negligence.

Most tort claims against social workers allege some form of malpractice (unintentional torts). The malpractice suit has its origins in early English common law. In fact, mention of physicians' professional liability dates to the thirteenth century (Hogan 1979). Since then a variety of landmark court cases have clarified the nature of malpractice. In a classic eighteenth-century (1767) case involving medical malpractice, for instance, the King's Bench stated in *Slater v. Baker and Stapleton*,

> He who acts rashly acts ignorantly; and although the defendants in general may be as skilful in their respective professions as any two gentlemen in England, yet the Court cannot help saying that in this particular case they have acted ignorantly and unskilfully, contrary to the known rule and usage of surgeons. (95 Eng. Rep. 860 at 863, 2 Wils. 359 at 362, cited in Hogan 1979:8)

The first malpractice case on record in the United States was *Cross v. Guthry* in 1794. In this case a physician was found liable in negligence related to surgery performed on a woman who later died (Hogan 1979).

The Elements of Malpractice and Liability

As described previously, four conditions must be satisfied to support a malpractice claim. These include evidence that the practitioner owed a duty to the injured party, that the practitioner was derelict in that duty, that the plaintiff suffered some sort of harm or injury, and that the injury was the direct and proximate result of the breach of the duty.

The first element—evidence that the practitioner had a legal duty to the injured party—is often the easiest to satisfy. In the example presented at the beginning of this chapter, for instance, the social worker employed at the family service agency unquestionably had a legal duty to the client.

Determining whether the practitioner was somehow derelict in that duty typically is much more complex. Here questions ordinarily arise that relate to the prevailing standard of care in the profession. The standard of care requires the practitioner to do what a "reasonable person of ordinary prudence" would do in the practitioner's place (Gifis 1991:460).

For many years courts defined *standard of care* by comparing a practitioner's actions with those of similarly trained professionals in the same community—what is generally known as the *locality rule*. The assumption here was that levels of expertise and training varied from community to community, as a function of local training programs and access to technology and treatment techniques. One practical consequence of the locality rule was that expert witnesses called upon to testify in a malpractice case were ordinarily expected to be drawn from the local community.

Over time, however, the locality rule has been overturned in many jurisdictions, either by judicial decision or legislation (Schutz 1982:4). The rationale has been that changes in modern communication, transportation, and education have provided practitioners with much greater access to updated information about developments in their profession. Consequently, courts now typically permit out-of-state expert witnesses to testify in malpractice cases. That is, the standard of care tends to be based on national, rather than local, norms in a profession.

Nonetheless, a plaintiff can find it exceedingly difficult to demonstrate that a social worker behaved in a manner inconsistent with the standard of care. Some departures from the standard of care are of course relatively easy to show. A social worker who discloses confidential information about a client to a client's neighbor, in casual conversation and without the client's permission, has clearly departed from the profession's standard of care. A social worker in a residential setting who neglects to record in case notes a client's obvious suicidal symptoms has clearly departed from the standard of care. These are the easy cases.

Far more common, however, are those cases in which reasonable people may disagree about the appropriateness of the practitioner's actions, that is, whether they in fact constituted a departure from the standard of care. The social worker in the opening example, for instance, might argue that it was essential for the client's lover to know about the client's HIV-positive status so that her welfare could be protected. This social worker might argue that the benefit of the disclosure, to which the client would not consent, outweighed the breach of the client's right to privacy.

Other social workers might find such an argument unpersuasive. They might argue that the social worker had an obligation to respect the client's right to confidentiality and that, without his explicit consent, disclosure to a third party was unacceptable and constituted a departure from the profession's standard of care.

Further, it is not hard to imagine that expert witnesses drawn from the social work profession might disagree. A jury in a civil suit concerning this case might be faced with thoughtful experienced experts who offer diametrically opposed views on the social worker's actions. One might support the social worker's claim to a duty to protect a third party from serious harm and that a breach of confidentiality under such circumstances is justifiable. Another expert witness might contend that the social worker's disclosure constituted a clear violation of professional ethics, particularly because the client never uttered an actual threat against his lover.

Courts recognize of course that professionals subscribe to various, sometimes competing, schools of thought. The idea that different schools of thought are permissible emerged in the nineteenth century, when physicians subscribed to different philosophies of practice, or schools, each with its own assumptions, principal concepts, and standards. Rather than try to determine which school of thought is most appropriate, courts have generally acknowledged the legitimacy of different schools of thought, so long as they are supported by a "respectable minority of the profession" (Hogan 1979:9). In instances in which it is difficult to determine whether a particular school of thought is endorsed by at least a respectable minority of a profession, a judge is likely to explore whether a professional association, relevant standards of practice, and ethical guidelines exist.

Practitioners are judged then according to the principles and doctrine endorsed by the school of thought to which they subscribe (*Force v. Gregory* 1893; *Nelson v. Dahl* 1928). As Slovenko (1978) notes with respect to psychotherapy,

> The courts tend not to pass judgment on the appropriate therapy or the efficacy of different forms of treatment (except sterilization, electroshock, and psychosurgery), a reflection of Justice Cardozo's observation that the law treats medicine with diffidence and respect. Thus, the court has refused to consider which "of two equally reputable methods of psychiatric treatment"—psychoanalysis as against a physiological approach—would prove most efficacious in a particular case. In *Tribby v. Cameron*, for example, the U.S. Court of Appeals for the District of Columbia said: "We do not suggest that the court should or can decide what particular treatment this patient requires. The court's function here resembles ours when we review agency action. We do not decide whether one agency has made the best decision, but only make sure it has made permissible and reasonable decision in view of the relevant information and within a broad range of discretion." (pp. 61–62)

It is important to note that if social workers present themselves as specialists within the social work profession—specializing in, for example, treatment of eating disorders, substance abuse, or post-traumatic stress disorder—they will be held to the highest standards of a specialist, even if the social worker's claim of expertise is a misrepresentation (Schutz 1982:4).

Although courts generally respect a profession's own determination of the standard of care, in principle, although perhaps not very likely, a court could rule that a profession has failed to properly define its own standard of care. As Schutz (1982) notes with respect to the practice of psychotherapy,

> As professionals practicing therapy, we have been given the privilege of largely setting the legal standards of conduct by in-house expert testimony. The privilege is not absolute. In some cases, the court has determined that the standards of a profession were not adequate safeguards for the public and that compliance with accepted standards was *persuasive but not conclusive* evidence against negligence. For instance, in *Helling v. Carey*, 519 P.2d 981 (Wash. 1974), the court

cited Justice Learned Hand in the *T. J. Hooper* case [60 F.2d 737 (2d Cir. 1932)]: "A whole calling may have unduly lagged in the adoption of new and available devices. It never may set its own tests, however persuasive be its usages. Courts must in the end say what is required; there are precautions so imperative that even their universal disregard will not excuse their omission." Hence, a therapist can be regarded as competent by his profession and still be found liable. However, the likelihood of such an unfortunate precedent is small. The courts have been chary about setting standards in our field. (p. 3)

Ordinarily, the burden of going forward with the evidence in a negligence case belongs to the plaintiff. However, in some cases the doctrine of *res ipsa loquitur* (the act speaks for itself) is introduced by the plaintiff to shift the burden of proof to the defendant. Under res ipsa loquitur the plaintiff argues that the negligence is so self-evident that any reasonable person can see it (Schutz 1982:4–5). Imagine, for example, a suit filed on behalf of a child who was injured by an abusive foster parent; the suit proffers evidence that the social service agency placed the child in the foster home without screening the foster parents, who had a known record of abuse.

The doctrine of res ipsa loquitur was first established in the British case of *Scott v. London and St. Katherine Docks Co.* (1865, cited in Hogan 1979:9–10). An English customs officer was hit on the head by several sacks of sugar that had fallen out of a warehouse window. The judges concluded that sacks of sugar do not fall out of second-story windows and hit pedestrians unless negligence is involved (Hogan 1979:318).

Three criteria must be met in order for a court to accept the doctrine of res ipsa loquitur: (1) the injury sustained does not ordinarily occur in the absence of negligence; (2) elements within the exclusive control of the defendant must have caused the injury; and (3) the injury must not have been the result of any voluntary action or contribution on the plaintiff's part (although states that recognize the concept of *comparative negligence*, described later, may dispose of the third criterion and apportion liability according to the percentage contributed by the plaintiff and defendant). The procedural effect of successfully invoking the doctrine of res ipsa loquitur is to shift the burden of going forward with the evidence, which normally belongs to the plaintiff, to the defendant, who is thereby charged with introducing evidence to refute the presumption of negligence (Gifis 1991:416).

Demonstrating the third element—that the client suffered some harm or injury—can also be difficult in social work. Unlike medicine, for example, where injuries resulting from malpractice are sometimes easy to document (when a fracture is set improperly and evidence of this appears on an X ray), in social work the injuries alleged are often difficult to document empirically. In many instances plaintiffs claim they have experienced some form of emotional injury or harm, as opposed to some form of physical injury. In these cases the plaintiff may have some difficulty substantiating the injury. Expert testimony may be required in order to present a strong case.

This suggests of course that a plaintiff can find it difficult to satisfy the fourth element—that the harm or injury was directly and proximately caused by the social worker's dereliction of duty. Even plaintiffs who can document that they sustained some sort of injury—emotional distress or depression, physical harm—can have difficulty demonstrating that the social worker's alleged dereliction of duty was the direct and proximate cause of the injury (Slovenko 1978:61–63). There may be strong evidence, for example, that a client manifested symptoms of depression after a social worker inadvertently released confidential information without the client's permission. The social worker's attorney might argue, however, that this client had a longstanding history of depression and that a variety of other stressful events in the client's life at the time of the inadvertent disclosure may account for the depression.

As Rothblatt and Leroy observe in relation to demonstrating the causal connection between a psychiatrist's breach of a duty and the injury of emotional harm,

> besides proving that the psychiatrist has breached the requisite standard of care in some specific detail, the plaintiff must also demonstrate causation and damage. Because the natural pathological development and prognosis of mental disease is not well known, it is frequently difficult to state to a reasonable degree of medical certainty whether the application or omission of a particular procedure at a specified time caused mental injury to the patient. Thus, it is often difficult for the plaintiff to prove the element of causation. The task

is simplified, however, if the alleged negligence in some manner caused or encouraged the patient to sustain or inflict tangible physical injuries upon himself or others. Indeed, this characteristic is typical of almost every successful suit. In this situation, proof of the injuries in addition to proof that ordinary prudent therapeutic techniques would have prevented the damage may sustain the burden of proof.

The plaintiff who complains of exclusively mental injuries may also have a difficult time proving the element of damages. Not only are his allegations intangible and difficult to demonstrate to the judge and jury, but they also tend to be somewhat speculative because of the state of knowledge about mental illness. Even where improper procedures have been used to institutionalize a person in need of mental care, the courts may absolve physicians from liability by finding that the patient was not injured by receiving the treatment he needed. (1973:264, cited in R. J. Cohen 1979:49–50)

Consider the opening example. Assume for the moment that the client sues you and your agency, alleging that you violated his right to confidentiality. Through his attorney your client (now presumably your former client) claims that you had a duty to respect his right to privacy and breached this duty by disclosing to his lover details of his HIV-positive status. In particular your former client asserts that you violated principle II.H of the National Association of Social Workers' *Code of Ethics* (1990:5): "The social worker should respect the privacy of clients and hold in confidence all information obtained in the course of professional service."

In addition, your former client claims that as a result of your disclosure of confidential information about him he suffered significant harm. Specifically, your former client alleges that he suffered serious emotional distress and symptoms of depression and anxiety. He spells out in detail how his lover fled the relationship following your disclosure and how he had to seek psychiatric help at considerable expense as a result. Finally, your former client claims that he lost time at work and wages as a result of this emotional injury.

You can imagine how controversial your former client's claims would be. In his mind, perhaps, is a clear, direct, and unambiguous connection between your alleged violation of his right to privacy and the emotional injury he claims to have suffered. From your point of view serious questions can be raised about this connection. In your defense your attorney may argue that your former client has a history of depression and anxiety symptoms and that he has missed work in the past as a result of his emotional difficulties. Further, at the time of your disclosure to your former client's lover—which you do not deny—your former client also complained of significant stress in his life because of conflict with his supervisor at work and financial problems. Hence, your attorney might argue that your disclosure of information cannot be demonstrated conclusively to be the direct cause of your client's subsequent symptoms of depression and anxiety, missed work, or lost wages. A number of other factors could account for these difficulties.

Your lawyer also might question whether your former client's claims of injury are valid (in relation to element 3). Although missed days of work and lost wages are easy to document—recognizing that the cause may be uncertain—claims of emotional injury can be difficult to substantiate—emotional injuries do not show up on X rays or laboratory tests. Evidence often takes the form of self-report and evaluations conducted by mental health professionals. As social workers know quite well, even seasoned practitioners may disagree about the validity of evidence presented to substantiate claims of emotional injury.

In many cases involving liability risks social workers can be sued no matter what course of action they take. In the case example, for instance, the social worker might be sued for disclosing confidential information without the client's permission. A social worker also could be sued for *failure* to disclose confidential information without a client's permission (here the distinction between *acts of commission* and *acts of omission* is clearly relevant). Imagine that you decide to honor your client's request for privacy. You believe your client's claims that he will engage in safer sex and will not engage in any activity that could threaten his lover's health. Moreover, you do not believe that violating your client's right to privacy without his permission would be ethical.

Six months later your client's lover becomes infected with HIV during one act of unprotected intercourse with your client. In a tear-filled conversation your client tells his lover that he struggled with his decision about whether to tell her about his HIV-positive status and even discussed the decision with you, his social worker. At that point your client's lover learns that you knew about your client's HIV-positive status and did not take steps to inform her. Your client's lover is so distressed about this news and feels so betrayed that she consults an attorney who sues you, alleging that you were obligated to take steps to protect her client's health, including warning her of your client's HIV-positive status. Specifically, the lover's attorney argues that you violated principle II.H.1 of the NASW (1990) *Code of Ethics*: "The social worker should share with others confidences revealed by clients, without their consent, *only for compelling professional reasons*" [pp. 5–6, emphasis added]. The attorney claims that the risk to her client's health clearly constituted a compelling professional reason to violate confidentiality and that you were remiss in not taking steps to protect her.

In your defense you argue that you did not have sufficient reason to violate your client's right to privacy. First, you argue, your client never actually issued a verbal threat against his lover. On the contrary, he reiterated his deep love and affection for her. Second, you have no evidence to prove that your client and his lover tend to engage in high-risk practices. Therefore, you claim it would have been irresponsible to divulge such confidential information without the client's consent.

Process Versus Outcome and the Standard of Care

The opening case also illustrates how difficult it can be to prove malpractice.

Some malpractice cases in social work are relatively clear cut. A social worker in a residential setting who simply forgot to enter into the record that a client displayed evidence of suicidal ideation may clearly be liable if staffers on the next shift were not alerted to the suicide risk, consequently failed to monitor the resident closely, and the client was injured seriously in an actual suicide attempt. Similarly, a social worker in private practice who neglects to discuss informed consent with a client, fails to have the client sign a consent form, and then discloses diagnostic information to the client's employer, clearly may be liable if the employer then fires the client. In these instances malpractice and negligence may be relatively easy to establish.

In general social workers will agree that a practitioner should never strike a client physically (except perhaps in extreme cases requiring self-defense) and that a practitioner should always obtain informed consent from a client before disclosing confidential information (except in rare cases involving genuine emergencies). The opening case example, however, illustrates a common phenomenon—reasonable practitioners disagree about what the social worker should have done and whether those actions departed from the standard of care in the profession. Some social workers might argue, for example, that you were ethically obligated to take steps to protect your client's lover from harm and that this might include disclosing confidential information about his HIV-positive status against his wishes. They probably would cite the well-known *Tarasoff* case, discussed more fully later in this book, to support their argument.

Other social workers might argue with equal force that you had an obligation to respect your client's right to privacy, that you did not have sufficiently compelling evidence to warrant disclosure of confidential information against his wishes. Such conflicting arguments about this very set of circumstances have in fact been presented by thoughtful experienced social workers (Reamer 1991a, 1991b).

What this suggests is that in many liability cases the court can find it quite difficult to determine what, exactly, constitutes the standard of care in the profession with regard to a social worker's actual decision and actions. Attorneys and expert witnesses often present strong arguments in conflicting directions.

What can happen, however—and this is a remarkably important point—is that debate about the standard of care may shift from the social worker's actual decision and actions related to the substantive issue at hand or the outcome of the decision (in this instance whether the social worker should have divulged confidential information to the client's lover against the client's wishes) and toward the *process* and *procedures* the social worker followed in order to make the decision. That is, the line of questioning may focus instead on the steps the social worker took to make a sound decision. Part of the standard of care in social work entails knowing when and how to obtain professional consultation. Consultation skills are taught in the profession, and substantial literature about the phenomenon is available to practitioners. Failure to obtain consultation might constitute a departure from social work's standard of care.

During a deposition (a method of pretrial discovery that consists of a witness's statement and responses to questioning under oath) or actual trial an opposing attorney in the case example might ask which supervisors the social worker consulted about the decision. Were these supervisors the most appropriate ones to consult, given their areas of expertise? Did the social worker bring the issue up in peer supervision? Did the social worker consult a lawyer about the legal implications of the decision? Did the social worker consult professional literature for guidance? Did the social worker document these various forms of consultation? Does the case record include evidence that the social worker actually took these various steps?

What I am suggesting here is that the standard of care in social work can be viewed in two ways. First, the standard of care may focus on a social worker's specific decisions or actions pertaining to the professional duty, such as the handling of confidential information, physical contact with clients, informed consent, and suicide prevention. Second, the standard of care may focus on the process and procedures the social worker followed in making the relevant decision or pursuing the controversial course of action (i.e., the social worker's use of supervision, consultation, research).

With regard to the process and procedures, documenting any supervision or consultation that social workers obtain or research they conduct is extremely important. Should some question arise about a social worker's particular decision or actions, being able to demonstrate the kind of prudent supervision and consultation that the social worker obtained can be quite useful. I have heard many malpractice and liability attorneys say, "If it's not written in the case record, it didn't happen."

Damages in Liability Cases

If the social worker loses the suit, two kinds of damages can be awarded, compensatory and/or punitive. In general damages include monetary compensation, which the law awards to the party injured by the action of another. *Compensatory, or actual, damages* include those directly related to the breach of duty and cover losses that can be readily proved to have been sustained and for which the injured party should be compensated as a matter of right, such as past or future earnings lost or the cost of mental health care.

Punitive, or exemplary, damages provide compensation in excess of compensatory or actual damages. They essentially constitute a form of punishment to the wrongdoer and excess compensation to the injured party. They are ordinarily awarded in instances of reckless, malicious, or willful misconduct (R. J. Cohen 1979; Gifis 1991). Punitive damages are awarded much less frequently than compensatory damages (Meyer, Landis, and Hays 1988:14).

Monetary awards against social workers may be adjusted based on the concepts of joint liability, comparative negligence, contributory negligence, or assumption of risk. Under the doctrine of *joint liability* a court might find that a social worker *and* another party are responsible for the injury to the plaintiff. Imagine a social worker who is sued by a former client who alleges that he was placed in a psychiatric hospital against his wishes, in part because of inaccurate information provided to the committing psychiatrist by the social worker. If the plaintiff's claim has merit, a finding of joint liability could result—both the committing psychiatrist and the social worker who interviewed the client are held responsible.

This is in contrast to comparative negligence. According to the doctrine of *comparative negligence,* responsibility for damages can be distributed between the plaintiff and defendant, based on the relative negligence of the two, particularly when the plaintiff's conduct contributed to the injury sustained as a result of the social worker's negligence (known as *contributory negligence;* the client's own actions fell below the standard of self-care that an ordinary reasonable person would exercise under the same or similar circumstances). As a result the amount of damages awarded to the plaintiff may be reduced. Over the years the rather strict standard associated with the doctrine of contributory negligence—where a plaintiff who acted negligently may be barred from recovering damages—has given way to the broader doctrine of comparative negligence, where negligent plaintiffs may find their damages reduced by the proportion by which their negligence contributed to their injury (Litan and Winston 1988).

Imagine a client who sues a social worker, claiming failure to provide adequate protection in a group home. The client was assaulted by another resident and claims that the social worker—the group home director—should have had at least one other staff person working on that shift. The plaintiff alleges that an additional staff person would have provided the supervision necessary to prevent such an assault. The court could find the social worker liable in failing to have an adequate staff-to-client ratio but might also find that the plaintiff was negligent because his behavior provoked the assault. Damages may be awarded accordingly, taking into account the comparative negligence of the parties involved.

The concept of assumption of risk can also influence the outcome of a liability claim. In tort law defendants can use *assumption of risk* to claim that plaintiffs were aware of a condition or situation obviously dangerous to them and yet voluntarily exposed themselves to the hazard or failed to take steps to avoid known danger. Thus, contributory negligence arises when a plaintiff fails to exercise due care, while assumption of risk arises regardless of the care used and is based on the concept of *consent* (Gifis 1991).

Consider, for example, a client who voluntarily signs a statement, while being admitted to an inpatient psychiatric treatment program, that acknowledges that the discussion of personal problems during treatment might trigger emotional distress, depression, and other psychiatric symptoms. If the client subsequently sues the treatment staff and program, alleging that their treatment approach created more psychological symptoms than it alleviated, the defendant might argue that the client assumed the risk.

State legislatures use *statutes of limitation* to restrict the time period during which someone can file a negligence suit and seek damages. In some cases the period specified in the statute of limitations may begin at the date of the actual injury, while in other cases it may begin at the date the person learned of the injury. Typically, minors' right to sue begins when they reach the age of majority. Thus, adults can sue for injuries sustained during their childhoods for a significant number of years after they reach the age of majority. The effective statute of limitations, as applied to the treatment of minors, is eighteen years plus the relevant state's statute (Schutz 1982:8).

Relatively few lawsuits actually reach court. Most malpractice and other professional liability claims (in the vicinity of 85 to 90 percent) are settled out of court (Meyer, Landis, and Hays 1988:14). Settlement of a case does not imply that the defendant admits responsibility or was in any way culpable. Defendants may simply decide to cut their losses and settle out of court to avoid further legal and other expenses.

For those cases that actually reach court, rulings can be based on statutory law and constitutional law but are often based on common law. Common law, frequently known as *case law*, is established by prior court decisions. Under the doctrine of stare decisis (to stand by that which was decided) a judge determines whether a particular case falls within the ruling set forth in the earlier case. The judge may also generate a new law, or precedent, based on this particular case (Hogan 1979).

Fortunately, social workers can obtain comprehensive liability insurance. Policies are available that cover individual practitioners, social service agencies, corporations, and schools or departments of social work. These liability policies typically contain options with regard to the amount of coverage (for example, the amount of coverage for each wrongful act, or series of related wrongful acts, and the amount of aggregate coverage during a given policy period), coverage during extended reporting periods (that is, coverage for claims filed against a social worker after the end of the policy period), and coverage of employees (as in a group private practice). The coverage provided by the NASW Insurance Trust, for example, is a claims-made policy, which means that the coverage is limited to liability for only those claims that are first made against the policy holder and reported to the company *during the period the policy is in force.* Social workers who also want to be insured for claims made after terminating the policy need to pay an additional premium for extended reporting period protection.

Professional liability policies also typically contain certain exclusions. The policy offered by the NASW Insurance Trust, for instance, excludes coverage for any dishonest, criminal, fraudulent, or malicious act or omission; fee disputes; a variety of wrongful acts of a managerial or administrative nature; any claim arising from any business relationship or venture with a former or current client; and a number of other specific activities enumerated in the policy. In addition, the policy contains a special provision regarding coverage for sexual misconduct. Under this policy the company places a ceiling on the amount it will pay for damages arising from actual or alleged sexual misconduct.

Even social workers employed in settings that provide group liability coverage should seriously consider obtaining their own individual coverage. When both a social worker and the worker's employer are named in a liability claim, the employer could argue that the social worker, and not the employing agency, was negligent. Individual coverage would thus protect workers who find themselves at odds with their employers in relation to a liability claim.

Liability claims and lawsuits are being filed against social workers with greater frequency. Thus contemporary social workers must have a keen understanding of legal concepts related to malpractice, negligence, and liability (Kurzman 1991). Fortunately, most malpractice and liability claims are preventable.

2 | Confidentiality and Privacy

The concept of privacy is central to social work practice. In clinical work especially, social workers have always had a deep-seated respect for their clients' need for confidentiality. The trust between social worker and client, so essential to effective help, typically depends on the worker's assurance of privacy. Clients' willingness to disclose intimate, deeply personal details about their lives is understandably a function of their belief that their social worker will not share this information with others.

But privacy is also relevant in other social work domains. Social work administrators need to understand the limits of confidentiality as they pertain to personnel matters or sharing of information with colleagues in other agencies (insurance companies, accrediting bodies, government departments). Protective service workers need to avoid invasion of privacy while investigating reports of child abuse and neglect. Social workers involved in community organizing need to appreciate the nature of privacy when they meet with local residents who air grievances about public officials. Social workers in social policy positions need to understand the tension between confidentiality rights and local open-meeting statutes, which may allow the public and media to attend sensitive high-level meetings.

The concept of privacy in professional practice to a great extent is rooted in pronouncements by the Pythagoreans in the fourth century B.C. and was later incorporated in the Hippocratic oath: "Whatever I see or hear, in the life of men, which ought not to be spoken of abroad, I will not divulge, as reckoning that all such should be kept secret." The concept of privacy was also an important component of ancient Jewish law, as conveyed in the Talmud. Early English common law also acknowledged the right to privacy associated with the concept of *honor among gentlemen* (Meyer, Landis, and Hays 1988:51).

Privacy rights were codified legally in 1791 in the Fourth and Fifth Amendments to the U.S. Constitution. Not until 1828, however, was there a legal basis for medical privacy, when New York State established the physician-patient privilege. In the United States the first formal statement of the legal concept of privacy appeared in an 1890 essay, "The Right to Privacy," written by Samuel Warren and Louis Brandeis. This seminal journal article ultimately served as the foundation for many court decisions and statutes. Warren and Brandeis defined *privacy* as the right to be left alone or elect not to share information about private matters, habits, and relationships (Meyer, Landis, and Hays 1988). Since then the concepts of privacy and confidentiality have assumed a prominent place among clients' most venerable rights (Donnelly 1978; Meyer, Landis, and Hayes 1988).

Clarifying the meaning of and differences between *privacy* and *confidentiality* is important. Privacy refers to the right to noninterference in individuals' thoughts, knowledge, acts, associations, and property. Confidentiality rights arise when individuals entrust others with private information, usually because of a "vital need to share. It requires the explicit or implicit mutual understanding that this second individual will use it only for the first individual's vital need, and not make it available to a third party without the first person's consent" (Grossman 1978:139).

Schutz argues further that an invasion of privacy "is a violation of the right to be left alone. It requires that private acts be disclosed to more than a small group of persons, and such disclosure must be offensive to a reasonable person of ordinary sensibilities" (1982:11).

Most contemporary social workers recognize that confidentiality cannot be absolute. Widely accepted exceptions related to protection of third parties (for example, mandatory reporting of child abuse or neglect) sometimes require disclosure of confidential information. Hence clients have a right to *relative* (versus *absolute*) confidentiality (Cohen 1979; Meyer, Landis, and Hays 1988).

Many of the earliest legal actions against professionals alleging breach of confidentiality involved physicians. The first recorded decision in the U.S. courts involving a physician's alleged breach of a patient's confidence was decided in 1920 (*Simonsen v. Swenson* 1920). In this instance the court ruled that the doctor had a privilege to disclose information required to prevent the spread of a contagious disease (M. B. Lewis 1986:594).

Over time most jurisdictions in the United States have recognized legal actions against psychotherapists and other social service professionals in breach-of-confidence cases. The number of cases alleging wrongful disclosure of confidential information has grown, especially since 1958. Courts have varied, however, with respect to the legal theory on which they have based their rulings. Suits alleging wrongful disclosure of confidential information have been based on theories of (1) invasion of privacy, (2) express or implied statutory violations, (3) breach of implied contract, and (4) tortious violation of the duty to maintain confidentiality (M. B. Lewis 1986). In *Hammonds v. Aetna Casualty & Surety Co.* (1965) the court stressed the necessity of privacy in therapeutic relationships when it concluded that "the preservation of the patient's privacy is no mere ethical duty upon the part of the doctor; there is a legal duty as well. The unauthorized revelation of medical secrets or *any* confidential communication given in the course of treatment, is tortious conduct which may be the basis for an action in damages" (243 F. Supp. 793 at 801–2). In *Horne v. Patton* (1974) the court was even more explicit about invasion of privacy; it concluded that disclosure of confidential information concerning a patient's mental health may constitute "unwarranted publicization of one's private affairs with which the public has no legitimate concern such as to cause outrage, mental suffering, shame or humiliation" (cited in M. B. Lewis 1986:597). The concept of invasion of privacy was also cited in *Doe v. Roe* (1977), in which the court ruled that a patient's privacy rights were violated when a therapist published a book containing verbatim information that the patient disclosed during therapy sessions.

Some courts have also ruled that wrongful disclosure of confidential information can be based on the theory of express or implied statutory violations, specifically statutes related to licensing, testimonial privilege, and limiting the availability of medical information. In *Simonsen v. Swenson* (1920) the Nebraska Supreme Court held that a physician's disclosure of confidential information—where the disclosure could not be justified by a privilege—violated the state's licensing statute. In *Berry v. Moench* (1958) the court ruled that patients may sue physicians when confidential information is disclosed in violation of a statute that implicitly mandates confidentiality. In *Alberts v. Devine* (1985) the Supreme Judicial Court of Massachusetts ruled that a psychiatrist could be held liable for breach of confidence, based in part on a state statute limiting the availability of hospital records.

Several court decisions have cited the theory of breach of an implied contract (M. B. Lewis 1986; Meyer, Landis, and Hays 1988). In *Hammonds*, for example, the court ruled that a physician's disclosure of confidential information constituted a breach of an implied contract between physician and patient. The court held that a simple contract is formed whenever a doctor-patient relationship is established and that one condition of this contract is that information learned during the course of the relationship will not be disclosed without the patient's permission. The court also stated that within the context of such a relationship patients have the right to rely on the professional's "warranty of silence." Similar references to the theory of implied contract also appear in *Horne* and *Doe v. Roe*.

Finally, some courts have cited the theory of breach of fiduciary duty in their opinions in cases involving wrongful disclosure. In *Alexander v. Knight* (1962), *Hague v. Williams* (1962), and *MacDonald v. Clinger* (1982), for example, courts held that medical professionals have a fiduciary duty to their patients that entails protecting confidential information and that a breach of that duty is actionable as a tort. Tort actions in breach of confidentiality were also recognized in *Vassiliades v. Garfinckel's* (1985), *Alberts v. Devine* (1985), and *Fedell v. Wierzbieniec* (1985).

Liability and malpractice problems in social work related to privacy and confidentiality usually fall into two broad categories. The first includes deliberate disclosure of confidential information, such as sharing with a third party threats made by a client against that person or filing a report of child abuse against a client's wishes. The second includes inadvertent or accidental disclosure of confidential information, as in leaving sensitive information about a client exposed on a table in a semi-public area or discussing a client's circumstances in the hallway of the agency.

The Duty to Protect

> Judy S. was a social worker at the Ocean State Family Service Agency. Her client, Alan F., had sought treatment three months earlier for symptoms of depression. Alan F. reported that for years he has had low self-esteem, ever since his bitter divorce.
>
> Alan F. was particularly agitated during one recent session. He told Judy S. that he and his former wife were in the middle of a big dispute about visitation and custody rights. Alan F. claimed that in spite of provisions in their divorce settlement his former wife has been "doing everything she can to keep me from seeing the kids."
>
> During the counseling session Alan F. went on and on about how his former wife was tormenting him. He was clearly distraught. Toward the end of the session Alan F. said, "I can't begin to tell you how much I hate that woman. She's ruining my life. You have no idea how much I'd like to get rid of her. Maybe I just ought to do it."

Nearly every clinical social worker can identify with the general circumstances presented in this case, a client who may pose a threat to a third party. In some instances the threat is clear and unambiguous, such as when a client explicitly announces an intention to harm a third party. By now there is considerable consensus that social workers and other mental health professionals need to take steps to protect such third parties and this may entail disclosure of confidential information against the client's wishes.

In other instances, however, the validity of the threat is less clear. Many clients make vague threats during an intense therapy session. Often such threats are nothing more than blowing off steam. Yet, as we have learned all too well in recent years, such threats sometimes are genuine and purposeful.

The *Tarasoff* Case

By now many social workers are acquainted with what is widely recognized as the red-letter precedent in so-called duty-to-warn and duty-to-protect cases: *Tarasoff v. Board of Regents of the University of California* (1976). In 1969 Prosenjit Poddar, an outpatient at Cowell Memorial Hospital at the University of California at Berkeley, informed his psychologist, Dr. Lawrence Moore, that he was planning to kill an unnamed young woman (easily identified as Tatiana Tarasoff) upon her return to the university from her summer vacation. After the counseling session during which Poddar announced his plan, the psychologist telephoned the university police and requested that they observe Poddar because he might need hospitalization as an individual who was "dangerous to himself or others." The psychologist followed the telephone call up with a letter requesting the help of the chief of the university police.

The campus police took Poddar into custody temporarily but released him based on evidence that he was rational; the police also warned Poddar to stay away from Tarasoff. At that point Poddar moved in with Tarasoff's brother in an apartment near where Tarasoff lived with her parents. Shortly thereafter the psychologist's supervisor and the chief of the department of psychiatry, Dr. Harvey Powelson, asked the university police to return the psychologist's letter, ordered that the letter and the psychologist's case notes be destroyed, and directed that no further action be taken to hospitalize Poddar. No one warned Tarasoff or her family of Poddar's threat. Poddar never returned to treatment. Two months later he killed Tatiana Tarasoff.

Tarasoff's parents sued the Board of Regents of the university, several employees of the student health service, and the chief of the campus police, along with four of his officers, because their daughter was never notified of the threat. A lower court in California dismissed the suit on the basis of sovereign immunity for the multiple defendants and the psychotherapist's need to preserve confidentiality. The parents appealed, and the California Supreme Court upheld the appeal and later reaffirmed the appellate court's decision that failure to protect the intended victim was irresponsible. The California Supreme Court ultimately held that a mental health professional who knows that a client plans to harm another individual has a duty to protect the intended victim. In the oft-cited words of the California Supreme Court,

> We recognize the public interest in supporting effective treatment of mental illness and in protecting the rights of patients to privacy and the consequent public importance of safeguarding the confidential character of psychotherapeutic communication. Against this interest, however, we must weigh the public interest in safety from violent assault. . . . We conclude that the public policy favoring protection of the confidential character of patient-psychotherapist communications must yield to the extent to which disclosure is essential to avert danger to others. The protective privilege ends where the public peril begins. (551 P.2d 334 at 336–37)

This landmark case was ultimately settled out of court for an undisclosed sum of money.

Tarasoff's Legacy

Since *Tarasoff* a number of important duty-to-protect and duty-to-warn cases have clarified the thinking of courts and legislatures about the circumstances under which mental health professionals should be obligated to disclose confidential information against clients' wishes. Some cases embrace and reinforce the court's reasoning in *Tarasoff*. Others challenge, extend, or otherwise modify the conclusions contained in the *Tarasoff* opinion. For example, in *McIntosh v. Milano* (1979) Lee Morgenstein, a patient of Dr. Michael Milano's, killed Kimberly McIntosh, a girl with whom Morgenstein once had had a relationship but who no longer wanted to be involved with him. Morgenstein had entered treatment with Dr. Milano at the age of fifteen; Morgenstein's parents had been referred to Dr. Milano by a school psychologist because of their son's drug use. In treatment Morgenstein had discussed how overwhelmed he was by his relationship with McIntosh and his intense feelings of jealousy since McIntosh had become involved with another boyfriend. Morgenstein had threatened McIntosh on a number of occasions, by firing a gun at her or her boyfriend's car and verbally threatening her and her dates. In addition, Morgenstein had brought a knife into a therapy session and had discussed fantasies of violent retribution against people who frightened him. Morgenstein was believed to have shot a BB gun at the home of McIntosh's parents.

One day Morgenstein approached McIntosh, forced her to enter his car, took her to a park, and shot her.

In suing Dr. Milano, McIntosh's parents argued that by not warning their daughter the therapist departed from the standard of care in the profession. An expert witness, a psychiatrist, supported the parents' position.

The defense argued that the *Tarasoff* guidelines should not be applied because the state of New Jersey did not have a duty-to-warn statute. In particular the defense maintained that

> there is no such duty by a therapist to third parties or potential victims, and that *Tarasoff* II should not be applied, and was wrongly decided in that it (a) imposes an "unworkable" duty on therapists to warn another of a third person's dangerousness when that condition cannot be predicted with sufficient reliability; (b) will interfere with effective treatment by eliminating confidentiality; (c) may deter therapists from treating potentially violent patients in light of possible malpractice claims by third persons; and (d) will result in increased commitments of patients to mental or penal institutions. (*McIntosh v. Milano*, 403 A.2d 500 at 505–6 [1979], cited in Austin, Moline, and Williams 1990:98]

Consistent with *Tarasoff*, however, the New Jersey Superior Court held that a therapist "may have a duty to take whatever steps are reasonably necessary to protect an intended or potential victim of his patient when he determines, or should determine, in the appropriate factual setting and in accordance with the standards of his profession that the patient is or may present a probability of danger to that person" (cited in Schutz 1982:56).

The logic of *Tarasoff* was also reinforced in *Davis v. Lhim* (1983). Dr. Yong-Oh-Lhim, a staff psychiatrist at Northville State Mental Hospital (Michigan), was sued by Ruby Davis, administrator of the estate of Mollie Barnes. Barnes, who was shot and killed by her son, John Patterson, had not been warned of a threat against her. Patterson had committed himself to the state hospital voluntarily several different times during a three-year period. His problems included depression, insomnia, and schizophrenia. On September 2, 1975, Patterson asked Dr. Lhim to release him from the hospital. Dr. Lhim complied and released Patterson to the custody of his mother. Patterson ended up staying with his aunt, Ruby Davis, because his mother was visiting her brother, Clinton Bell. As time passed, however, the mother found her son too hard to handle and drove him to Bell's home. Patterson entered the Bell home, found a handgun, and began shooting it. Patterson shot and killed his mother, Mollie Barnes, when she tried to take the gun from him.

The court concluded that Mollie Barnes was a foreseeable victim because Dr. Lhim knew of a threat Patterson had made against her. The Wayne Circuit Court found in favor of the plaintiff.

The *Tarasoff* decision also clearly influenced the outcome of *Chrite v. United States* (1983). In this case a Veterans Administration (V.A.) hospital in Michigan was sued by Warner Chrite, who alleged that no one had warned his wife, Catherine, about a threat posed by a V.A. patient, Henry O. Smith. Smith was released from the hospital under a state law that does not permit a patient to remain under supervision, without court permission, for more than sixty days. On the day he was released Smith wrote a note stating, "Was Henry O. Smith Here Yesterday. He is wanted for murder Mother in Law." Hospital staff recorded the note in Smith's chart but did not warn his mother-in-law, Catherine Chrite. Smith carried out his threat after being released. The court ruled in favor of Warner Chrite, concluding that hospital staff had an obligation to warn Catherine Chrite about the threat. Because of the details in the note, the court ruled, Catherine Chrite should have been considered a foreseeable victim.

Tarasoff also had a direct influence in *Jablonski v. United States* (1983). In this case the Veterans Administration Hospital in Loma Linda, California, was sued by Meghan Jablonski in the death of her mother, Melinda Kimball. Kimball was killed by Phillip Jablonski, her son-in-law, who was a patient at the hospital at the time of the slaying. Phillip Jablonski had gone to the V.A. hospital voluntarily for a psychiatric examination, after threatening Isobel Pahls, Kimball's mother, with a knife and attempting to rape her. The police spoke with the head of psychiatric services at the hospital and informed him of Phillip Jablonski's criminal record, including his obscene telephone calls to Pahls, and encouraged the medical staff to place Phillip Jablonski in an inpatient unit. In addition, Kimball informed another physician that Phillip Jablonski had once been convicted in a rape, had a prison record, and said that four days earlier Phillip Jablonski had attempted to rape her mother. The court found the government liable, saying that the staff should have concluded, based on the information and prior records available, that Kimball was a foreseeable victim.

The ruling in *Mavroudis v. Superior Court* (1980) further spelled out that the danger of violence to others must be an "imminent threat of serious danger to a readily identifiable victim" in order to justify a duty to warn. In *Thompson v. County of Alameda* (1980) the courts narrowed the requirement even further by suggesting that a duty to warn exists only when there are specific threats to identifiable victims. In this case a chronic juvenile sex offender, "James," informed authorities that he intended to kill whatever child he next accosted. In spite of this a juvenile counselor, who was also a licensed therapist, released the youngster, who ultimately carried out his threat. The parents of the slain youth, a five-year-old boy, sued the county authorities, alleging negligence because a dangerous juvenile was released into the community; they further claimed that supervision of James's legal custodian (his mother) was improper and that neither the local police, the neighborhood parents, nor James's mother had been warned of his violent tendencies. The court ruled that because the county officials could not have identified and warned a specific victim, the county had no duty to protect the child who was killed. The Superior Court of Alameda County dismissed the case, and the plaintiffs appealed. The Supreme Court of California affirmed the superior court's decision (Austin, Moline, and French 1990:100).

The courts further stressed the importance of foreseeable harm and an identifiable victim in *Leedy & Leedy v. Hartnett & Veterans Administration Hospital* (1981). Harrison and Gertrude Leedy sued the Veterans Administration hospital in Lebanon, Pennsylvania, after no one warned them that a patient, John Hartnett, had a tendency to get violent when drinking. Hartnett, a disabled veteran who received treatment at the hospital between 1956 and 1978, had been diagnosed as a paranoid schizophrenic and chronic alcoholic. Hospital staffers apparently were familiar with Hartnett's violent tendencies during at least a ten-year period. On September 26, 1977, Hartnett discharged himself from the hospital and told hospital staffers he would be staying with the Leedys. On March 31, 1978, Hartnett and the Leedys went to a club to celebrate Hartnett's birthday. Hartnett drank twenty-four 12-ounce bottles or cans of beer. Early the next morning, at 2 A.M., Hartnett beat the Leedys at the Leedys' home.

The Leedys sued the hospital, claiming negligence because no one warned them of Hartnett's violent tendencies. The hospital argued that it could not be held responsible for Hartnett's actions because he never informed the staff of his intent to harm the Leedys. The court ruled in favor of the hospital, concluding that the Leedys were in no greater danger than anyone else who came into contact with Hartnett. The court ruled that Hartnett did not make *specific* threats at the time of discharge and his actions therefore were not foreseeable (Austin, Moline, and French 1990:101).

The Colorado courts used similar reasoning when they dismissed *Brady v. Hopper* (1983), in which victims of John Hinckley's assault on President Ronald Reagan sued, alleging negligence. Hinckley had been brought to Dr. John Hopper by his parents after Hinckley attempted to commit suicide. During his treatment with Dr. Hopper, Hinckley never specifically mentioned his intention to kill the president. Moreover, the defense argued, Hinckley had no history of violence and no previous hospitalizations because of violence. The court determined that Hinckley's therapist, Dr. Hopper, did not have a duty to protect the victims because Hinckley did not make explicit threats against these specific victims (Meyer, Landis, and Hays 1988:44).

The absence of specific threats against victims also influenced the decision in *Cairl et al. v. State of Minnesota et al.* (1982). In this case Steven J. Cairl, who was the owner of a small apartment building, sued the state of Minnesota, the Ramsey County Welfare Department, and Bruce Hedge, the community reentry facilitator at the Minnesota Learning Center, because residents of the building, including Mary Ann Connolly and her two daughters, were not warned of Connolly's son's dangerous tendencies. Tom Connolly, a resident at the Minnesota Learning Center who had an IQ of 57, was released to his family's home for the Christmas holiday; such home visits were consistent with the center's treatment philosophy. Learning Center staffers knew that Tom Connolly had set fires but concluded that "the fires Mr. Connolly had set while at the center were not sufficient to cause concern" (Austin, Moline, and Williams 1990:107). Mary Ann Connolly had been informed of the home visit plan, and on December 21, 1977, Hedge drove Tom Connolly to her home. On December 23, 1977, Tom Connolly set fire to the living room couch; one of his sisters was severely burned, another died of her injuries, and Cairl's property was destroyed.

At the initial trial in the District Court of Ramsey County the court ruled that the hospital staff was not negligent in failing to warn the building's residents because Tom Connolly had not specifically stated that he would injure any of them; further, the court concluded, Mary Ann Connolly was aware of her son's firesetting history. The plaintiffs appealed the district court ruling, which was affirmed by the Supreme Court of Minnesota (see also *Perreira v. State* 1989; *Schuster v. Altenberg* 1988; and *Naidu v. Laird* 1988).

The absence of a specific threat also influenced the outcome of *Rogers v. South Carolina Dept. of Mental Health* (1989). A woman had been admitted to psychiatric hospitals on nine occasions. She had a substantial record suggesting a longstanding delusion of persecution by her family. After her release from one of her hospitalizations, the woman claimed that her sister was trying to poison her. Two weeks later she shot and killed her sister. The personal representative of the sister's estate filed a wrongful death suit against the patient's psychiatrist, alleging that the doctor had a duty to warn the sister that the patient might harm her. The appeals court concluded in part that because there was no evidence that the patient had made specific threats against her sister while being treated by the psychiatrist, the psychiatrist had no duty to warn the sister ("Psychiatrist Did Not Owe Duty to Warn," 1989:3).

At least one case (*Currie v. United States* 1986) suggests that therapists may have a duty to commit to hospitalization potentially dangerous clients in an effort to protect potential victims. In this case a patient at a V.A. outpatient clinic who was in treatment to address post-traumatic stress syndrome threatened to blow up a building owned by IBM, his former employer. The therapist involved in the case believed that the patient posed a threat and contacted IBM officials, the FBI, local police officials, and the U.S. attorney's office. The therapist did not, however, believe that the patient met the commitment criteria under North Carolina law. Some time later the patient took homemade explosives and a gun to an IBM office and killed an employee.

The victim's estate sued the V.A., claiming that it had not warned all potential victims and alleging negligence in not seeking the man's commitment. The defense argued that the duty to protect did not pertain because the victim was one of many IBM employees and hence could not have been identified. The defense also argued that there was no duty to commit because the patient did not meet the involuntary commitment criteria. In an important ruling the U.S. District Court held that patients who act out at random or in only broadly predictable ways do in fact create a duty for therapists. The court also ruled that the therapist wrongly interpreted the state's commitment criteria and that the patient was indeed committable (Meyer, Landis, and Hays 1988:45–46).

These findings contrast, however, with the rulings in *Lipari & the Bank of Elkhorn v. Sears, Roebuck & Co. & the United States* (1980). The plaintiff, Ruth Ann Lipari, sued Sears, Roebuck because a psychiatric patient, Ulysses L. Cribbs, had bought a gun at one of its stores; also named in the suit was the federal government because Cribbs was a patient at a V.A. hospital. One night Cribbs entered an Omaha nightclub and fired shots into the room, killing Dennis Lipari and seriously wounding Ruth Ann Lipari. Once the suit was filed, Sears, Roebuck and Ruth Ann Lipari sued the V.A. hospital because Cribbs had not been detained or committed. Court papers disclosed that Cribbs had been committed to a mental institution and started treatment in a day program at the V.A. hospital approximately two months before the shooting. The court denied the government's motion for a summary judgment and agreed with the plaintiffs' argument that the Veterans Administration was negligent by virtue of failing to commit Cribbs.

In recent years many states have adopted the guidelines, in the form of statutes, established in *Tarasoff* and other duty-to-warn or duty-to-protect cases (Kopels and Kagle 1993). However, a Maryland court did not accept the reasoning in *Tarasoff* in *Shaw v. Glickman* (1980). In this case Leonard Billian, his wife Mary Ann, and her lover, Dr. Daniel Shaw, were all in treatment with a team led by Dr. Leonard Gallant (Glickman was named as a defendant because he was the personal representative of the estate of the late Dr. Gallant.) After learning of the affair between his wife and Shaw (Shaw, a dentist, and Mary Ann Billian were both nude and asleep in the same bed when Leonard Billian entered Shaw's home at 2 A.M.), Leonard Billian shot Shaw five times. The plaintiff, Shaw, argued that Gallant, the team leader, was negligent because Shaw had not been warned of Leonard Billian's "unstable and violent condition and the foreseeable and immediate danger that it presented to Dr. Shaw." The Superior Court of Baltimore City ruled in the defendant's favor—concluding that Dr. Gallant did not have a duty to warn—and granted the defendant a summary judgment. This decision was appealed by Shaw. The appellate court affirmed the lower court decision, concluding that because Leonard Billian never stated his intent to kill or injure Shaw and Shaw assumed the risk of injury when he went to bed with Mary Ann Billian, Gallant did not have a duty to warn. Moreover, the court argued that it would have been "a violation of the statute for Dr. Gallant or any member of his psychiatric team to disclose to Dr. Shaw any propensity on the part of Billian to invoke the old Solon law and shoot his wife's lover" (cited in Schutz 1982:57).

A Florida court, too, apparently challenged the *Tarasoff* doctrine in *Boynton v. Burglass* (1991). In this case the plaintiff sued a psychiatrist, alleging that the psychiatrist had a duty to warn and did not do so. The plaintiff's son was killed by a patient of the psychiatrist. The suit alleged that the psychiatrist had a duty to warn the intended victim, the victim's family, or law enforcement officials of the threat of violence and that the slaying resulted from the breach of that duty. The suit stated that the patient had threatened to kill the plaintiff's son during a therapy session.

The Florida trial court dismissed the suit because it failed to state a claim (i.e., the plaintiff failed to set forth sufficient facts to entitle recovery against the defendant, should the plaintiff win the case); the plaintiffs appealed. The appellate court affirmed the trial court's decision, concluding that "it would be fundamentally unfair to impose a duty to warn upon psychotherapists because psychiatry is an inexact science and a patient's dangerousness cannot be predicted with any degree of accuracy" (cited in "Psychotherapist Has No Duty to Warn," 1992:3). In addition, the appellate court concluded that the psychiatrist would have violated both his duty to his patient and Florida's statutory psychotherapist-patient privilege had he disclosed the patient's alleged threat to harm the victim. The court opinion also expressed concern about the possibility that patients' trust and confidence would be undermined if a clinician were required to warn potential victims whenever a patient expressed hostile feelings toward a third party.

Courts have been reluctant to extend the *Tarasoff* reasoning to cases involving suicide. In *Bellah v. Greenson* (1978), for instance, a therapist's patient committed suicide and the family members claimed they should have been warned of this possibility. The court held, however, that the clinician had no duty to warn unless there was a risk of "violent assault to others" (cited in Meyer, Landis, and Hays 1988:43). Although the ruling did not conclude that therapists *cannot* provide such warnings, it did assert that therapists are not *required* to violate confidentiality.

Clearly, the *Tarasoff* decision unleashed considerable debate and controversy concerning the limits of clients' right to confidentiality. Proponents argue that it is naïve to believe that the right to confidentiality is inviolable. Public safety, they assert, sometimes needs to trump privacy rights, particularly when a third party is at risk of serious or violent harm.

Critics, however, argue that *Tarasoff*-like guidelines are like the camel's nose under the tent. Once the perimeter has been compromised, the entire structure is at risk. One commonly cited concern is that mental health practitioners have relatively poor records of predicting clients' violent behavior (Kopels and Kagle 1993; Schutz 1982:55, 59–60). Thus, it makes little sense to base a practitioner's obligation to disclose confidential information to protect third parties on the assumption that professionals are in fact able to predict future violence accurately. Grossman (1978) has been one of the most ardent critics. Referring to the California court that handed down the *Tarasoff* decision, Grossman states,

> The court also keeps using statements such as "to *predict* that Poddar presented a serious danger of violence . . . [and] did in fact *predict* that Poddar *would* kill." It indicates that the *amicus* brief introduced by national professional organizations did bring to their attention from the authoritative source of the treating professions that therapists can *not* predict a violent act. The statistics of studied experiences ran approximately one eventual violent act out of 100 "predictions." None of these studies compared these to the average population incidence of violence. Nor was mention made that therapists can detect thought and emotional processes having a violence theme. At times they may detect a weakening of the ordinary restraints that keep such themes from overt expression, but they certainly cannot predict the future external events that may trigger such an increased weakening of control of the violent emotion or thought that leads to either a verbal or physical assault. They cannot predict whether an act that may take place, should control break, will be verbally or physically assaultive. (pp. 159–60)

In addition, critics question the assumption that providing a warning to a potential victim is likely to, in and of itself, prevent a violent act. According to Grossman, the belief that such warnings are likely to provide real protection to potential victims is naïve:

Approximately 50 people interested in *Tarasoff* were informally asked, "If you were warned under these circumstances—a psychiatric patient on the loose, who had threatened your life during therapy—how would you protect yourself?" Most first answered, "I'd call the police." When told of the above cases [where warnings seemed not to be effective], they gave one of these replies: "I would hate going into hiding"; "I don't know"; and "I'd kill him if he came near." The warning offers no protection and may well harm the supposed victim. (1978:163)

Balancing Confidentiality and Protection

The various duty-to-protect cases that have been litigated over the years have helped to clarify the precarious trade-offs between social workers' obligation to respect clients' right to confidentiality and their simultaneous duty to protect third parties from harm. Although some rulings in these cases are inconsistent and contradictory, the general trend suggests that ordinarily four conditions should be met to justify disclosure of confidential information to protect a third party from harm. First, the social worker should have evidence that the client poses a threat of *violence* to a third party. As the court said in *Tarasoff*, "[W]hen a therapist determines, or pursuant to the standards of his profession should determine, that his patient presents a serious danger of violence to another, he incurs an obligation to use reasonable care to protect the intended victim against such danger" (17 Cal. 3d 425 at 431). Although courts have not provided precise definitions of *violence*, the term ordinarily implies the use of force—by use of a gun, knife, or other deadly weapon—to inflict harm.

Second, the social worker should have evidence that the violent act is *foreseeable*. That is, the social worker should be able to present evidence that suggests significant risk that the violent act will occur. Although courts recognize that social workers, and other human service professionals, cannot make foolproof predictions, social workers must be able to demonstrate that they had good reasons for believing that their client was likely to carry out the violent act.

Third, the social worker should have evidence that the violent act is *imminent*. That is, the social worker should be able to present evidence that the act was impending or likely to occur relatively soon. Here, too, the courts have not provided clear unambiguous guidelines. *Imminence* may be defined differently by different practitioners, ranging from minutes to hours to weeks from the moment of decision. Ultimately, the social worker needs to be able to make a strong case to defend her or his definition of imminence.

4. Finally, a number of court decisions—although not all (see, for example, the discussion of *Lipari v. Sears*)—suggest that a practitioner must be able to identify the probable victim. The rationale here is that disclosure of confidential information against a client's wishes should not occur unless the social worker has specific information about the client's apparent intent. This would include knowledge of an actual potential victim. As M. B. Lewis observes,

> Though not stated in either opinion, it appeared that both *Tarasoff* and *McIntosh* required that there be a particular or readily identifiable potential victim in order to impose liability for negligent failure to warn. In *Thompson v. County of Alameda*, the California Supreme Court clarified this requirement. The *Thompson* court found no cause of action where the threats uttered by a juvenile offender to county officials did not constitute specific threats against particular individuals, but rather, were directed to an entire class. The court concluded that the county could not be liable for negligent failure to warn or to take other steps to protect an entire class of children to whom the juvenile posed a threat. (1986:588–89)

It should be noted, however, that when a social worker can infer the identity of a foreseeable victim from case-related material—even if the client has not specifically named the potential victim—a duty to warn may exist (Austin, Moline, and Williams 1990:119).

The Ambiguity of *Duty to Warn*

Despite the rulings in *Tarasoff* and subsequent duty-to-warn cases, practitioners and lawyers continue to disagree about the wisdom of the general guidelines for disclosing confidential information and about their application to various cases. By now they generally agree that a social worker whose client makes a clear threat to violently injure an identifiable victim within the next several hours has a duty to take steps to protect the potential victim. This may include disclosing confidential information against a client's wishes. Other cases, however, are less clear.

Consider, for example, the case that opened this book, the young man who was HIV-positive and seemed to pose a threat to his partner, who was not aware of his infection. This set of circumstances is complicated, and there has been considerable disagreement about the relevance of the *Tarasoff* and other duty-to-protect guidelines that have evolved since that decision. When the *Tarasoff* case was decided, no one anticipated its eventual application to AIDS cases. In fact, the final *Tarasoff* decision in 1976 preceded by five years the first AIDS case identified in the United States. Since then, however, the debate about the relevance of *Tarasoff* to AIDS cases has been vigorous. Some argue, for example, that *Tarasoff* is not an adequate precedent because people with AIDS may not specifically and explicitly threaten a third party with an act of violence. People who are HIV-positive usually are concerned about their partners and willing to practice safer sex, although they may be unwilling to disclose their HIV-positive status to their partners. In addition, the threat to third parties may not always be imminent, and the victim may not be identifiable (Kain 1988). As Francis and Chin argue,

> Maintenance of confidentiality is central to and of paramount importance for the control of AIDS. Information regarding infection with a deadly virus, sexual activity, sexual contacts and the illegal use of IV drugs and diagnostic information regarding AIDS-related disease are sensitive issues that, if released by the patient or someone involved in health care, could adversely affect a patient's personal and professional life. (1987:1364)

However, some claim that the fact that an HIV-positive individual merely *poses* a threat to another party is sufficient to rely on *Tarasoff* and related cases as precedents (Lamb et al. 1989). As Gray and Harding (1988) conclude, "A sexually active, seropositive individual places an uninformed sexual partner (or partners) at peril, and the situation therefore falls under the legal spirit of the *Tarasoff* case and the ethical tenets of 'clear and imminent danger' " (p. 221).

Although precise unequivocal guidelines governing disclosure of confidential information to protect third parties do not exist, liability risks can be minimized (Austin, Moline, and Williams 1990; Schutz 1982). For example, faced with a client who may pose a threat to a third party, the social worker should

- consult an attorney who is familiar with state law concerning the duty to warn and/or protect third parties (state laws vary on the obligations of mental health professionals; some states have adopted *Tarasoff*-like guidelines, and some have not);
- consider asking the client to warn the victim (unless the social worker believes this contact would only increase the risk);
- seek the client's consent for the social worker to warn the potential victim;
- disclose only the minimum amount necessary to protect the potential victim and/or the public;
- encourage the client to agree to a joint session with the potential victim in order to discuss issues surrounding the threat (unless this might increase the risk);
- encourage the client to surrender any weapons he or she may have;
- increase the frequency of therapeutic sessions and other forms of monitoring;
- be available or have a backup available, at least by telephone;
- refer the client to a psychiatrist if medication might be appropriate and helpful or a psychiatric evaluation appears to be warranted; and
- consider hospitalization, preferably voluntary, if appropriate.

Throughout this process social workers should seek relevant consultation from colleagues who have experience in dealing with dangerous clients and should document this consultation, the nature of their own thinking about the case, and the rationale for whatever decision the social worker ultimately makes.

Most important, clients must be informed at the beginning of service that while the right to confidentiality is ordinarily respected, legal limits do exist. Social workers might consider including a brief explanation of confidentiality limits on an information sheet prepared for clients. The form would provide clients with a summary of agency policy concerning disclosure of confidential information: compliance with the law, the circumstances under which the social worker has a duty to warn or protect, reimbursement policies and legal actions that may require disclosure, and emergencies. Other items on this list might pertain to service hours, fees, instructions in case of emergency, and the fact that success in treatment cannot be guaranteed. Clients might be asked to sign a copy of this document, to be inserted in the client's file, attesting that they read it, understand its content, and were given an opportunity to ask questions.

When a social worker concludes that disclosure is necessary, who should be warned is not always clear. Schutz (1982) offers sage advice in these circumstances:

> Generally, it is suggested that the authorities and/or the intended victim should be warned. Warning the authorities makes the most sense when the intended victims are the patient's children, since a warning to the victim is ordinarily useless, and the child protective agency often has broader powers than the police—who might say that they cannot detain the patient (particularly after a failed commitment) because he has not done anything yet. If one decides to warn the victim—who is naturally shocked and terrified by the news that someone intends to kill him—and if nothing occurs, one could be liable for infliction of emotional distress by a negligent diagnosis. One way to reduce this risk might be to include as a part of the warning a statement of professional opinion about the nature and likelihood of the threat; to recommend that the victim contact the police, an attorney, and a mental health professional for assistance to detain (or try to commit) the patient; to inform the victim of his legal rights; and to offer assistance with the stress of such a situation. (p. 64)

One pitfall of course is that social workers' concern about liability could lead them to overreact. That is, to avoid risk social workers might disclose information too quickly or seek civil commitment of individuals who do not in fact require confinement. Such excessive caution can create its own problems. Unnecessary intrusion and violation of clients' rights can trigger legal claims alleging defamation of character, negligent diagnosis, infliction of emotional distress, false imprisonment, invasion of privacy, and malicious prosecution.

In the end social workers must use their judgment in the tension between protecting clients' right to confidentiality and protecting third parties from harm. Explicit, unambiguous guidelines for these decisions cannot be drawn. As M. B. Lewis notes, "It must, however, be recognized that psychotherapy is an imperfect science. A precise formula for determining when the duty to maintain confidentiality should yield to the duty to warn is, therefore, beyond reach" (1986:614–15). Although court decisions provide some guidance, social workers ultimately must rely on thoughtful judgment based on prudent consultation. After reviewing case law and statutes on the issue, M. B. Lewis goes on to say,

> The acceptance by many jurisdictions of the duty imposed on psychotherapists to warn or take other reasonable steps for the protection of their patients' potential victims, viewed contemporaneously with an increasing recognition that patients have a right to sue for damages for unauthorized disclosure of confidential information, places mental health professionals in an unenviable predicament. *Tarasoff* and its progeny established that persons harmed by individuals undergoing therapy may sue that patient's psychotherapist for negligent failure to protect them from the patients' dangerous propensities. Case law also makes it clear that mental health professionals have duty to maintain the confidential nature of their relationships to those to whom they are rendering treatment. A breach of either duty may result in civil liability. The inquiry that arises out of this conflict is whether therapists can uphold a duty of reasonable care with respect to potential victims while continuing to exercise reasonable care toward their patients. (1986:605–6)

The Concept of Privileged Communication

The *Tarasoff* case and other duty-to-protect cases that have been litigated since *Tarasoff* raise a variety of complex issues concerning the limits of clients' right to privacy, particularly when third parties appear to be at risk. As I noted earlier, privacy and confidentiality are essential ingredients in therapeutic relationships. Nonetheless, we also know clients' rights to privacy and confidentiality have limits. Mandatory reporting laws related to child abuse, for instance, are now widely accepted by social workers.

To understand the limits of privacy and confidentiality social workers must be familiar with the doctrine of *privileged communication*. The right of privileged communication—which assumes that a professional cannot disclose confidential information without the client's consent—originated in British common law, under which no "gentleman" could be required to testify against another individual in court. Among professionals the attorney-client relationship was the first to be granted the right of privileged communication. Over time other groups of professionals, such as physicians, psychiatrists, psychologists, and clergy, sought legislation to provide them with this right. Social work is one of the most recent professions to actively seek such legislation (Wilson 1978).

Social workers need to understand the distinction between *confidentiality* and *privilege*. *Confidentiality* refers to the professional norm that information shared by or pertaining to clients will not be shared with third parties. *Privilege* refers to the disclosure of confidential information in court proceedings. As Meyer, Landis, and Hays state,

> The terms confidentiality and privilege, though often confused, actually refer to different legal concepts. Confidentiality refers to the broad expectation that what is revealed in a private or "special" relationship based upon trust will not be shared with third parties. Obviously, the kind of information revealed by individuals in therapy fits into this category. Privilege is a narrower concept that concerns the admissibility of information in a court of law, though in practice it really refers to whether courts may legitimately compel revelation of confidential information for the purpose of legal proceedings. (1988:51–52)

Various groups of professionals have argued that they and their clients or patients must be protected by statutes from requests to reveal confidential information. As a result many states have

enacted legislation that permits practitioners to withhold information shared by a client in confidence.

Four conditions, originally proposed by the jurist John Henry
Wigmore, are commonly accepted as necessary in order to consider information privileged:

1. the communication must originate in a confidence that it
   will not be disclosed;
2. the element of confidentiality must be essential to the full
   and satisfactory maintenance of the relationship between the
   parties;
3. the relation must be one which in the opinion of the community ought to be sedulously fostered; and
4. the injury that would inure to the relation by the disclosure
   of the communication must be greater than the benefit thereby gained for the correct disposal of litigation. (Wigmore
   1961:52)

Regarding the first condition, social workers can reasonably
assume that most clients expect that information they share will
be kept confidential. As Hamilton (1951) argued,

> It is part of the attributes of a profession that the nature of the confi-
> dential relationship assumes significance. In lay intercourse inti-
> mate things are told at the teller's own risk. Under authoritative
> external pressures or prosecution it is assumed that a person is not
> obliged to incriminate himself, but in law, medicine, and religion it
> is imperative for successful treatment that the person put himself
> unreservedly into the hands of his counselor or practitioner or priest.
> In a general way this is true of social work, and as professional com-
> petence has increasingly developed skill in the interviewing process,
> the client tends to yield himself fully, trusting in the worker's under-
> standing and skill to help him. (p. 39)

Further, a central tenet of social work practice is that effective
casework depends on clients' willingness to trust workers with
the most personal details of their lives and that such trust is necessary for, as Wigmore's second condition states, "the full and
satisfactory maintenance of the relationship between the parties." In addition, the assumption that relations between clients
and practitioners are important and valuable is generally accept-

ed by the community at large, thus satisfying Wigmore's third condition. The fourth condition, that the injury caused by disclosure of confidential information is greater than the benefit gained from disclosure, is ordinarily the most difficult to satisfy and triggers the greatest debate:

> Against these facts and speculation as to the harm that results from forced disclosure and the frequency with which disclosure occurs, society's interest in the correct disposal of litigation must be balanced. That interest is obviously great, but does not seem to have a constant value, i.e., society as a whole has a greater interest in the correct disposal of a charge of murder than it has in a charge of peace disturbance arising from a marital quarrel. Thus the answer to Wigmore's fourth requirement can be viewed as depending upon the facts of a particular case rather than a predetermined evaluation. For example, the correct disposal of the murder charge probably outweighs any injury that would inure to the social worker-client relation. But the desirability of preserving a marriage of thirty years seems to override the benefit which would be gained by the correct disposal of the charge of peace disturbance. ("Note: Social Worker-Client Relationship," 1965, cited in Wilson 1978:114–15)

Over the years courts have identified a number of exceptions to the client's right of privileged communication (note that it is the *client* who holds the right, not the practitioner). A number of these exceptions pertain to judicial proceedings, such as when a client introduces in court the fact that she or he has received counseling for emotional problems resulting from an automobile accident that has led to a suit for damages or when a social worker's testimony about a client is required so the social worker can defend against a suit filed by the client. Disclosure of privileged information may also be permissible in cases in which a client threatens to commit suicide, shares information in the presence of a third person, is a minor and is the subject of a custody dispute, is involved in criminal activity or has been abused or neglected, is impaired and may pose a threat to the public (an actively alcoholic airline pilot or bus driver), has not paid his or her fees and a collection agency is retained, threatens to injure a third party, or has informed the social worker about having committed a serious unsolved crime

(Lakin 1988; VandeCreek, Knapp, and Herzog 1988; Wilson 1978).

Cases in which clients admit or confess to commission of a crime can be particularly troublesome. On the one hand social workers may want to avoid undermining clients' trust by disclosing confidential information. After all, many clients seek out social workers in the first place for the express purpose of addressing their guilt feelings and sense of remorse about misdeeds. Practitioners may not want to discourage these constructive efforts. At the same time, however, social workers can understand the legitimate claim by the public that it has a right and need to know who perpetrated serious unsolved crimes.

Although statutes are clear that social workers must disclose information shared by clients concerning child abuse or neglect, they offer less guidance with respect to other crimes committed by clients. In *Missouri v. Beatty* (1989) a psychiatrist's patient admitted during a therapy session that she had robbed a local service station earlier in the day. The psychiatrist placed an anonymous telephone call to the local Crime Stoppers office and without identifying his patient indicated that the offender had been employed at the restaurant where she worked. The Crime Stoppers staff passed this information on to the police, who eventually arrested the patient.

The patient argued in court that her psychiatrist violated her confidentiality rights and that any related evidence should not be admissible. The Missouri appeals court upheld the patient's conviction, ruling that the psychiatrist had not violated the physician-patient privilege because the law creating that privilege applied only to a psychiatrist's in-court testimony ("Psychiatrist's Crime Tip," 1990:1).

In a California case (*California v. Kevin F.* 1989) a resident at a substance abuse treatment facility confessed to his psychotherapist that six months earlier he had set fire to a friend's home, knowing that people were inside, in an attempt to hide evidence of a theft. A friend of the client's mother and her son were seriously injured. Several months later the psychotherapist referred to the confession in a report to the client's probation officer. The client was eventually charged with arson and placed in a juvenile correctional facility. He appealed his adjudication, arguing that disclosure of his confession by the psychotherapist violated the state's privileged communication statute. The appeals court ruled, however, that the confession fell under a statutory exception that permitted disclosure when a psychotherapist had reason to believe an individual posed a danger to himself or others ("No Violation of Confidentiality," 1990:4).

Social workers who facilitate group, couples, or family treatment must be especially alert to privileged communication guidelines. Some professionals argue that a client who discloses information to third parties in group, couples, or family treatment forfeits the right to the privilege (because of the client's willingness to share this information with others). Others argue, however, that this sort of disclosure should not invalidate the privilege. At least one court case (*Minnesota v. Andring* 1984) acknowledges that group therapy does involve an expectation of privacy and that the privilege should apply (Meyer, Landis, and Hays 1988). In a case involving marital therapy (*Cabrera v. Cabrera* 1990), the appeals court rejected the husband's argument that confidential information shared by the wife with the couple's psychologist was not privileged and should have been disclosed in court. The husband had appealed the outcome of divorce and custody proceedings and wanted to introduce the psychologist's testimony to support his arguments. The husband claimed that the disclosures made by the wife occurred during marital counseling rather than psychological counseling and therefore were not privileged. The appeals court held that the wife's communications were privileged and, because she had not waived the privilege, the psychologist could not testify about her sessions with the wife or her sessions with the couple. The court concluded that "it would make no sense . . . to divide visits to a psychologist in a case such as this into marital counseling versus psychological counseling and assign privileged status to the latter but not the former" (cited in Psychologist-Patient Privilege," 1991:5). Because statutes vary from state to state and because case law sometimes is inconsistent, social workers should consult a lawyer to determine the current status of a particular client's right to privileged communication.

Social workers should also be careful to seek clients' permission or a court order before disclosing privileged information.

Otherwise, the social worker might be found liable in violating clients' right to privacy and confidentiality. In *Cutter II v. Brownbridge* (1986) a licensed clinical social worker, Robert Brownbridge, prepared a written document concerning the diagnosis and prognosis of his client, Newell Cutter, in response to a request from the client's former wife. Brownbridge apparently prepared the document in the absence of a subpoena or other court order. Eventually, the document was filed by the client's former wife's attorney as evidence in a dispute between the Cutters concerning visitation rights involving their children. Brownbridge's client sued the social worker, alleging that Brownbridge had violated his constitutional and common law right to privacy, breached an implied covenant of confidentiality, and intentionally inflicted emotional distress. The California Superior Court held that the social worker had "violated his client's right to privacy and confidentiality by voluntarily publishing material concerning his client without first resorting to prior judicial determination" (cited in Austin, Moline, and Williams 1990:70).

Responding to Court Orders

Social workers who are subpoenaed by a court may face a special dilemma concerning the disclosure of privileged information. If the social worker practices in a state in which laws grant the right of privileged communication, avoiding compliance with the subpoena may be easier because the legislature has acknowledged the importance of the privilege. Also, contrary to many social workers' understanding, a legitimate response to a subpoena is to argue that the requested information should not be disclosed or can be obtained from some other source. A subpoena itself does not require a practitioner to disclose information. Instead, a subpoena is essentially a request for information, and it may be without merit. As Grossman has said, "If the recipient knew how easy it was to have a subpoena issued; if he knew how readily the subpoena could demand information when there actually was no legal right to command the disclosure of information; if he knew how often an individual releases information that legally he had no right to release because of intimidation—

he would view the threat of the subpoena with less fear and greater skepticism" (1978:245). Further, Grossman says, "In private discussions attorneys admit that the harassing tactic of using these writs is as important in court contests as the legal 'right to the truth' " (1978:145).

Resisting disclosure of confidential information is appropriate, particularly if social workers believe the information is not essential or if they can argue that the information can be obtained from other sources. According to Wilson (1978),

> When data sought by the court can be obtained through some other source, a professional who has been subpoenaed may not have to disclose his confidential data. If the practitioner freely relinquishes his confidential though non-privileged data with little or no objection, the courts may not even check to see if the information can be obtained elsewhere. If the professional resists disclosure, however, the court may investigate to see if it can get the data from some other source. (1978:138)

Social workers should be aware of various guidelines concerning the service of and response to a subpoena:

- Do not release any information unless you are sure you have been authorized in writing to do so.
- If you do not know whether the privilege has been waived, you must claim the privilege to protect your client's confidentiality.
- Should you employ a registered assistant or trainee, it would be wise to claim the privilege to protect confidentiality even though the court might rule that unlicensed practitioners are not covered by the privilege.
- You need to determine who served you with the subpoena. You need to arrange for any witness and travel fees before going to court.
- At a deposition, where there is no judge, you might have your own attorney present or choose to follow the advice and direction of your client's attorney.
- If you feel your information about your client is embarrassing, damaging, or immaterial, you might consider getting written permission to discuss the situation with your client's attorney.

- Unless you are required to produce records only, and are providing all your client records, you must appear at the location stated in the subpoena. (Austin, Moline, and Williams 1990:18)

Despite a local privileged communication statute and a social worker's attempts to resist a subpoena and disclosure of confidential information, a court of law could formally order the practitioner to reveal this information. For example, in New York state a social worker whose client was presumably protected by the right of privileged communication was ordered to testify in a paternity case after the court ruled that "disclosure of evidence relevant to a correct determination of paternity was of greater importance than any injury which might inure to relationship between social worker and his clients if such admission was disclosed" [*Humphrey v. Norden* 359 N.Y.S.2d 733 at 734 (1974), cited in Wilson 1978:100].

In *Belmont v. California State Personnel Board* (1974), a social worker was suspended from her job at the California Department of Social Welfare for willful disobedience of an order to disclose information to the department concerning her clients. The department had requested the information for inclusion in a new computerized database. The social worker, who had provided services to emotionally disturbed clients who were receiving public assistance, refused to share the information and was suspended for five days without pay. The appellate court ruled that social workers employed in this setting do not have a privilege to refuse to disclose confidential information. The court concluded that "the Department's and the Legislature's purpose to make 'maximum use of electronic data processing' in the handling and storage of welfare recipient information, under the facts embraced by appellants' offer of proof, flouted neither the 'right of privacy' nor other Fourth Amendment principle" (R. J. Cohen 1979:146).

In *in re Lifschutz* (1970) a teacher, Joseph F. Housek, sued John Arabian for damages, alleging that Arabian assaulted him. In a deposition Housek testified that he received counseling services for approximately six months from a psychotherapist, Joseph E. Lifschutz. Dr. Lifschutz, however, refused to testify in response to a subpoena, even with respect to whether he had treated Housek. Dr. Lifschutz claimed that information about any relationship he has with a client is privileged. Both lower and appellate courts ruled that Dr. Lifschutz was in contempt because the psychotherapist privilege in California does not apply when clients introduce to the court proceedings their emotional or mental condition (Grossman 1978). Further, the privilege belongs to the client, not the therapist.

The California Supreme Court refused to hear the case, and Dr. Lifschutz continued to refuse to testify. Eventually, he was jailed for contempt of court. After a hearing on Dr. Lifschutz's challenge of the contempt finding, the California Supreme Court ruled that he was indeed obligated to testify. The court concluded that Dr. Lifschutz's client waived the privilege by openly testifying that he had been treated by Dr. Lifschutz. The court also rejected various arguments presented by Dr. Lifschutz concerning, for example, the extent to which his livelihood would be threatened by disclosure of confidential information and the claim that Dr. Lifschutz did not receive equal protection under the clergy-penitent-litigant act. This case is particularly important because it recognized that no previous cases had applied the patient-litigant exception to the psychotherapist-client privilege (Austin, Moline, and Williams 1990:47).

A mental health clinician was also found in contempt of court for refusing to disclose confidential information in *Caesar v. Mountanos* (1976). Dr. George Caesar, a psychiatrist, was providing treatment to Joan Seebach following injuries she allegedly sustained in an automobile accident. Despite Seebach's willingness to waive in writing the psychotherapist-patient privilege, Dr. Caesar refused to answer a number of questions concerning the relationship between Seebach's emotional condition and the accident. Dr. Caesar contended that disclosure of this confidential information could be harmful to Seebach. The California Court of Appeals affirmed the judgment of the district court, concluding that there needs to be "a proper balance between the conditional right of privacy encompassing the psychotherapist-patient relationship and [California's] compelling need to ensure the ascertainment of the truth in court proceedings" [542 F.2d 1064 at 1070 (9th Cir. 1976), cited in Austin, Moline, and Williams 1990:52–53).

Unique issues can emerge when clients share confidential information with student interns. Social workers must determine whether their state's statutes extend the concept of privileged communication to clients seen by student interns. In *California v. Gomez* (1982) the court concluded that privileged communication pertains only to licensed professionals, not to student interns. This case involved information John Gomez shared with two student interns about his intention to kill a man with whom his wife had become involved. Gomez argued that the trial court erred by allowing the student interns to testify concerning his comments about wanting to kill his wife's lover. Gomez claimed that the psychotherapist-patient privilege should apply. Since the *Gomez* decision, however, the California legislature has passed laws that extend the psychotherapist-patient privilege to some registered interns who are completing their practicum requirements (Austin, Moline, and Williams 1990:55).

Unintentional Disclosure of Confidential Information

Clearly, in many instances social workers have to make a deliberate decision about whether to disclose confidential information to third parties. Cases involving the duty to protect, suicide, child abuse, and fee collection, for instance, sometimes call for difficult judgments about the limits of privacy and the need for others to know details of a client's life.

Far more common, however, are cases in which confidential information about a client is disclosed unintentionally, with no deliberate intent to breach a client's right to privacy. In these instances a social worker typically has simply been absent-minded, careless, or sloppy.

Bev E., a social worker at a local family service agency, had an 11 A.M. appointment to meet with another social worker, Carl F., at a nearby community mental health center. Bev E. and Carl F. were members of a subcommittee of the state NASW chapter charged with planning the chapter's annual meeting. Bev E. and Carl F. agreed to meet in Carl F.'s office to map out details related to the keynote address, workshop topics, scheduling, and so on.

Bev E. arrived at the community mental health center about ten minutes early. She took an elevator to the fourth floor office, walked into the waiting room, and introduced herself to the receptionist. The receptionist told Bev E. that Carl F. would be with her momentarily, offered her a cup of coffee, and invited her to take a seat. Bev E. sat on a nearby chair and began skimming a magazine. Several minutes later one of the center's other social workers walked out of her office and through the waiting room, leaving the agency's suite. The receptionist noticed this other worker and said, "Oh, Mary, Sue Smith called a few minutes ago. She said she won't be able to keep her two-thirty appointment. Apparently she has a child care problem. She said she'd call back to reschedule."

This reminded Bev E. of her own afternoon schedule. She glanced at her appointment book and realized she should call a colleague with whom she was planning to meet that afternoon in order to get driving directions. Bev E. asked the receptionist whether she could use a telephone to make the call. The receptionist said she needed to run down the hall to make a photocopy and invited Bev E. to use her telephone. "Just dial nine for an outside line," the receptionist said.

Bev E. made her telephone call and searched around the desk for note paper on which she could write directions. As she glanced down at the desk, Bev E. noticed an open case record on which the receptionist was working. To avoid staring at the record, Bev E. turned away from the desk, only to find herself staring at a partially typed letter on the receptionist's computer monitor.

At that point Carl F. walked into the waiting room area to greet Bev E. They met in Carl F.'s office to discuss details concerning the upcoming NASW conference. After about twenty minutes Carl F.'s telephone rang. He placed his hand over the mouthpiece and asked Bev E. whether she minded if he took the call. He explained that one of his clients was moving to another state and he was transferring the client to a social worker in that state. Bev E. indicated that he should take the call. Before long Bev E. heard Carl F. give the caller identifying information about the client's age, family circumstances, treatment history, and presenting problems. During the conversation Bev E. also gazed around the office and eventually noticed several case records sitting on top of Carl F.'s desk, with clients' names exposed on the files' labels. As soon as Carl F. hung up the telephone, an exasperated colleague knocked on his door and said he needed to get some advice about the delivery of services to one of the agency's clients, an illegal alien.

After the telephone call Carl F. and Bev E. finished a rough draft of the conference schedule. They walked down the hall to make a photocopy. When Carl F. opened the photocopy machine cover, he found part of a case record that one of his colleagues had left in the machine. While Carl F. made a photocopy of the conference schedule, Bev E. glanced down at the waste basket sitting next to the machine. On top of the pile of discarded paper was a slightly crumpled copy of the face sheet of a client's record. Apparently, it had been copied on the wrong size paper and thrown out.

At that point Carl F. asked Bev E. whether she had time for a quick bite to eat at a nearby deli. Bev E. accepted the offer, and the two proceeded to the building's elevator. When they got on the elevator, they were greeted by three other agency workers, who proceeded to animatedly discuss a case in which they were all involved. Bev E. heard one staffer mention the name of a client involved in the case.

Bev E. and Carl F. then walked to the local deli for lunch. They sat at their table and continued to discuss the upcoming conference. Before long, however, Bev E. could not help but overhear the three staff members who had been on the elevator continuing their discussion of the case while seated at a nearby booth.

After lunch Bev E. went on her way and Carl F. returned to his office. At the end of the day Carl F. gathered two case records he wanted to work on at home, tidied up his desk, and went to catch the 5:15 P.M. bus. On his way home on the bus Carl F. pulled out one case record. As he reviewed it and made some notes, a passenger seated next to him began reading the exposed material, unbeknown to Carl F.

Carl F. continued working on the case when he got home. When his wife got home, Carl F. left the record on the kitchen table, and he and his wife went out to a dinner meeting, leaving their children with a babysitter. While Carl F. and his wife were out, the hungry babysitter sat down at the kitchen table to have a snack. She began flipping through the case record.

At about 9 P.M. that evening a custodian entered Carl F.'s office to empty the trash, straighten the furniture, and dust. As the custodian was dusting Carl F.'s desk, he noticed the name on the case record that Carl F. had left on top of the desk. It was the name of the custodian's second cousin, and the custodian proceeded to sit down and thumb through the record.

Although this case example has been fictionalized, I have witnessed every component of the vignette. My guess is that many details will be familiar to readers.

Unfortunately, daily pressures in social work settings can exacerbate inadvertent disclosures of confidential information. In these instances practitioners mean no harm. They do not make deliberate decisions to violate clients' right to privacy. These breaches of confidentiality are mistakes.

Social workers can take a number of steps to prevent these mistakes and the liability risks they involve. An important step is to provide systematic routine training to all agency staffers. Including professional and nonprofessional staff members (secretaries, clerks, cooks, and maintenance staff in a program) is especially important because both have access to confidential information. Because of the turnover in social service agencies the training on confidentiality should be offered periodically. This produces knowledgeable staff and enhances protection of clients' and staff members' rights, and it provides some measure of protection to the agency because it can demonstrate its efforts to ensure that staff members understand how to handle confidential information. The same recommendation pertains to private practitioners, of course.

Training on confidentiality should include two major components: written material and verbal communication of information related to clients. Written confidential material can take several forms, including such case record items as intake forms, assessment and diagnostic reports, progress notes, insurance forms, and correspondence. Social workers need to be acquainted with guidelines concerning access to case records by (1) third parties outside of the agency (other service providers, insurance companies), (2) staff within the agency, (3) clients, and (4) clients' families, guardians, executors and/or significant others. In general, contents of case records should not be released to parties outside the agency without the client's informed consent (see chapter 3 for a discussion of informed consent procedures). Although some exceptions are permissible (life-threatening emergencies, for example), clients' informed consent ordinarily is essential. Social workers need to be especially careful when asked for confidential material by close friends or colleagues employed in other agencies who may feel entitled to information because of their unique relationship.

Sharing of information between public agencies can also be a special problem. Staffers at a state public welfare department may feel entitled to case record material located in a state child welfare agency when a particular client is involved with both agencies. Unless a clear memorandum of agreement has been negotiated between the agencies, releasing confidential information without the client's consent is inappropriate.

Agency-based social workers must also be careful about releasing confidential information to other staff members *within* the organization. Staffers sometimes mistakenly assume that their mere employment in an agency entitles them to information contained in clients' records. Certainly, in many cases various staff members in an agency should have access to the record. In a community mental health center, for example, giving a variety of professionals access to confidential material may be appropriate.

In some instances, however, access by staff should be limited. On occasion, staff members who are not directly involved in a client's care may be curious about a case, as when an agency is providing services to a celebrity or notorious individual. The governing principle should be that access is provided only to staff members who are involved in the client's case and have a need to know the confidential information in order to carry out their duties. Staffers who cannot satisfy the need-to-know criterion should not have access.

Social workers also need to be clear about clients' rights to their own records. Professionals' thinking about this changed dramatically over time. Once, few practitioners believed clients should be able to examine their own records. Records were typically viewed as agency property and for staffers' eyes only. More recently, however, social workers and other professionals have come to appreciate why clients may need or want to see their records and that such disclosure can indeed have therapeutic value if handled properly. As Wilson (1978) observes,

> Only a few short years ago, the social work profession simply assumed that a record was the private property of the professional or the agency, and that was that. A few therapists occasionally advocated client participation in recording as part of the therapeutic process, and others began using the video-recorded interview as a means of allowing the individual to study how he communicates and to provide feedback regarding the therapist's effectiveness. However, such procedures were considered experimental rather than routine. . . . [T]here will be increasing pressure from consumers (and also as a result of the ethical philosophy of the social work profession) for all settings to be more open in sharing record materials with clients. (pp. 83, 85)

Many agencies and private practitioners have developed policies concerning clients' access to records. Clients may be allowed to have photocopied portions of the record, for instance, or may examine the record while in the presence of a staff person. Such policies often spell out the circumstances in which clients may be denied access, such as when there is reason to believe that the client would be harmed emotionally. In these instances an alternative is to release the information to the client's legal representative. Of course, social workers must be careful not to share the contents of a client's case record with family members, significant others, or guardians without proper consent or legal authorization.

Written information about clients can also be released quite accidentally, as demonstrated by the case example involving Bev. E. Both professional and clerical staff members need to be careful not to leave confidential information on desk tops and conference tables to which others may have visual access; provide visual access to computer monitors that contain confidential information; leave confidential material in a photocopier; discard confidential information in a way that risks exposure (that is, social workers should tear up or shred confidential material before disposing of it); allow passengers on buses, trains, or airplanes to read confidential information over one's shoulder; leave confidential information exposed to family members or visitors at home; or mail material to a client's home with the social worker's name and title on the envelope (unless the client says that he or she is not concerned about this form of disclosure). Many social workers and agencies omit the practitioner's or agency's name from envelopes mailed to a client in order to protect the client's right to privacy.

Widely available technology such as facsimile, or fax, machines also poses special problems. Although the social worker who sends the information may not intend for anyone other than the recipient to read the written communication, fax machines are often located in areas in which others have access to the material. Social workers who fax confidential material should be sure that the recipient is available to retrieve the information immediately and should include a confidentiality notice on the cover sheet. This is one example:

> The documents accompanying this facsimile transmission contain confidential information. The information is intended only for the use of the individual(s) or entity(ies) named above. If you are not the intended recipient, you are advised that any disclosure, copying, distribution, or the taking of any action based on the contents of this information is prohibited. If you have received this facsimile in error, please notify us immediately by telephone at the above number to arrange for return of the original documents.

As the case example also illustrated, inappropriate release of confidential information via verbal communication is a common problem. Unfortunately, a great deal of confidential information is divulged inadvertently when third parties seated in waiting rooms hear staff members greet clients by name; third parties hear staffers discuss clients in a hallway, in a waiting room or elevator, at a social gathering, or in a restaurant or other public facility; and when third parties are seated in social workers' offices while social workers discuss a case on the telephone. Social workers must also be careful to edit the messages they leave at a client's workplace and home.

Answering machines can also pose a problem. Although a practitioner may believe that the client or a professional colleague is the only one who will listen to the confidential message, others may have access to the answering machine. Similarly, social workers should be careful not to discuss confidential information using portable or cordless telephones because scanners have been known to pick up what are essentially radio transmissions from these devices.

Several other circumstances also warrant special attention to confidentiality. In group or marital therapy and family counseling, social workers must be careful to respect clients' wishes concerning the disclosure of confidential information. In several cases social workers have inadvertently divulged confidential information without their clients' consent.

Marriage or couples counseling can pose other problems as well, particularly when one partner contacts the social worker individually and shares confidential information that she or he does not want disclosed to the other partner. Some social workers permit such confidential disclosures, or secrets, and do their best to respect the confidence. Other social workers prohibit such secrets, usually for therapeutic reasons. This is a complicated professional debate, one that I cannot settle here. Suffice it to say that social workers should always be clear ahead of time how they would handle such circumstances, and they should clearly present their policy on this issue to their clients. Those practitioners who permit such secrets ought to share this policy with clients at the beginning of treatment. Clients can then state whether they are comfortable with the arrangement. Social workers who prohibit secrets should inform clients of this policy.

Even such clear policies do not prevent problems, however. In one case a social worker was providing marriage counseling to a couple. The wife was particularly distressed about the husband's drinking and insisted that he seek treatment. To save the marriage the husband sought alcohol treatment and talked about his progress in sessions with his wife and the social worker. Several months after treatment began, the social worker was attending a professional conference at a local hotel and encountered the husband outside the hotel bar. The husband was clearly inebriated.

The husband pleaded with the social worker not to tell his wife about his drunk state. The social worker had to decide whether he had an obligation to share this information with the wife, particularly when the husband refused to do so himself. The social worker felt uncomfortable participating in therapy sessions in which he knew the husband was actively deceiving his wife. The social worker also felt he was colluding with the husband and reinforcing the husband's lying and deception. The social worker resolved the matter by agreeing to work with the husband individually over a four-week period to help the husband acknowledge his problem to his wife during subsequent joint counseling sessions.

A final problem has to do with statements about confidentiality that appear on agencies' or private practitioners' public relations materials, such as brochures, pamphlets, and client's rights statements. Many agencies provide brochures that briefly describe agency services, hours, staff, and fees. Often they contain statements such as this one, which appears on a family service agency brochure: "All counseling sessions are held in strict confidence." In addition, many agencies and practitioners distribute client's rights statements that spell out confidentiality policy among other policies related to civil rights, grievances, medication, fees, and cancellations. The following is a statement that appears on the client's rights statement prepared by a community mental health center:

> Your privacy is very important to us. No one will be told that you are a client at XYZ Agency without your written permission. Your case record is a confidential document and is protected by federal and state laws. It will only be accessible to clinical staff members responsible for your treatment and support personnel as required during normal business hours. During other times, the medical record is secured in a locked room. No information about you will be obtained or given out to anyone, including your family or private doctor, without your written authorization.

After reading the statement on the first agency's brochure and on the second agency's client's rights form, clients might reasonably expect that *everything* they reveal in counseling would be considered confidential. They might be quite surprised to learn of the various exceptions, such as social workers' need to comply with mandatory reporting laws related to child and elder abuse and legal guidelines in cases in which a client threatens to harm third parties (duty-to-protect guidelines). Therefore, clarifying that there are legal limits to clients' right to confidentiality is important. Although spelling out these limits on these documents may not be appropriate, at the very least the statements should state that such limits exist. I advise adding a phrase along the lines of "All information in your record will be considered confidential *to the extent permitted by law.*" At an appropriate time early in the relationship, social workers should spell out, as gently and diplomatically as possible, the nature of these limits.

In sum, formulating comprehensive policies to prevent inappropriate disclosure of confidential information is important. Such policies should address a variety of topics and issues, including

1. disclosure of information over the telephone and fax machine;
2. access to agency facilities and clients by outsiders (for example, to attend meetings or participate in a tour);
3. physical safeguarding of records;
4. record retention and destruction;
5. access to client records by staff, clients, significant others, and legal representatives;
6. disclosure of information to outside agencies;
7. audio and video recording of clients;
8. photocopying of confidential information;
9. display of confidential information on computer terminals in public or semipublic areas;
10. discussion of confidential information in waiting rooms, hallways, offices, elevators, and other public and private settings;
11. use of answering machines and cordless or portable telephones;
12. statements concerning confidentiality on agency brochures and documents; and
13. disclosure of confidential information to the news media and law enforcement officials.

Social workers can consult a variety of documents to help them formulate confidentiality policies, including state and federal laws, accreditation standards, union policies, licensing regulations, agency policies, insurance company policies on disclosure, professional literature, and codes of ethics.

Clearly, respect for clients' rights to privacy and confidentiality is among the most enduring of social work values. Privacy and confidentiality are essential ingredients in effective social work practice. Practitioners know, however, that various circumstances may warrant or require disclosure of confidential information. In other instances social workers may disclose confidential information unintentionally or inadvertently. Awareness of the various ways in which confidentiality can be breached appropriately and inappropriately can help social workers avoid liability risks.

3 | Service Delivery: Improper Treatment

Social workers provide a wide variety of services in a wide variety of settings. Practitioners who work in family service agencies, community mental health centers, psychiatric hospitals, and private practice provide individual, family, and group counseling. Social workers in public social service agencies—such as mental health, child welfare, public assistance, corrections, and elderly affairs departments—may be involved in casework, program evaluation, and administration. Social workers in local grassroots agencies may be involved in advocacy, community organizing, and needs assessments.

Fortunately, most social workers are competent professionals who provide sound interventions. Unfortunately, on occasion liability claims are filed against social workers alleging that their interventions were somehow flawed. Ordinarily, these claims allege that the social worker's intervention departed from the standard of care in the profession. The claimant, often a client or family member, sometimes alleges that the social worker carried out his or her duties in a negligent or illegal fashion (acts of misfeasance or malfeasance) and sometimes that the social worker

2

failed to carry out her or his duties (acts of nonfeasance). Whatever the setting and whatever the practice method, social workers need to be concerned about the malpractice and liability risks associated with flawed treatment.

Statistically, most malpractice and liability claims alleging improper treatment stem from some sort of direct practice, that is, social work with individuals, families, or treatment groups. Some claims also involve social work administration, usually related to personnel matters. Relatively rarely, malpractice and liability claims pertain to community organizing and research.

The focus in this chapter is primarily on malpractice and liability risks related to direct practice. In particular, the chapter discusses risks related to informed consent, assessment and intervention, undue influence, suicide, commitment proceedings, protective services, and defamation of character.

Informed Consent

Social workers have always recognized the central importance of clients' consent, whether to services, release of information, medication, or audio/video recording. Because of social workers' longstanding commitment to the principle of client self-determination, informed consent has been a centerpiece of professional practice (Bernstein 1960; Keith-Lucas 1963; Perlman 1965; McDermott 1975; Reamer 1987c).

The historical roots of informed consent have been traced to Plato, who in *Laws* compares the Greek slave-physician who gives orders "in the brusque fashion of a dictator" with the free physician who "takes the patient and his family into confidence . . . [and] does not give prescriptions until he has won the patient's support" (quoted in President's Commission 1982:5). The medieval French surgeon Henri de Mondeville also stressed the importance of obtaining a patient's consent and confidence, although he also urged his colleagues to "compel the obedience of his patients" by selectively slanting information provided to them (President's Commission 1982:4–5).

By the late eighteenth century European and American physicians and scientists, such as Condorcet, Mirabeau, Cabanis, Volney, Chaussier, Virey, Rush, Gregory, and Young, had begun to develop a tradition that encouraged professionals to share information and decision making with their clients. The first major legal ruling in the United States on informed consent is found in the 1914 landmark case of *Schloendorff v. Society of New York Hospital*, in which Judge Benjamin Cardozo, then on the New York Court of Appeals, set forth his oft-cited opinion concerning an individual's right to self-determination: "Every human being of adult years and sound mind has a right to determine what shall be done with his own body" (cited in Pernick 1982:28–29). To do otherwise, Cardozo argued, is to commit an assault upon the person.

Revelations that followed World War II of medical experiments performed without consent of the subjects and that followed the civil rights movements of the 1960s helped form the foundation for current informed-consent legislation and guidelines. The red-letter event during this era was the 1957 case of *Salgo v. Leland Stanford Jr. University Board of Trustees*, in which the phrase *informed consent* was introduced. The plaintiff in this case, who became a paraplegic following a diagnostic procedure for a circulatory disturbance, alleged that his physician did not properly disclose ahead of time pertinent information regarding risks associated with the treatment.

Although the concept of informed consent has its origins in medicine and health care, it has recently been applied legislatively, judicially, and administratively to a wide range of other client groups. Social workers regularly provide services to such client groups as the mentally ill and retarded, minors, elderly, hospital patients, prisoners, and research subjects. In agencies that provide mental health services, for example, social workers must be familiar with consent requirements related to voluntary and involuntary commitment and the rights of institutionalized and outpatient clients regarding the use of psychotropic medication, restraints, aversive treatment measures, isolation, sterilization, and psychosurgery (Schutz 1982).

Social workers in agencies that serve children must keep pace with rapidly changing standards regarding consent of minors. Consent issues arise in relation to abortion counseling, contraception, treatment of sexually transmitted diseases, mental health services, substance abuse treatment, and foster care. In

Dymek v. Nyquist (1984), for example, a father had been awarded custody of his nine-year-old son. His former wife took the boy
to a psychiatrist, who treated him for one year without his
father's knowledge and consent. The suit alleged that the psychiatrist knew the mother was not the custodial parent and that
permission to treat had not been obtained from the court. The
court found in the plaintiff's favor, ruling that the psychiatrist
had no authority to provide psychotherapy to the child (Austin,
Moline, and Williams 1990:187).

Traditionally, minors have not been considered capable of
giving informed consent or entering into contracts; the consent
of parents or someone standing in loco parentis has typically
been required, unless it is a genuine emergency (Cowles 1976;
Rozovsky 1984). Especially since the 1970s, however, a number
of states have begun to recognize the concepts of *mature* or
emancipated minors, which imply that certain minors are in
fact capable of providing their own consent in their relationships with professionals. *Mature minors* are those who are
"judicially recognized as possessing sufficient understanding
and appreciation of the nature and consequences of treatment
despite their chronological age" (Rozovsky 1984:240). *Emancipated minors* are those who have obtained the legal capacity of
an adult because they are self-supporting, living on their own,
married, or in the armed forces.

States vary considerably in the extent to which they grant
minors autonomy and the right to consent. For example, with
respect to abortion services, substance abuse treatment, dispens-
ing contraceptives, and treatment of sexually transmitted diseases, some states permit professionals to treat minors without
obtaining parental consent; some require that parents be notified, that their consent be obtained, or both; and some merely
permit agency staff members to notify parents, obtain their consent, or both. State laws also are different in the extent to which
parental consent is required to place a child in an inpatient or
outpatient mental health program.

Consent issues related to the care of medical patients have
received considerable attention recently, especially regarding the
care of hospital patients and their right to die, be informed of
medical risks, refuse treatment on religious grounds, consent to

experimental treatment, participate in research, and donate organs. Once again states vary considerably in the amount of autonomy they grant patients and the procedures health-care staff members are expected to follow when patients fail to provide consent or request controversial treatment. In the famous *Quinlan* case (1976), the Supreme Court of New Jersey required hospital staff to consult with a hospital ethics committee, rather than a court of law, concerning the decision to remove extraordinary treatment. However, in *Superintendent of Belchertown v. Saikewicz* (1977) the Massachusetts Supreme Judicial Court rejected the New Jersey approach, with its reliance on administrative procedures, in favor of court approval of decisions concerning life-prolonging care of incompetent patients.

Debate concerning client consent to participate in research has also received much attention. Discussion has been especially vigorous with respect to clients whose competence to consent is considered questionable or who are considered especially vulnerable. Particular attention has been paid to the right of the mentally ill, elderly, minors, and prisoners to consent to participate in research related to drugs, treatment techniques, and program evaluation (Rozovsky 1984).

Obtaining Valid Consent

Although states and local jurisdictions have different interpretations and applications of informed-consent standards, what constitutes valid consent by clients is agreed upon in light of prevailing legislation and case law. In general for consent to be considered valid six standards must be met: (1) coercion and undue influence must not have played a role in the client's decision; (2) clients must be capable of providing consent; (3) clients must consent to specific procedures or actions; (4) the forms of consent must be valid; (5) clients must have the right to refuse or withdraw consent; and (6) clients' decisions must be based on adequate information (Cowles 1976; President's Commission 1982; Rozovsky 1984).

Absence of coercion and undue influence. Social workers frequently maintain some degree of control over the lives of their

clients. Access to services, money, time, and attention are but a
few of the resources social workers control. That social workers
not take advantage of their positions of authority to coerce a
client's consent, subtly or otherwise, is especially important
(Giordano 1977;Reamer 1979). Practitioners who want clients to
agree to enter or terminate a program, release information to
third parties, participate in a research project, or take medication, for example, need to be aware that clients may be particularly susceptible to influence, which would jeopardize the validity of their consent.

The inappropriate use of coercion is illustrated in *Reif v. Wein-*
berger (1974), in which a judge in the District of Columbia ruled
that the expenditure of federal funds should be enjoined in some
sterilization cases because of the use of coercion. The evidence
in this case indicated that a number of welfare clients had been
coerced into agreeing to sterilization procedures; they had been
told that a portion of their welfare benefits would be withheld
unless they agreed to the proposed procedures.

Capacity to consent. Although professionals widely agree that
only competent clients are capable of giving informed consent,
they are in much less agreement about the determination of
competence. According to Applebaum and Roth (President's
Commission 1982), practitioners must consider the ability of
clients to make choices, comprehend factual issues, manipulate
information rationally, and appreciate their current circumstances. Olin and Olin (President's Commission 1982) argue for
a single standard, the ability to retain information, whereas
Owens (President's Commission 1982) emphasizes the ability to
"test reality." In contrast the President's Commission for the
Study of Ethical Problems in Medicine and Biomedical and
Behavioral Research stated in its prominent 1982 report that
competency is determined by the client's possession of a set of
values and goals, ability to communicate and understand information, and ability to reason and deliberate.

Despite the unsettled debate about determining competence,
practitioners seem to agree that incompetence should not be presumed for any particular client group, such as children, the elderly, the mentally ill, or mentally retarded, except for those who

are unconscious. Rather, clients in some categories—perhaps children or severely retarded adults—should be considered to have a greater *probability* of incapacity. Assessments of a client's capacity should at least consist of such measures as a mental status exam (which accounts for a person's orientation to person, place, time, situation, mood and affect, content of thought and perception), the ability to comprehend abstract ideas and make reasoned judgments, any history of mental illness that might affect current judgment, and the client's recent and remote memory. In instances in which clients are judged incompetent, practitioners should be guided by the principle of *substituted*, or *proxy judgment* (Buchanan and Brock 1989), in which a surrogate attempts to replicate the decision that the incapacitated person would make if able to make a choice (President's Commission 1982). An important point for social workers to consider is that clients whose competence fluctuates may be capable of giving or withdrawing consent during a lucid phase (Rozovsky 1984:18).

Consent to specific procedures. Social service agencies often have clients sign general consent forms at a first or second appointment or at the time of admission to a residential program. In a number of precedent-setting cases, however, clients have challenged in court such blanket consent forms, claiming that they lacked specificity and failed to authorize interventions introduced subsequently. In *Winfrey v. Citizens Southern Natl. Bank* (1979), a woman challenged her physician's authority to perform a complete hysterectomy, based on her consent to an exploratory operation. In *Darrah v. Kite* (1969) the father of a young child challenged a neurosurgeon's authority to conduct a ventriculogram on the child when the consent form referred only to "routine brain tests" and a "workup." Professionals are thus advised not to assume that general consent forms are valid. Rather, consent forms should include specific details that refer to specific activities or interventions. As Rozovsky has observed, "Reliance on a general consent form may be of questionable merit. Courts have been known to examine the circumstances of a specific case to determine whether the general consent was broad enough to permit the treatment in question" (1984:26).

Social workers and agency staff should also refrain from having clients sign blank consent forms; this is a practice occasionally used to avoid having to contact clients in person for their signatures at a later date. If challenged in court, these consent forms might not be considered valid, given the absence of information related to treatment or intervention at the time the clients' signatures were obtained. Having clients sign blank forms clearly violates the spirit of the concept of informed consent.

In addition, the language and terminology that appear on consent forms must be understandable to clients, and clients should be given ample opportunity to ask questions. Practitioners should avoid as much as possible the use of complex and technical jargon. Particular care must be taken with clients who do not have good command of English; social workers should be aware that some clients who are able to speak English reasonably well (expressive language skill) may not be equally capable of understanding the language (receptive language skill). Having access to an interpreter in such instances is important. In addition, social workers should be certain that clients who have auditory or visual impairments are provided with the assistance they need in order to provide informed consent.

Valid forms of consent.   Many states authorize several forms of consent. Consent may be written or verbal, although some states require written authorization. In general, consent obtained verbally is considered valid, providing that all other criteria for valid consent have been met. In addition, consent may be expressed or implied. *Expressed consent* entails explicit authorization by a client for a specific intervention or activity such as admission to a residential facility or the release of specific information to a third party. *Implied consent* occurs when consent is inferred from the facts and circumstances surrounding a client's situation. An example is a client who answers questions that are part of an anonymous, mailed, and voluntary client-satisfaction survey. A reasonable assumption is that the client has consented to the activity.

Right to refuse or withdraw consent.   While developing sound procedures for obtaining valid consent from clients is important for social workers and agencies, practitioners also should plan for the possibility that clients will refuse or withdraw consent. Of course, clients who do so also should be considered legally and mentally capable of such a decision, and their decisions need to be informed by details shared by practitioners concerning the risks associated with refusing or withdrawing consent. Taking psychotropic medication or being disabled to some degree by mental illness does not by itself provide grounds for being denied the right to refuse or withdraw consent. Rather, clients' capacity should be judged in terms of the ability of the clients to think clearly, grasp details relevant to their conditions, understand the extent to which their psychiatric history is likely to affect their current judgment, and understand the extent to which they pose a public health risk. Ordinarily, the best interests of social workers are served by having their clients sign a release form absolving them, or their agencies, of responsibility for any adverse consequences stemming from a decision not to give consent. If a client refuses to sign such a form, detailed notes describing the client's decision and the negotiation should be placed in the client's record.

Adequate information. Professionals generally agree about the topics that should be covered in discussions with clients before obtaining consent. Commonly cited elements of disclosure include the nature and purpose of the recommended service, treatment, or activity; the advantages and disadvantages of the intervention; substantial, probable, or significant risks to the clients, if any; potential effects on clients' families, partners, jobs, social activities, and other aspects of their lives; alternatives to the prospective intervention; and anticipated costs to be borne by clients and their relatives. This information must be presented to clients in understandable language, without coercion or undue influence, and in a manner that encourages clients to ask questions (President's Commission 1982; Rozovsky 1984). Consent forms should also be dated and should include an expiration date. Many social workers' forms state that the consent is valid for a period of 90 or 120 days, unless the client withdraws the consent at an earlier date. Consent forms without an expiration date may be considered invalid if the original signature was obtained long before the form was actually used.

Social workers must also consider that obtaining informed consent entails more than having clients sign a form. Consent is a process that includes the systematic disclosure of information to a client over time, along with an opportunity to discuss with the client the forthcoming treatment and service. As part of this process social workers must be especially sensitive to clients' cultural and ethnic differences related to the meaning of such concepts as *self-determination, autonomy,* and *consent.* Hahn observes that, for example, "the individualism central in the doctrine of informed consent is absent in the tradition of Vietnamese thought. Self is not cultivated, but subjugated to cosmic orders. Information, direct communication, and decision may be regarded as arrogant" (President's Commission 1982:55–56). In contrast, Harwood (President's Commission 1982:56) suggests that mainland Puerto Rican Hispanics expect to be engaged in the therapeutic process and have a strong desire for information and for information given without condescension. That social workers be cognizant of such cultural beliefs and preferences is essential if they are to obtain informed consent effectively and sensitively.

Exceptions to informed consent.   In a variety of circumstances professionals may not be required to obtain informed consent before intervention (Rozovsky 1984:114–23). These include instances involving emergencies, client waiver, and therapeutic privilege. In genuine emergencies, for example, professionals may be authorized to act without the client's consent. According to many state statutes and much case law, an emergency entails a client's being incapacitated and unable to exercise the mental ability to make an informed decision. Interference with decision-making ability must be a result of injury or illness, alcohol or drug use, or any other disability. In addition, a need for immediate treatment to preserve a life or health must exist. As Rozovsky has noted, it is important for practitioners not to assume "that a person who has consumed a moderate amount of alcohol or drugs or who has a history of psychiatric problems is automatically incapable of giving consent: the facts and circumstances of individual cases are essential to such determinations" (1984:89).

Further, many statutes authorize practitioners to treat clients without their consent in order to protect them or the community from harm. Cases involving substance abusers, prisoners, and people with sexually transmitted diseases are examples (President's Commission 1982:195; Rozovsky 1984:41–51). As social workers have come to learn, they may be obligated to disclose information to third parties without clients' consent if they have evidence that serious injury to others or to the state might otherwise result. As chapter 2 explained, the *Tarasoff* case and other duty-to-protect and duty-to-warn cases included circumstances in which a mental health professional was expected to disclose confidential information to third parties. Instances involving abuse and neglect and when minors request social services also are relevant.

Both statutes and case law have recognized the right of clients to request that they not be informed of the nature of risks associated with impending treatment or services (see, for example, *Holt v. Nelson* 1974; *Ferrara v. Galluchio* 1958). In these instances clients may decide that they are better off not knowing what the services or treatment will entail and thus waive their right to give informed consent. Professionals are generally advised to document such a waiver and to consider having clients sign a waiver form.

The most controversial exception to informed consent concerns the concept of *therapeutic privilege*. In several statutes involving the physician-patient relationship, for example, states have permitted practitioners to withhold information if they believe that disclosure would have a substantially adverse effect on a patient's welfare. These statutes allow considerable discretion by professionals and thus have led to extensive debate about the possibility of misuse of the privilege by physicians and other health and mental health professionals. This controversy has been fueled by the growing trend to avoid paternalism and toward full disclosure to patients and clients by the professionals who care for them (Reamer 1983b). In general, practitioners are cautioned to exercise the exception of therapeutic privilege

only in extreme circumstances that can be thoroughly documented. As Schutz wisely notes,

> Once the therapist invokes the therapeutic privilege, he must accept
> the burden of proof that a full disclosure would have harmed the
> patient. Otherwise, he faces a potential charge that the incomplete
> disclosure was abuse of duty. On the other hand, if he does make a
> full disclosure, he faces the charge that the statements given caused
> an injury or caused the patient to refuse a treatment and that, as a
> result, the patient suffered an injury. (1982:39)

Clinical Assessment and Intervention

Social workers in direct practice settings—such as family service
agencies, community mental health centers, psychiatric hospitals, and private practice—routinely assess clients in an effort to
formulate an intervention plan. Particularly in work with individual clients and families, social workers draw on a wide array
of assessment and diagnostic frameworks, reflecting different
theoretical orientations. Some practitioners may favor psycho-
dynamically oriented assessments and interventions, while others may favor cognitively or behaviorally oriented assessments
and interventions. By now most social workers agree that no one
theoretical perspective can claim a monopoly. Although practitioners may favor one view or approach over another, many draw
on the strengths of various perspectives while keeping in mind
their respective limitations and biases.

Whatever the social worker's ideological or theoretical perspective with respect to assessment and intervention frameworks, every social worker must be mindful of a range of malpractice and liability risks. As I discussed in chapter 1, claims
alleging malpractice or negligence ordinarily argue that the
social worker somehow departed from the standard of care associated with contemporary practice. Courts typically avoid ren-
dering opinions about the relative merits or demerits of one practice approach versus another; so long as a significant minority
within the profession embraces an approach, courts tend to be
respectful of a professional's right to pursue it. Rather, what matters is whether there is evidence that the practitioner's use and
implementation of that approach was somehow flawed or below

par (the breach of professional duty) and resulted in injury to the plaintiff (usually the client or the client's legal representative).

Social workers need to be aware of several potential problems related to assessment and intervention, including failure to diagnose or assess properly and incompetent delivery of service.

Failure to Assess

Well-trained social workers are expected to have the skill to "diagnose" (a medical term I prefer to avoid) or assess a variety of client problems. Although not every social worker may be skilled in all areas of assessment, most practitioners involved in direct practice are trained to assess common mental health disorders and problems in living.

Problems can arise, however, when social workers do not conduct thorough assessments consistent with the standard of care in the profession or make erroneous assumptions based on the data available to them. Imagine a client with symptoms of depression who seeks help from a social worker. During the first interview the client also mentions that she has chronic headaches. The social worker conducts a cursory assessment and neglects to ask additional questions about the headaches—their intensity, frequency, duration, and so on. As a result the social worker does not recommend that the client consult a physician who is trained to assess the organic causes or correlates of headaches. The client turns out to have a brain tumor, and she sues the social worker, alleging negligence. The client does not expect the social worker to be able to diagnose a brain tumor, of course. She can claim, however, that the social worker should ask detailed questions about somatic complaints and, if appropriate, refer her to a physician.

In *Kogensparger v. Athens Mental Health Ctr.* (1989), the court held a mental health center liable in failing to consider the possibility that organic problems caused a patient's symptoms, which included behavioral disorders and complaints of abnormal discomfort in his head. Staff members maintained that the symptoms, which included consuming excessive amounts of food and water, were caused by schizophrenia. The patient, who had been hospitalized for more than three years, suffered a grand mal seizure and died one week later. An autopsy disclosed a brain tumor. Experts agreed that the tumor was slow growing and must have been detectable for several years before the patient died; the court ruled that the center's failure to provide appropriate care was the proximate cause of death ("Mental Health Center's Failure," 1992:2).

A number of important legal precedents related to failure to diagnose come from the field of medicine. Most concern problems of misdiagnosis, missed diagnosis (the failure to identify a problem), and improper treatment. Over the years physicians have been held liable when they have not used a standard and well-accepted diagnostic test (*Narcarato v. Grob* 1970, *Smith v. Yohe* 1963; *Estate of Davies v. Reese et al.* 1977), interpreted test data incorrectly (*Green v. State, Southwest Louisiana Charity Hospital* 1975), and have not responded to a patient's adverse reaction to a diagnostic test (*Dill v. Miles* 1957). Doctors have also been held liable for the consequences of inaccurate test results, although they can avoid liability if the misdiagnosis does not affect treatment or if the misdiagnosis is followed by correct treatment) (R. J. Cohen 1979; Cohen and Mariano 1982:150–51).

Other failure-to-diagnose suits have been filed alleging failure to pursue information that seemed relevant and turned out to be essential. In *Merchants National Bank v. United States* (1967), a psychiatrist was found to be negligent in not pursuing a patient's allegation that her husband had attempted to harm her. Mental health professionals also have been held liable in the failure to forward significant information to another therapist. In *Underwood v. United States* (1966) an Air Force psychiatrist, who was being transferred off base, did not inform his patient's new psychiatrist of the patient's threats to kill his wife. The new therapist permitted the patient to return to duty and draw a firearm, which he then used to kill his wife. The victim's father won his suit alleging that the psychiatrist's failure to forward the information constituted negligence (Schutz 1982:25–26).

Not surprisingly, many cases involving failure to diagnose involve allegations that a mental health professional did not exercise sound judgment and that as a result the client or patient suffered an injury. In *Chatman v. Millis* (1975) a psychologist was sued by the ex-husband of a woman who sought to terminate his visitation rights with their two-and-a-half-year-old child by alleging that the husband had sexually molested the boy (R. J. Cohen 1979). The psychologist interviewed the mother and son but not the father. As a result of the assessment the psychologist concluded that the father's visitation rights should be terminated or, at the very least, that his visits with the child should be supervised. Although the court ruled that a negligence suit could not be brought because a doctor-patient relationship never existed between the husband and the psychologist, one judge issued a strong dissenting opinion:

> Defendant was negligent and careless in making such diagnosis by failing to exercise the degree of skill and care, or to possess the degree of knowledge, ordinarily exercised or possessed by other psychological examiners or psychologists engaged in this type of practice . . . in that he failed and neglected to ever interview the plaintiff and in fact did not even know him, failed to administer any diagnostic tests . . . or to use any of the proper methods that psychologists use in exercising ordinary care to protect others from injury or damage; the defendant acted in a manner willfully and wantonly in disregard to the rights of the plaintiff. (R. J. Cohen 1979:164)

Courts do not expect absolute precision in professionals' assessments. Judges recognize the inexact nature of assessment. What they do expect is conformity with the profession's standard of care with regard to assessment procedures and criteria. Although the outcome of a case may be tragic and the social worker's assessment may be wrong, the practitioner may not have been negligent. To be considered negligent a diagnosis must be wrong (an error in judgment) *and* determined in a negligent fashion (Schutz 1982:25). An error in judgment is not by itself negligent.

Many failure-to-diagnose cases involve suicide attempts. Typically, the plaintiff (ordinarily, a client who failed in an attempt to commit suicide and was injured in the process or a family member of a client who committed suicide) alleges that the social worker (or other mental health professional) did not properly diagnose the potential for suicide. In *Hardy a/k/a McDermott v. Perry & Jack, Inc. and Adventist Health System*, the plaintiff, a thirty-one-year-old woman, who was admitted to the defendant's hospital by two friends who were concerned about her substance abuse and recent suicide attempt, contended that the hospital staff did not properly assess her suicide risk. During the initial assessment a hospital staff member noted recent slash marks on the plaintiff's left wrist but accepted her explanation that the cuts were accidental. The staff had not interviewed the plaintiff's friends and therefore did not know of the recent suicide attempt. Shortly after the plaintiff's admission to the New Hampshire hospital she was found hanging in a bathroom. She suffered permanent anoxic brain damage, although it was unclear whether the damage was entirely the result of the hanging or of a preexisting condition aggravated by the hanging ("Patient Admitted to Hospital," 1990:2). The case was settled for $175,000.

In *Young et al. v. United States*, a U.S. District Court found a V.A. hospital in Tennessee liable for failure to properly assess the risk of suicide. The plaintiff was a thirty-three-year-old veteran who had been diagnosed with chronic paranoid schizophrenia and whose records indicated that he had drunk as much as a fifth of alcohol per day. The man was taken to the V.A. hospital by ambulance, the trip ticket for which stated that the patient had been seeing demons and intended to kill himself. The V.A. nurse testified during the trial that she had placed the trip ticket on the chart; however, the resident psychiatrist stated that she did not see the trip ticket when she examined the patient later that afternoon. The resident psychiatrist examined the patient, "who was a little nervous but rational," and the patient was sent home. The next morning the patient was found dead from a self-inflicted shotgun wound. The court found that the V.A. hospital deviated from the standard of care, either by failing to transmit the ambulance trip ticket or failing to consider its contents, and that the psychiatrist failed to take an adequate history ("Hospital Liable for Failure to Admit," 1991:4).

The Iowa case of *Baker v. United States* (1964) demonstrates the difference between an inaccurate judgment and negligence. The suit was filed by the wife of Kenneth Baker. Mrs. Baker served as guardian for her husband, a psychiatric patient receiving care at the V.A. Hospital in Iowa City. He attempted suicide by leaping into a thirteen-foot-deep window well located on the grounds of the hospital. He was seriously injured, suffering a variety of fractures and complete paralysis of his right side. Mrs. Baker alleged in her suit that the physician who admitted her husband to the hospital failed to properly diagnose his mental illness. According to Mrs. Baker, she had conferred with the acting chief of the neuropsychiatric service at the hospital and had informed him of her husband's suicidal tendencies. She also told the physician that she had found a gun her husband had hidden several weeks earlier. Mr. Baker was subsequently placed on an open ward; the physician did not think he was a suicide risk.

The U.S. District Court ruled that the admitting physician was not negligent and "exercised the proper standard of care required under the circumstances." In addition, the court concluded, "Diagnosis is not an exact science. Diagnosis with absolute precision and certainty is not possible" (cited in Austin, Moline, and Williams 1990:167).

Similar issues related to professional judgment arose in *Boyer v. Tilzer* (1992). The police took a man into custody and transported him to a state mental health facility where he was involuntarily admitted for a period not to exceed ninety-six hours. An emergency room report described the patient as combative, hyperreligious, and manic. He was apparently hearing voices, seeing demons, and thinking he was God. A psychiatric resident diagnosed the patient as suffering from alcohol abuse and probable PCP (phencyclidine) psychosis and recommended substance dependency treatment.

The hospital released the patient after three days. One week later he began having hallucinations and delusions. He stabbed his girlfriend's hand with a knife and fatally stabbed a third party who had come to her assistance. The patient was arrested and diagnosed as having paranoid schizophrenia.

The dead woman's estate sued the psychiatric resident, alleging that the patient had been incorrectly misdiagnosed and released. The trial court found in favor of the resident, concluding that there was no proof the resident had acted in bad faith or in a grossly negligent fashion. The estate appealed, and the Missouri appeals court also found no evidence that the psychiatric resident had not performed his duties in good faith and without gross negligence ("Psychiatrist Not Negligent," 1992:1).

Negligent Intervention

Fortunately, most social workers provide skilled service to clients that is consistent with prevailing standards in the profession. Unfortunately, on occasion social workers are negligent. In these instances their intervention approaches or techniques deviate from the standard of care in the profession. As I noted in chapter 1, many liability judgments against social workers stem from genuine mistakes (speaking about confidential matters too loudly in an agency hallway) or good intentions (disclosing privileged information without a client's consent in order to protect third parties). Other judgments, however, are triggered by what lawyers refer to as "wanton and willful misconduct." Wanton and willful misconduct is more fully addressed in chapter 4. The emphasis here is on liability risks that pertain to negligent departures from the standard of care.

Social workers' intervention approaches and techniques can be negligent in many ways. In some instances social workers may use techniques for which they have not received proper training, such as biofeedback or hypnosis, or carried them out in some flawed fashion. A social worker who uses such techniques improperly and whose lack of skill causes injury to a client may be found liable for abuse of the psychotherapeutic process.

Using nontraditional approaches can also trigger liability claims. Although social workers should not feel compelled to conform entirely to commonly used techniques endorsed by the majority of colleagues or to completely avoid experimentation, they should be wary of radical departures from common practices in the profession. As Austin, Moline, and Williams urge,

> If you are using techniques that are not commonly practiced, you will need to have a clear rationale that other professionals in your field will accept and support. It is important to consult colleagues when you are using what are considered to be nontraditional approaches to treatment. This is primarily because it is not difficult to prove deviation from average care. Some examples of what may be considered nontraditional therapeutic techniques might include ask-

ing clients to undress, striking a client, or giving "far-out" home-work assignments. (1990:155–56)

In *Hammer v. Rosen* (1960), for example, Alice Hammer and her father sued her psychiatrist, Dr. John Rosen. Dr. Rosen had treated Alice Hammer, who had been diagnosed with schizo-phrenia. The plaintiffs claimed that Dr. Rosen beat Alice Ham-mer during treatment sessions. According to court records, Dr. Rosen treated his schizophrenic patients by also acting in a schizophrenic manner at times. Ultimately, the court of appeals reversed the lower court decision and Dr. Rosen was found liable for improper treatment and malpractice (Austin, Moline, and Williams 1990:156–57).

Several similar issues were raised in *Miller v. Martin, One-sian, Macomb Cty. Community Guidance Ctr. and St. Joseph Hospital of Mt. Clemens*. The plaintiff was a legal secretary who went to St. Joseph Hospital in Michigan with symptoms of panic disorder and agoraphobia. One of the defendants (Martin) was a social worker. The plaintiff alleged that she was discharged to outpatient treatment without being informed of the diagnosis or given an explanation of her condition. She claimed that attempts to treat her condition were limited to comments about less painful methods of suicide and New Age spiritual guidance. The case was settled for $100,000 ("Patient Improperly Treated," 1992:6).

A number of novel issues related to what were once nontradi-tional intervention techniques were raised in *Solano County Department of Social Services v. Ron B.* (1987). The case began when the Solano County (Calif.) department of social services filed a petition alleging that Ron B. sexually molested his three-year-old daughter, Amber B., and that his one-year-old daughter, Teela B., was at risk of sexual abuse. The court eventually ordered that the two girls be placed in the custody of their moth-er. Ron B. appealed the ruling, challenging the testimony given by a court-appointed psychologist, Dr. Henry Raming. Dr. Ram-ing had been instructed to assess Amber for sexual abuse.

Ron B. challenged Dr. Raming's method in determining that Amber had been sexually abused. He claimed that Amber's reports of abuse and behavior with anatomically correct dolls were interpreted by a new scientific method that had *not* been shown to satisfy what is known as the *Kelly-Frye test of admissibility* (Austin, Moline, and Williams 1990:159). The Kelly-Frye test requires that

> a new scientific method of proof is admissible only upon showing that the procedure has been generally accepted as reliable in the scientific community in which it was developed. . . . The test does not apply to mere expert testimony as distinguished from scientific evidence. When a witness gives his [her] personal opinion on the stand—even if he [she] qualifies as an expert—the jurors may temper their acceptance of his [her] testimony with a healthy skepticism born of their knowledge that all human beings are fallible. (cited in Austin, Moline, and Williams 1990:159)

The court of appeals found that the trial court had erred when it did not require evidence that the psychologist's techniques were generally accepted in the relevant scientific community, consistent with the Kelly-Frye test.

Another potential source of problems is advice giving. If social workers give clients advice that departs from the standard of care—such as advising clients about psychotropic medication doses—they could be held liable (in this instance for practicing medicine without a license). In a widely publicized case a New Jersey social worker employed at a mental health clinic, Hackensack Medical Center, told the New Jersey State Board of Medical Examiners in January 1988 that social workers were being allowed to refill patients' medication prescriptions because of a shortage of psychiatrists. The social worker said that she and other clinic social workers would order prescriptions by telephone, and staff psychiatrists would later sign the prescription forms. She also alleged that social workers occasionally would change patients' medication—including antipsychotic and antidepressant drugs—and modify dosages without consulting a physician. After she blew the whistle, the social worker said, "I knew that [social workers] prescribing medications was wrong, and I was surprised something like this could be going on, but I was really getting involved in my [psychotherapy] cases and I enjoyed the group I was leading, so I thought I would try to change things from within" ("Member Blows Whistle," 1990:11).

The board investigated and in 1990 reprimanded the clinic's consulting psychiatrist, finding that she had inadequately supervised patients who were on prescription drugs. She admitted no wrongdoing but faced $8,000 in penalties. The clinic was to be monitored for two years by an independent consultant.

In addition, social workers and the agencies for which they work can be sued for mistreating clients, for example, in the form of verbal or emotional abuse. Consider what happened in *Gorman v. Lifespring, Inc.* The plaintiff was a thirty-six-year-old attorney who participated in a five-day program that included lectures, "guided fantasies," and experimental psychological exercises. The plaintiff experienced psychotic symptoms (hallucinations) during the training, along with hyperactivity and sleep deprivation. He was hospitalized for five days, discharged, and about three months later was readmitted to the hospital, where he was then treated for about three more months. The attorney had no prior history of mental illness. He sued, claiming intentional infliction of emotional distress, negligence, and fraud (in the form of an introductory session that he alleged was misleading). The District of Columbia jury found in favor of the defendant with respect to intentional infliction of emotional distress but found in favor of the plaintiff with regard to the allegations of negligence and fraud. The plaintiff was awarded $297,387 ("Attorney Suffers Psychotic Breakdown," 1991:1).

In *Aprilliano v. Webb, d/b/a The Training*, the plaintiff sued sponsors of EST-like seminars, alleging that their treatment caused several psychological problems and a suicide attempt. Lynne Aprilliano, who had a history of abuse and psychological difficulties, was recovering from an automobile accident and was depressed because of her injuries. She claimed that during the sessions she was told by the trainer and other participants that the automobile accident was really her fault and that she "chose" to be in the accident. Aprilliano claimed that the sponsors should have had a procedure to screen out individuals who were in treatment elsewhere. The Utah case was settled for $50,000 ("Woman Claims Psychological Problems," 1992:6).

Of course, many lawsuits alleging negligent intervention are not successful. In *Hess v. Frank* (1975) a patient sued his psychiatrist, claiming that the doctor used abusive language and that such language caused anguish and serious injury to the patient. The plaintiff sued for $100,000 in damages and $20,000 previously paid to the psychiatrist for treatment but lost the case. The court did not find in favor of the patient (R. J. Cohen 1979:164).

Undue Influence

On occasion liability problems arise in the delivery of social work services because of the phenomenon of undue influence. *Undue influence* occurs when social workers use their authority improperly to pressure, persuade, or sway a client to engage in an activity that may not be in the client's best interest or that may pose a conflict of interest. Undue influence may take several forms. Examples include persuading an elderly client to include the social worker in her or his will, influencing a minor in a way that is contrary to his or her parents' wishes, and convincing a client to include the social worker, during treatment, in a lucrative investment or business partnership. Gifis offers the legal definition of undue influence:

> It is established by excessive importunity, superiority of will or mind, the relationship of the parties (e.g., priest and penitent or caretaker and senior citizen) or by any other means constraining the donor or testator [one who makes and executes a testament or will] to do what he is unable to refuse. . . . The elements of undue influence are susceptibility of testator/donor to such influence, the exertion of improper influence, and submission to the domination of the influencing party. (1991:508)

Geis v. Landau (1983) illustrates how subtle issues involving undue influence can be (Austin, Moline, and Williams 1990:224–25). Dr. Jon Geis, a clinical psychologist, had provided counseling services to Betsy Landau for approximately eight years. During this period Landau was going through a divorce and explained to Dr. Geis that it was difficult for her to pay his fees. When the therapy terminated, Landau had an outstanding bill of $8,000. Dr. Geis sued Landau for the unpaid fees. In her defense Landau contended that Dr. Geis, who allowed her fee to build up unpaid, failed to discuss with her the fact that she was "getting in over her head." At one point Dr. Geis wrote Landau a note stating "not to worry about the bill"; according to testimony, Dr. Geis had confidence that Landau would eventually pay the bill. According to court records, Dr. Geis also stated that he decided it was unwise to refer Landau to a low-cost mental health clinic. According to the court, Dr. Geis "made a unilateral decision that only he could help the defendant." The judge ruled that Dr. Geis had

> exercised excessive power over his client, who was dependent upon him for resolution to her problems. The judge stated that he had doubts that there was no other alternative (low-cost clinic) available to Mrs. Landau that would have been able to assist her with further treatment. The judge stated that his decision to grant judgment to the defendant (Mrs. Landau) did not mean that a therapist can never "extend credit to a patient," but, when a therapist knows that the client has no means by which to pay the account, such credit is not considered fair. (Austin, Moline, and Williams 1990:225)

A case involving a social worker who exerted undue influence was reported widely in the *New York Times* (1979). A social worker in New York City was convicted of killing his sixty-eight-year-old client after stealing a substantial sum of money from her and then throwing the woman's weighted body into the East River after persuading the woman to withdraw more then $13,000 from a bank. He was sentenced to a minimum of twenty-five years in prison (Besharov 1985:180).

Undue influence can be difficult to prove, as illustrated by the classic case of *Patterson v. Jensen et al.* (1945). Although this case involves a physician rather than a social worker, it contains many issues broached in undue influence cases. Mary Faulks named her personal physician, Dr. Patterson, as the primary beneficiary in her will. In addition to serving as her physician, Dr. Patterson had borrowed money from Faulks to buy a house. Faulks had also given Dr. Patterson money for an airplane hangar, partial payment on an airplane, and a family vacation. In response to one of the gifts Dr. Patterson promised Faulks that he would attend to her medical needs for the rest of her life. The man whom Faulks and her husband had raised as a young boy, Will Jensen, objected to the relationship between his guardian and Dr. Patterson. He argued that it was not in her best interest and that she was "susceptible to undue influence." The court ruled that Faulks was not impaired when she had her last will drafted and that it had no clear evidence that Dr. Patterson influenced the contents of the will or became the primary beneficiary as a result of undue influence. The court concluded that influence that resulted from kindness and affection was not undue "if no imposition or fraud be practiced, even though it induced the testator (Mrs. Faulks) to make an unequal and unjust disposition" (cited in Austin, Moline, and Williams 1990:223–23).

Fortunately, lawsuits against social service professionals alleging undue influence are rare. Nonetheless, social worker-client relationships certainly pose the potential for the exercise of undue influence.

Suicide

Sadly, many cases alleging improper assessment and intervention involve suicide. As discussed earlier, a distressingly large number of liability cases allege that a mental health professional did not adequately assess for suicide risk and therefore did not take proper precautions to prevent a suicide. In *Grossman v. United States*, the plaintiff's husband was admitted to a hospital after showing signs of depression and slitting his wrists. The man was released about two-and-a-half weeks later after receiving medication and psychotherapy. Several months later the man was admitted to a V.A. hospital after buying a shotgun with the intention of killing himself. The hospital staff made no attempt to obtain the patient's earlier records or contact the physicians who had treated him. In addition, staff members did not take a complete history at the time of admission and did not conduct a thorough interview with the patient's family about his prior history. The patient then attempted suicide for the third time, unsuccessfully, by jumping in front of a truck while out of the hospital on a weekend pass. Two months after his admission to the V.A. hospital the patient walked out of the facility and committed suicide by throwing himself under the wheels of a bus directly in front of the hospital and on the hospital grounds. The V.A. hospital was found liable, and the plaintiff was awarded $570,841 in Washington, D.C. ("$570,841 Judgment Returned," 1991:3).

In another important case raising similar issues (*Arriaza v. Harvard Community Health Plan* 1990), a suit was filed against a psychiatric facility, two psychiatrists, two psychiatric nurses, and a psychiatric social worker in Massachusetts. The plaintiff, a nineteen-year-old patient who jumped from the sixth floor of a psychiatric facility, alleged that the defendants did not properly diagnose his suicidal ideation and did not take precautions to prevent a suicide attempt. Before his suicide attempt the patient had a one-year history of psychiatric illness and previous psychiatric hospitalization. He had hallucinations, delusions, and symptoms of depression. One of the nurses' notes reported that the patient had stated he had given his body to Satan.

Three days after his admission the patient was released on a pass to attend a psychiatric group therapy session on the sixth floor of the building. After the therapy session the patient was left momentarily unattended. He walked to an open atrium foyer and jumped. He suffered severe injuries, including hip and leg fractures, brain damage, and loss of an eye, kidney, and spleen. The trial was divided on liability and damages. The jury found the defendants 85 percent negligent and the plaintiff 15 percent contributorily negligent; the plaintiff ultimately settled for $3 million during the damages phase of the trial ("Psychiatrists Liable," 1991:1).

As chapter 5 discusses more thoroughly, in still other cases plaintiffs allege that social service staff members did not provide adequate supervision of a suicidal client. As Meyer, Landis, and Hays (1988) conclude,

> While the law generally does not hold anyone responsible for the acts of another, there are exceptions. One of these is the responsibility of therapists to prevent suicide and other self-destructive behavior by their clients. The duty of therapists to exercise adequate care and skill in diagnosing suicidality is well-established (see *Meier v. Ross General Hospital*, 1968). When the risk of self-injurious behavior is identified an additional duty to take adequate precautions arises (*Abille v. United States*, 1980; *Pisel v. Stamford Hospital*, 1980). When psychotherapists fail to meet these responsibilities, they may be held liable for injuries that result.
>
> Not every completed suicide or gesture is cause for liability—only those which could reasonably have been prevented. Demonstrating

negligence requires proof that the patient should have been identified as suicidal based on widely recognized criteria used by most other therapists of the same training. (p. 38)

As Meyer, Landis, and Hays suggest, *Meier v. Ross General Hospital* (1968) sets an important precedent in litigation involving suicide. The widow and children of the patient, Kurt Meier, brought a wrongful death suit against the hospital and Dr. James Stubblebine, director of the psychiatric unit, after Meier committed suicide while a patient in the hospital. The family had brought the patient to the hospital after he had attempted suicide by cutting his wrists. The hospital had what it described as an "open door" policy for its psychiatric patients in order to provide a homelike atmosphere. The patients were free to move about the hospital and even to leave if they so wished. Staff members recognized that this open door policy lessened security and exposed potentially suicidal patients to greater risk, but they believed that ultimately the enhanced freedom of movement improved the prospects for rehabilitation (R. J. Cohen 1979:106–7).

Approximately one week after Meier slashed his wrists, he committed suicide by jumping head first from an open window in his second-floor room. The trial court found in favor of the hospital and psychiatrist. On appeal to the California Supreme Court, however, the decision was reversed, and the court ordered a new trial. The court opinion contains important language concerning professionals' responsibility when they perceive a risk of suicide:

> If those charged with the care and treatment of a mentally disturbed patient know of facts from which they could reasonably conclude that the patient would be likely to harm himself in the absence of preclusive measures, then they must use reasonable care under the circumstances to prevent such harm [*Wood v. Samaritan Institution* (1945) 26 Cal. 2d 847, 853, 161 P.2d 556]. Given this duty and the fact that defendants placed decedent, following an attempted suicide, in a second floor room with a fully openable window, the jury could find from the fact of decedent's plunge through this window that defendants more probably than not breached the duty of care owed to decedent. Even in the absence of expert testimony which describes the probability that the death or injury resulted from negligence, the

jury may competently decide that defendant more probably than not breached his duty of care when the evidence supports a conclusion that the cause of the accident (here, the openable window) was not inextricably connected with the course of treatment involving the exercise of medical judgment beyond the common knowledge of laymen. (cited in Cohen and Mariano 1982:156)

Similar reasoning appears in *Sayes v. Pilgrim Manor Nursing Home* (1988). This case involved a police officer who was injured when he dived into the water in an effort to rescue an emotionally disturbed nursing home patient who was attempting suicide by wading toward deep water. In his suit against the nursing home the police officer alleged that his injury was caused by its care of the woman and that that care was negligent. The appeals court ultimately held that the nursing home was negligent in allowing the woman to leave the facility unattended. In its ruling the appellate court made three main points:

First, the nursing home's voluntary acceptance of the resident, after her release from a state mental hospital, with full knowledge of her mental and physical disorders, obligated it to take extra care and precautionary measures to assure that she would not injure herself or others.

Second, the nursing home had allowed the resident complete freedom to leave the home's premises, despite the fact that she had been rehospitalized on four occasions due to her violent and/or destructive outbursts.

Third, immediately preceding the suicide attempt, the resident had exhibited behavior that should have placed the nursing home on notice that she was likely to engage in violent, combative and destructive behavior. These warning signs were ignored. (cited in "Nursing Home Liable," 1990:1)

As is often the case, courts do not expect mental health professionals to have the ability to always predict accurately whether a client is likely to commit suicide. Rather, what is required is competent assessment, consistent with the standard of care in the profession and a good faith effort to protect the client from harm.

Porter v. Maunnangi (1988) illustrates this reasoning concerning good-faith effort. A former state hospital patient's mother filed a wrongful death suit alleging that psychiatrists at the hospital to which her son had been involuntarily committed did not diagnose his suicidal condition and did not provide adequate psychiatric treatment for him. The hospital won the suit because state law provided that licensed physicians cannot be civilly liable so long as their decisions are made "in good faith and without gross negligence" (cited in "Psychiatrists Not Liable," 1989:2). The plaintiffs had not alleged that the psychiatrists had acted in bad faith or were grossly negligent.

A number of suicide cases allege that staff in a psychiatric facility did not remove from a client's possession or supplied patients with dangerous objects—particularly those that could facilitate suicide. *Tomfohr v. the Mayo Foundation* (1989) is prototypical. In this case a forty-two-year-old man appeared at a hospital emergency room and reported that he was fantasizing about killing his parents, his family, and himself. He had been depressed because his employer had transferred him to another city. He agreed to be admitted to the locked psychiatric unit of the hospital, where his room was checked every thirty minutes. The nurse who interviewed him shortly after admission removed his safety razor, nail clippers, and cologne bottle. She did not, however, take away a thirty-inch leather shoulder strap that could be detached from his personal luggage. At that point the nurse decided the man should be placed on suicide precautions with fifteen-minute room checks. During the evening after he was admitted, staff members noted that the patient was pacing the room, wringing his hands, clenching his fists, holding his head, and sighing. A nurse also observed the man hunched over and rigid. Staff members administered Haldol and left the man alone. Ten minutes later staff members found the patient hanging by his luggage strap.

A wrongful death suit was filed, alleging that hospital staff did not take reasonable precautions to prevent suicide. The plaintiffs argued that the staff should have removed the luggage strap and the patient should have been placed on constant observation or in a room where self-destructive behavior would be minimized or eliminated. The hospital argued that belts and straps are less lethal than sharp objects and to take the former away might antagonize patients and interfere with the patient-staff relationship. The Minnesota jury awarded $940,000 to the plaintiffs ("Hospital Liable for Failure to Prevent Suicide," 1990:2).

Poplin v. Willingway Hospital (1989) raises similar issues. A forty-nine-year-old nurse with a history of severe psychiatric problems, for which she had been hospitalized several times, had been admitted to a drug and alcohol abuse treatment hospital. For several weeks before her admission the patient had experienced hallucinations and had attempted suicide. She also stopped taking the medication she had been prescribed. The patient's family took her to the drug and alcohol abuse treatment hospital where she was placed in a single room. According to testimony, the patient was not treated for depression, despite signs of depression. About one week after she was admitted, the hospital staff provided the patient with a hair dryer, which had a long extension cord that the patient used to commit suicide. A suit brought against the hospital claimed that the staff did not properly diagnose and monitor the patient and that staffers had provided the extension cord. The Georgia jury awarded the plaintiff $750,000.

Zercher & Zercher v. Timberlawn Psychiatric Hospital also involved allegations that the hospital should not have permitted a suicidal patient access to a dangerous object, but the defense was rather novel. The plaintiff's twenty-seven-year-old son, who had a history of schizophrenia, was admitted to the hospital for psychiatric treatment for suicidal ideations. About six months after admission the patient committed suicide by hanging himself with fishing line that his treating psychiatrist permitted him to keep in his room. The hospital denied any negligence, claiming that because the patient was an outdoorsman the fishing line was therapeutic. The Texas case was settled for $320,000 ("Schizophrenic Patient Hangs Self," 1991:6).

To prevent malpractice and liability claims related to suicide social workers should take a number of precautions and preventive steps (Austin, Moline, and Williams 1990; Meyer, Landis, and Hays 1988; Schutz 1982):

- Social workers should be familiar with their agency's manual containing policies and guidelines for dealing with suicidal clients. Agencies that do not have a manual containing policies and guidelines should develop one.

- Social workers in private practice should obtain regular peer supervision that reviews guidelines and policies for dealing with suicidal clients.
- Early in the therapeutic relationship social workers should obtain information from clients about significant others who should be contacted in case of emergency. Clients should also be asked to sign a written consent form, giving their social worker permission to contact these individuals should the social worker determine that the client is or may be suicidal. In general clients should be informed when the social worker contacts significant others about the client's risk of suicide.
- Social workers should use a formal assessment form to assess the likelihood or probability of suicide. The assessment should obtain information related to the client's treatment history and history of suicidal thoughts and/or attempts. The social worker can explain that completion of the intake form is standard procedure used with every new client. This may help to avoid situations in which clients conclude that the social worker is worried that the client is suicidal. (For examples of criteria to consider in a suicide assessment, see Meyer, Landis, and Hays 1988:278–79 and Schutz 1982:68–72.)
- All the social worker's observations, impressions, and courses of action related to suicide risk should be documented in writing in the case record.
- Social workers dealing with minors should consider having each minor and parent sign a written contract specifying the procedures to be followed if the social worker believes the client is suicidal.
- Social workers should obtain proper consultation when faced with a client who is or may be suicidal. Documenting the consultation sought and received is important.
- Social workers must be careful to ensure that suicidal clients with whom they have terminated treatment have access to competent care (see the discussion of abandonment in chapter 8).

- When the risk of suicide is high, social workers are obligated to take proper steps to "control" the client, as in seeking emergency treatment or hospitalization. The social worker should thoroughly document these efforts.
- Social workers should be familiar with local statutes concerning their duty to protect and duty to warn when a client is or may be suicidal.
- Social workers should explain and clarify their availability to clients and how to handle emergencies and absences during the practitioner's vacations or illness.
- Social workers should follow widely accepted guidelines for managing a suicidal client. The following, for example, is adapted from Schutz (1982:72–73):

  1. elicit from the client, if possible and credible, a promise that he will control his impulses or will call the therapist or a local emergency number (many social workers draw up a "suicide contract" with suicidal clients);
  2. make sure that any weapons in the client's possession are placed in the hands of a third party;
  3. increase the frequency of treatment sessions;
  4. contact significant others in the client's social network (with consent) and ask them to assist in supporting the client between sessions or in conjoint sessions;
  5. use a call-in system between sessions to monitor the client's stability;
  6. obtain psychiatric consultation in regard to the possibility of using medication as an adjunct to treatment. Bear in mind, however, that antidepressants may initially increase the risk because the seriously depressed client may become sufficiently energized to make an attempt. Also, a client may hoard the medication until a lethal dose is collected; and
  7. consider taking steps to have the client hospitalized, preferably voluntarily but, if necessary, involuntarily.

Involuntary Civil Commitment

Social workers are often involved in civil commitment decisions. Although they may not be authorized to sign the commitment papers, social workers are often consulted and relied on for information related to commitment proceedings. Cases involving potential suicide often lead in this direction.

The stakes in these cases are of course high. Hospitalization, whether voluntary or involuntary, can be traumatic. Clients' freedom is restricted, and they may experience significant emotional distress. Clients also could be abused in the process.

A substantial number of lawsuits in the mental health field are responses to attempts to commit clients to psychiatric facilities. Some suits allege that a mental health professional failed to conduct a proper thorough assessment and that the commitment therefore was inappropriate. This may constitute false imprisonment, which arises from the "nonconsensual, improper, or unlawful restraint or confinement of one person by another for any period of time" (Cohen and Mariano 1982:380). As Meyer, Landis, and Hays assert,

> Following the Supreme Court's decision in *Addington v. Texas* (1979), the burden of proof is on the petitioner and the state, who must demonstrate by "clear and convincing evidence" that the detainee meets the statutory criteria for commitment. This level of proof is a compromise between mere "preponderance" of the evidence, used in other civil matters, and "beyond a reasonable doubt," the standard in criminal proceedings, and reflects a balance of the need to protect individual rights against the presumably well-intentioned intervention by the state. The court determined that language in the Constitution requires significant due process protections, but not as much as in criminal matters. (1988:117)

Other cases allege that a mental health professional made an error in judgment about the client's mental health and vulnerability or relied on hearsay evidence. In *Kleber v. Stevens* (1964) the plaintiff claimed that a psychiatrist's commitment papers were improper because they were based on hearsay. The trial court awarded the plaintiff $20,000 in damages.

In addition, some suits allege that the mental health professionals involved did not confine a client in the least restrictive alternative. In the classic case of *Lake v. Cameron* (1966), Catherine Lake challenged her confinement at St. Elizabeths Hospital in the District of Columbia (Austin, Moline, and Williams 1990:199). A police officer had found her wandering the streets and took her to Washington, D.C., General Hospital. Twelve days later Lake filed a writ of verbal habeas corpus in U.S. District Court; a judge concluded that she was "of unsound mind" and authorized her transfer to St. Elizabeths Hospital. Staff concluded that Lake was a danger to herself and in need of care and supervision that her family was not able to provide.

At the District Court commitment hearing and the habeas corpus hearing, Lake testified that she was competent to be free. At the court of appeals hearing Lake also stated that, consistent with the newly enacted District of Columbia Hospitalization of the Mentally Ill Act, she would be willing to consider a less restrictive alternative to the psychiatric institution. The court ultimately concluded that "the government, while seeking to provide some sort of custodial care, could not compel Mrs. Lake to accept its help at the price of her freedom. She had a right to be treated with the least restrictive alternative" (cited in Austin, Moline, and Williams 1990:201; also see *Welk v. Florida* 1989).

Several important cases also demonstrate that hospitalized clients are entitled to treatment while detained. In *O'Connor v. Donaldson* (1975) the plaintiff, Kenneth Donaldson, then forty-nine, was civilly committed to the Florida State Hospital in Chattahoochee with a diagnosis of paranoid schizophrenia (Austin, Moline, and Williams 1990:203). He was confined to the hospital against his will for fifteen years. On several occasions during his hospitalization Donaldson unsuccessfully petitioned state and federal courts for his release, claiming that he did not pose a threat of danger, was not mentally ill, and that the hospital was not providing him with treatment.

In 1971 at the age of sixty-four, Donaldson filed suit again in U.S. District Court, alleging that the hospital's superintendent and staff had deprived him of his constitutional right to liberty. Evidence presented during the trial demonstrated that Donaldson received primarily custodial care rather than treatment. The jury found in favor of Donaldson. The appellate court's opinion stated that "regardless of the grounds for involuntary civil commitment, a person confined against his will at a state mental institution has 'a constitutional right to receive such individual treatment as will give him a reasonable opportunity to be cured or to improve his mental condition' " (cited in Austin, Moline, and Williams 1990:206; also see *Rouse v. Cameron*, 1966, and *Eckerhart v. Hensley* 1979).

Psychiatric patients also have a right to *refuse* treatment in some circumstances, particularly when coerced treatment violates their First Amendment rights to freedom of religion and speech or their Eighth Amendment rights to protection from cruel and unusual punishment. The right to refuse treatment was established in *Rennie v. Klein* (1978). Rennie, who had been hospitalized on twelve previous occasions, had refused to take medication ordered by his psychiatrist. A federal District Court ruled that involuntary psychiatric patients *may* have the right to refuse medication or other forms of treatment in the absence of an emergency, consistent with the constitutional right to privacy. In addition, the court ruled, due process must be followed in order to coerce medication. To overrule the patient's refusal four factors should be considered by an objective independent party: (1) the patient's capacity to decide on his particular treatment, (2) the patient's physical threat to other patients and staff, (3) whether any less restrictive treatment exists, and (4) the risk of permanent side effects from the proposed treatment. The court ultimately overruled Rennie's refusal, based on these four criteria. Nonetheless, this decision has been influential in right-to-refuse-treatment cases (Meyer, Landis, and Hays 1988:134).

Finally, some lawsuits contend that mental health staff members did not adequately monitor a client's progress and condition. In *Whitree v. State* (1968) a patient who had been hospitalized in a state institution for fourteen years alleged that he had been falsely imprisoned. The court found in his favor, noting in particular the infrequent examinations of the patient and the lack of depth of the examinations that were conducted. The court also concluded that "the lack of psychiatric care was the primary reason for the inordinate length of this incarceration, with the concomitant side effects of physical injury, moral degradation, and mental anguish" (cited in R. J. Cohen 1979:139). The plaintiff was awarded $300,000 in damages.

As Austin, Moline, and Williams (1990:207–8) suggest,

- Social workers should inform clients of their rights regarding detainment before seeking involuntary commitment.
- Social workers should develop a good working relationship with a psychiatrist who can be consulted when needed.
- Treatment plans should respect clients' right to be treated with the least restrictive alternative. Social workers should be familiar with available resources, both institutional and noninstitutional, the restrictions they impose, and their therapeutic value.
- Social workers should ensure that hospitalized clients are receiving proper treatment in addition to appropriate custodial care. They should also be familiar with clients' right to *refuse* treatment.
- Social workers should monitor the care clients are receiving in residential settings to which they have been admitted.
- Social workers should ensure that clients' progress is reviewed and updated regularly.
- Social workers should be familiar with local statutes concerning criteria for commitment (see Meyer, Landis, and Hays 1988:125–31, for example) and commitment procedures. Social workers should be particularly familiar with the role they are permitted to assume in commitment proceedings.

As Meyer, Landis and Hays state with respect to practitioners' involvement in commitment proceedings,

> Psychotherapists can serve as petitioners; in fact, in many states they may bypass some of the paperwork involved and arrange for the person to be taken to the hospital simply by calling the authorities. For example, if a client disclosed an intent to commit suicide, a licensed therapist can generally ask the police to take him or her to an inpatient facility immediately, leaving the paperwork for later. Practicing therapists should acquaint themselves with the pragmatics of commitment procedures in their communities *before* a crisis arises. Magistrates and clerks of court are usually very cooperative in explaining the relevant laws and procedures and may "walk

through" a petition to illustrate the entire process. Therapists should understand whom to call to arrange a mental health warrant, the criteria that apply in their jurisdiction, how and where to complete the necessary paperwork, and the location of the community evaluation center. Further, they should be able to explain all of the above to members of the community. (1988:120)

Protective Services

Many social workers face protective service issues during their careers. The most obvious circumstances are those encountered by child welfare professionals who have day-to-day contact with child abuse and neglect cases. Practitioners also have a much greater understanding of protective service issues involving other special populations, such as the elderly, mentally retarded, and mentally ill.

Even those social workers who are not employed directly in protective service positions are bound to have at least some indirect encounter with protective service issues at some point in their careers. Clinical social workers in a community mental health center, family service agency, juvenile correctional facility, school, a senior center, or in private practice are, like many other professionals, mandated reporters. Every state now has a statute obligating mandated reporters to notify local protective service officials when they suspect abuse or neglect of a child. In all states social workers are mandated reporters. States typically mandate reporting of suspected physical abuse, physical neglect, sexual abuse, emotional maltreatment, and institutional maltreatment of children, and a growing number of states mandate reporting of elder abuse and neglect. The terms used in states' statutes vary but usually include language such as *physical battering, physical endangerment, physical neglect, medical neglect, sexual abuse, sexual exploitation, emotional abuse, developmental neglect, emotional neglect, improper ethical supervision, educational neglect, abandonment,* and *institutional maltreatment* (Besharov 1985).

Not surprisingly, cases involving mandatory reporting and protective services are highly charged. Allegations of the strongest and most provocative kind are often leveled by and against family members and partners. Otherwise-trusted professionals may feel obligated to report suspected abuse or neglect against a client's wishes. Reports of abuse and neglect may also be used as a weapon in child custody disputes.

One consequence of the sensitive nature of protective services is that some individuals' threshold of tolerance for false allegations, harassment, and so on, is relatively low. As a result social workers need to be particularly knowledgeable about and sensitive to related liability and malpractice risks.

Social workers need to be aware of four broad areas of risk: (1) reporting of abuse and/or neglect, (2) inadequately protecting a child, (3) violating parental rights, and (4) inadequate foster care services (Besharov 1985).

Reporting of Abuse and/or Neglect

With respect to reporting of abuse and/or neglect, a common claim is failure to report. Since 1964 all states have passed laws that require the reporting of suspected child abuse and neglect. The list of mandated reporters varies from state to state (as do definitions of what constitutes reportable abuse and neglect); however, social workers (and teachers and most medical professionals) are mandated reporters in all states. In spite of this clear mandate the evidence is clear that human service workers, including social workers, fail to notify authorities of more than half the abused and neglected children whom they encounter (U.S. National Center on Child Abuse and Neglect 1981; Besharov 1985:24).

In addition to criminal penalties that may be imposed for failing to report suspected abuse or neglect, social workers risk civil penalties and lawsuits. In *People v. Noshay*, an Arizona social worker was accused of failing to report, even though she had urged the mother of the child to report to the police an allegation involving molestation. The social worker believed that urging the mother to report what happened complied with state law and that reporting it against the client's wishes might harm the client and jeopardize the therapeutic relationship. Although the charges were eventually dropped because the state's haphazard record-keeping system could not be relied on to prove that a report was not made immediately, the case makes clear the real possibility of criminal liability if a report is not made (Besharov 1985:28–29).

A number of important civil suits allege negligence on the part of mandated reporters stemming from failure to report. In *Robinson v. Wical* (1970), the plaintiff sued the police, two hospitals, and individual doctors after a child with severe injuries consistent with abuse was not reported. A five-month-old child had been taken to the hospital on several occasions with such injuries as a fractured skull, contusions, blood blisters on the penis, marked swelling and discoloration of the left arm and fingertips, burned fingers, puncture wounds and strangulation marks, and welts. The infant's father, who was separated from the mother, sued the defendants, claiming that the hospital did not report and that the lack of report was the cause of the infant's permanent brain damage. The California case was settled out of court for $600,000 (Besharov 1985:32–33)

Social workers can also be exposed to liability risks in wrongful reporting. All states grant immunity from civil and criminal liability to people who report. Almost all states require that professionals report suspected abuse and neglect *in good faith* if they are to be granted immunity from liability (Besharov 1985:39). Hence, "bad faith" reporting may expose social workers to liability. In *Austin v. French* (1980), for example, a suit against a Virginia physician accused the doctor of maliciously reporting a child who had various bruised knots on his body. The doctor berated the parents on two occasions for their treatment of the child and allegedly made "unnecessarily irresponsible and defamatory" remarks toward the parents. It was eventually demonstrated, however, that the bruising was the result of the child's hemophilia. The case was settled for $5,000 (Besharov 1985:41),

In contrast the mental health counselor sued in *Lux v. Hansen* (1989) for filing a report of child abuse was not found liable, even though her conclusion that the child had been sexually abused by her father was erroneous. The court concluded that the counselor had reason to suspect child abuse, in light of comments made by the child, and that under the qualified immunity doctrine, "liability may be found only if a defendant's conduct reflects bad faith or violates clearly established statutory or constitutional rights" ("Counselor Who Suspected Child Abuse," 1990:4).

Similar issues emerged in *Vineyard v. Craft* (1992), in which a Texas appellate court held that a psychotherapist who erroneously concluded that a child had been sexually abused by her father could not be sued by the father for harm to his family relationship, allegedly the result of the therapist's report to the child protection agency ("Psychotherapist May Not Be Sued," 1992:4). The court held that the risk of harm to the family's interests that may result from an erroneous child abuse report was outweighed by the public's interest in protecting children by obtaining professionals' opinions when sexual abuse is suspected.

Controversy surrounding reports of abuse and neglect can sometimes trigger what are known as *adverse employment action lawsuits*. An example would be a suit filed by a worker in a residential program who claims that actions she took to report institutional abuse that occurred in her program resulted in some form of disciplinary action against her by agency administrators. Besharov presents a compelling case summary of this phenomenon:

> I was fired from my position as the only social worker at [a center for the treatment of cerebral palsy] because I was advocating for a child who attended the center. The child, an eleven year old who was fully ambulatory, was tied into a wheelchair from 9 to 3 each day for the past three years in order to prevent his acting out self abusive behavior. A helmet was placed on his head and tied to the back of the wheelchair and his upper arms were tied behind him. No motion was possible. In addition, he was heavily sedated. On the basis of my previous, extensive work with handicapped children, examination of the reports in the child's file and discussions with my colleagues at the agency, I believed that the child had, in addition, been misdiagnosed as severely retarded and was in the wrong program at the Center. After trying, without success, for four months to convince the Center administration, the psychologist and the doctors to untie the boy, to reevaluate him and to plan a proper educational program for him, I contacted the Chairman of the Board of Trustees of our agency and asked him to intervene. Three weeks after contacting him, the

child's situation was unchanged and I then notified [the state agency that had placed the child and the state agency responsible for investigating reports of child abuse].

I did not seek support from the child's parents because staff members had reported that the child was tied and kept in a closet at home. I had met the mother and believed that she could not, at that time, be helpful to the child.

I then gave information to the [state agency] and was immediately suspended from my job. I received my salary for 55 days and was then fired, with a dismissal letter containing false statements that will totally damage my professional reputation as a social worker. I asked for an evaluation of my work at the agency the day I was fired and was refused. I also utilized all of the grievance procedures that were available to me according to the agency's written Personnel Policies, but my efforts were ignored. (1985:43–44)

The social worker accepted a $5,000 settlement after realizing that the legal fees generated by her suit might exceed the value of any additional payment she might receive.

Inadequately Protecting a Child

Social workers are frequently in a position to investigate reports of abuse and neglect and then arrange, provide, or monitor substitute care for children who have been abused or neglected. Such care may be provided in foster care, group homes, or other residential settings. Many public and private child welfare agencies are overwhelmed by this daunting task. In many programs budgets and resources cannot keep pace with ever-growing case loads.

One unfortunate correlate of strained programs and social workers is litigation related to protective service professionals not accepting a report for investigation. *Mammo v. Arizona* (1983) is a classic example. In this case the father of an infant filed a wrongful death suit against the Arizona Department of Economic Security, alleging that the department failed to carry out its duty to accept and investigate reports. The infant died as a result of an apparent homicide. Both the police and the father—the noncustodial parent—had contact with the department, conveying their concern about the possibility of child abuse. During two weekends the father had observed bruises on the bodies of the infant's two older siblings. After the father spoke with an intake unit supervisor in the department's child protective services division, the department took no action except to recommend that the father retain an attorney to contest the mother's custody of the children. The jury returned a verdict of $1 million in the father's favor, although the trial judge reduced the award to $300,000 (the judge believed the award was excessive).

Jensen v. Conrad (1984) illustrates a lawsuit alleging lack of proper investigation of a report. The county department of social services attempted to contact a woman named Clark after her child's school principal alerted the department to the possibility of child abuse. After numerous attempts to contact Clark by letters, telephone calls, and home visits, the department classified the case as unfounded and closed the investigation. About two months later the child's younger brother was killed by Clark's boyfriend, who was subsequently tried and convicted of murder.

Once protective services staff members are concerned about a child's safety, they have a responsibility to place a child in protective custody. They may be liable if they do not take proper steps to protect the child. In a case reported by Besharov , a Louisville, Kentucky, child protection worker and the worker's supervisor were charged with official misconduct involving the death of a three-year-old child. A physician attending the child was also indicted. The allegation was that the various professionals failed to take appropriate steps to protect the child by placing the child in protective custody. All charges were dismissed but only because the judge concluded, "It offends my sense of fairness that these three people were chosen [for prosecution] when everyone else who came into contact with the child could have been charged as well" (cited in Besharov 1985:66).

Issues related to inadequate protection of a child were central to the landmark case of *DeShaney v. Winnebago County Department of Social Services* (1989). In this case the U.S. Supreme Court ruled that the Winnebago County, Wisconsin, Department of Social Services and several of its social work staff members could not be held liable for damages in not protecting a child who had been severely abused by his father. *DeShaney* raised a number of important constitutional issues, primarily related to the Fourteenth Amendment to the U.S. Constitution, which forbids the state or its agents from depriving individuals of their right to life, liberty, or property without due process of law. The court of appeals held in this case that "the state's failure to protect people from private violence, or other mishaps not attributable to the conduct of its employees, is not a deprivation of constitutionally protected property or liberty" (*DeShaney*, 812 F.2d 298 at 301).

Social workers can also incur liability risks in returning at-risk children to dangerous foster parents and in providing inadequate case monitoring. Practitioners must be careful to ensure that children are returned home only when the evidence is substantial that the parents no longer pose a danger. They must also be sure to monitor children's progress carefully. In *Bugue v. Iowa* (1980), for example, the noncustodial father claimed that the department of social services was negligent in the monitoring of his thirty-four-month-old daughter's safety after he reported his suspicion of abuse. Although the staff had decided to leave the child in the home and provide supportive services, no follow-up visit to the family was made. The child was later killed by the mother's lover. The case was settled for $82,500 (Besharov 1985:70).

Violating Parental Rights

Protective service workers must be careful not to violate parents' rights while they conduct investigations and provide social services after reports of abuse or neglect. Because of the volatility of family emotions surrounding allegations of abuse and neglect, social workers must be particularly alert to any violations of parents' rights.

One potential problem is unnecessarily intrusive investigations in which social workers' investigative methods may be excessive, harassing, or constitute an invasion of privacy. In *Hale v. City of Virginia Beach*, for example, a father who was investigated sued two workers and the agency, alleging that the workers harassed him, threatened him with prosecution, and publicized false remarks about him to third parties. The Virginia case was settled for $4,000.

Of course, investigations of abuse and neglect sometimes result in the removal of children from the home. Often these placements are in the children's best interest and are not contested by the parents. On other occasions, however, parents vehemently object to the children's removal. In some cases parents sue, alleging wrongful removal. *Doe v. Hennepin County* illustrates this phenomenon. In this case parents sued the county, alleging that the child protection agency unjustly removed their child from the home. The court ruled that the parents had made a "sufficient showing that fact questions exist concerning whether defendants' actions were reasonable and in good faith" (cited in Besharov 1985:94).

Inadequate Foster Care Services

Once children are placed in foster care, social workers have a responsibility to ensure the safety and overall quality of this substitute care. Unfortunately, sometimes children are placed with abusive foster parents. Tragically, a number of court cases document this phenomenon (Besharov 1985:111–15).

Of course, foster children can also pose a risk to foster parents (Besharov 1985). Lawsuits against social workers and child welfare agencies have alleged that foster children have killed a foster parent (*Snyder v. Mouser* 1971; *Kreuger v. Louise Wise Services*, cited in Besharov 1985:109); damaged or destroyed property (*Seavy v. State* 1966), and infected a foster parent with a serious virus (*Vaughn v. North Carolina Department of Human Resources* 1979). Clearly, social workers must do their best to identify risks foster children may pose and either inform potential foster parents of the risk or seek alternative placements.

Once children are placed in foster care, social workers may be held accountable if they do not provide proper treatment services to the children and in some cases their parents. Although relatively few lawsuits make these allegations, some do. In *Little v. Utah State Division of Family Services* (1983), for example, the state agency was found liable after an autistic little girl died; the court found the agency had failed to adequately train the girl's foster parents and other substitute caretakers, make timely evaluations of her condition, provide appropriate safety equipment (such as headgear), and arrange for proper supervision. In *Cameron v. Montgomery County Child Welfare Services*, one of the claims of the plaintiff, a foster child, was that the child welfare agency had prevented parental supervision and failed to provide services to the mother that might have helped the child return home. The case was settled for $5,000 (Besharov 1985:120).

Defamation of Character

Social workers involved in protective services have to be particularly careful to avoid defamation of parents' character. Practitioners must avoid unwarranted characterizations of parents—whether oral or written—that might be considered defamatory. But social workers in all settings must be careful about defamation.

Defamation occurs as a result of "the publication of anything injurious to the good name or reputation of another, or which tends to bring him into disrepute" (Gifis 1991:124). Defamation can take two forms: libel and slander. *Libel* occurs when the publication is in written form. *Slander* occurs when the publication occurs in oral form. More specifically, social workers can be liable for defamation if they say or write something that is untrue, they knew or should have known to be untrue, and caused some injury to the plaintiff. The social worker's defense against an allegation of defamation is that the statement was true, the client signed a valid consent form authorizing the release of information, or the social worker had a legal responsibility to disclose the information, for example, to comply with a mandatory reporting law (Schutz 1982:10).

In the well-known case of *Berry v. Moench* (1958), Dr. Moench, a psychiatrist, was sued by Berry because Dr. Moench wrote a letter that Berry alleged included false and derogatory information about him. Berry had been Dr. Moench's patient seven years before. Dr. Moench had written a letter to a Dr. Hellewell concerning Berry's emotional stability and background. The daughter of former patients of Dr. Hellewell, who had requested the letter from Dr. Moench, was engaged to Berry. In his letter to Dr. Hellewell, Dr. Moench made the following comments about Berry:

> He was treated here in 1949 as an emergency. Our diagnosis was Manic [sic] depressive depression in a psychopathic personality. . . . The patient was attempting to go through school on the G.I. bill. . . . Instead of attending class he would spend most of the days and nights playing cards for money. . . . During his care here, he purchased a brand new Packard, without even money to buy gasoline. . . . He was in constant trouble with the authorities during the war. . . . He did not do well in school and never did really support his wife and children. . . . My suggestion to the infatuated girl would be to run as fast and as far as she possibly could in any direction away from him. (331 P.2d 814 at 816 [1958], cited in Austin, Moline, and Williams 1990:91)

Dr. Moench acknowledged that much of the information contained in the letter was based on information obtained from Berry's former wife, his referring doctor, and his former wife's sister. The court ruled that Dr. Moench had committed libel.

Social workers involved in protective services must be especially aware of defamation issues. In the *Austin* case involving the child with hemophilia, for example, the physician accused of wrongful reporting of child abuse was accused of making "unnecessarily irresponsible and defamatory" remarks toward the parents (Besharov 1985:41). Similar allegations were made in the *Hale* case, discussed earlier in relation to unnecessarily intrusive investigations. In this case the plaintiffs alleged that the workers "maliciously and falsely addressed remarks to third persons, the substance of which were [sic] that the plaintiff was an alcoholic; that the plaintiff was mentally unstable and was a 'very sick man'; that he was guilty of child molestation; that they were going to take his child or children away from him; and that he would be prosecuted criminally" (cited in Besharov 1985:79).

Allegations of defamation can occur even when practitioners think they were being careful, as in *Gasperini v. Manginelli* (1949), in which the plaintiff, the father of the patient discussed in an order for psychiatric hospitalization, claimed that libel occurred when the physician failed to attach *Jr.* to the name on the medical report. Of course, in some cases allegations of defamation are brought because of explicit labels attached to clients, as in *Iverson v. Frandsen* (1956), in which a psychologist was sued for stating in his psychological report that the plaintiff's nine-year-old daughter was "feeble-minded" and "a high-grade moron." Other cases have involved allegations that defamation occurred when professionals used phrases such as "pathological character" and "criminal elements" (see *McDermott v. Hughley* 1989) and "longstanding personality disorder" (*Roth v. Tuckman* 1990). Although such defamation suits often are unsuccessful, mounting a defense usually is costly and burdensome.

4 | Service Delivery: Impaired Social Workers

Some liability claims against social workers are the result of honest mistakes. Careless oversight, such as forgetting to get a client to complete an informed-consent form before releasing confidential information to another agency, can lead to a lawsuit. Other liability claims may result from well-intentioned, deliberate decisions, as when a social worker decides to breach a client's privacy in order to protect a third party from harm. And unfortunately, many liability claims result from incompetent practice carried out by impaired social workers.

> George M., M.S.W., was the director of clinical services at Family Services Associates, Inc., a local family service agency. He had been clinical director for six years, after having been a caseworker and family counselor at the agency for five years. George M. had also worked for three years as a mental health coordinator at a local community mental health center. George M. was in the process of divorcing his wife.
>
> In addition to supervising clinical staff, George M. usually carried three or four cases of his own. One involved a twenty-six-year-old woman who sought counseling for anxiety symp-

toms and problems with self-esteem. George M. conducted the initial intake interview and decided to handle the case himself. George M. and his client spent a number of weeks fruitfully exploring a number of family-of-origin issues that concerned the client.

During the eighth week of treatment the client mentioned that she wanted to talk about an event that occurred when she was seventeen years old, when she had been sexually molested by her older brother. In her judgment a considerable portion of her present-day anxiety could be traced to that event and subsequent sexual contact with her brother. George M. and his client spent several weeks exploring these issues.

At the end of the twelfth session the client began crying, following some discussion about the sexual assault. George M. got up from his chair and embraced the client. He also began to kiss her. George M. then said that he thought he could be very helpful to his client by showing her what unconditional sincere lovemaking was like. He dimmed the lights in his office and made love to his client.

George M. and his client continued to have sexual contact for about two months, at which point the relationship became strained. The client began treatment with a new social worker in a different agency. The client disclosed to the social worker that she and George M. had been sexually involved during the course of their professional relationship. After considerable discussion with her client, the social worker encouraged her client to file an ethics complaint against George M. and to consult an attorney about suing him.

The Nature of Impairment

In recent years various professions have begun to pay increased attention to the problem of impaired practitioners (portions of this discussion are adapted from Reamer 1992a). In 1972, for example, the Council on Mental Health of the American Medical Association released a statement that said that physicians have an ethical responsibility to recognize and report impairment among colleagues. In 1976 a group of attorneys recovering from alcoholism started Lawyers Concerned for Lawyers to address chemical dependence in the profession, and in 1980 a group of recovering psychologists inaugurated a similar group, Psychologists Helping Psychologists (Kilburg, Nathan, and Thoreson 1986; Knutsen 1977; Laliotis and Grayson 1985; McCrady 1989). In 1981 the American Psychological Association held its first open forum on impairment at its annual meeting (Stadler et al. 1988).

Social work's first national acknowledgment of the problem of impaired practitioners came in 1979, when the NASW released a public policy statement on alcoholism and alcohol-related problems (NASW 1987a). By 1980 a small nationwide support group for chemically dependent practitioners, Social Workers Helping Social Workers, had formed (by 1987, however, it had only sixty-five members; see NASW 1987a). In 1982 NASW established the Occupational Social Work Task Force, which was charged with developing a "consistent professional approach for distressed NASW members" (NASW 1987a:7). In 1984 the NASW Delegate Assembly issued a resolution on impairment, and in 1987 NASW published the *Impaired Social Worker Program Resource Book*, prepared by the NASW Commission on Employment and Economic Support, to help practitioners design programs for impaired social workers. The introduction to the resource book states:

> Social workers, like other professionals, have within their ranks those who, because of substance abuse, chemical dependency, mental illness or stress, are unable to function effectively in their jobs. These are the impaired social workers. . . . The problem of impairment is compounded by the fact that the professionals who suffer from the effect of mental illness, stress or substance abuse are like anyone else; they are often the worst judges of their behavior, the last to recognize their problems and the least motivated to seek help. Not only are they able to hide or avoid confronting their behavior, they are often abetted by colleagues who find it difficult to accept that a professional could let his or her problem get out of hand. (1987a:6)

Organized efforts to address impaired workers began in the late 1930s and early 1940s after the Alcoholics Anonymous emerged and during World War II's need to retain a sound work force. These early occupational alcoholism programs eventually led, in the early 1970s, to the emergence of employee assistance programs (EAPs), designed to address a broad range of problems experienced by workers.

More recently, strategies for dealing with professionals whose work is affected by problems such as substance abuse, mental illness, and emotional stress have become more prevalent and visible. Professional associations and informal groups of practitioners are convening to examine the extent of impairment among colleagues and to organize efforts to address the problem (Bissell and Haberman 1984; Prochaska and Norcross 1983).

Ironically, however, in contrast to a number of other helping professions, the social work literature contains little discussion of impaired professionals. The subject index of *Social Work Research & Abstracts* does not include a discrete heading concerning impaired professionals. In addition, a search (up through 1991) of such headings as *alcoholism, drug use, mental illness, ethics and values,* and *burnout* produced only two articles in social work journals that were devoted primarily to the problem of impairment among social workers (Bissell, Fewell, and Jones 1980; Fausel 1988). Not until 1992 was a widely disseminated article on the subject of impairment in the profession published in a major social work journal (Reamer 1992a). Since 1985, however, *Psychological Abstracts* has had a separate heading that lists a large number of publications on impaired practitioners in other social services and health-care professions, including medicine, psychiatry, psychology, and counseling.

This review of literature suggests that although a number of other professions have begun extensive discussions in journals and books of the problem of impaired practitioners—a major means of educating members and preventing malpractice and liability claims—social work has not. Despite the occasional discussion of specific forms of impairment among practitioners—most notably alcoholism—in the social work literature, there is a paucity of discussion of the general problem of impairment (U.S. Department of Health and Human Services 1989). At this point in its history social work knows little about the prevalence of impairment within its ranks, and the profession's efforts to address the problem and prevent liability claims are nascent at best (Berliner 1989; Reamer 1992a, 1992b).

Extent of Impairment

Both the seriousness of impairment among social workers and the forms it takes vary. Impairment may involve failure to provide competent care or violation of the ethical standards of the profession. It may also take such forms as providing flawed or inferior psychotherapy to a client, sexual involvement with a client, or failure to carry out professional duties as a result of substance abuse or mental illness. Lamb et al. (1987) provide a comprehensive definition of *impairment among professionals*:

> Interference in professional functioning that is reflected in one or more of the following ways: (a) an inability and/or unwillingness to acquire and integrate professional standards into one's repertoire of professional behavior; (b) an inability to acquire professional skills in order to reach an acceptable level of competency; and (c) an inability to control personal stress, psychological dysfunction, and/or excessive emotional reactions that interfere with professional functioning. (p. 598)

Unfortunately, no precise estimates of the extent of impairment among social workers are available. No comprehensive surveys have been conducted. Only rough estimates (at best) of the extent of the problem have been made. For example, in the foreword to the *Impaired Social Worker Resource Book* published by the NASW Commission on Employment and Economic Support (1987a), Ruth Antoniades, who chaired the commission, states, "Social workers have the same problems as most working groups. Up to 5 to 7 percent of our membership may have a problem with substance abuse. Another 10 to 15 percent may be going through personal transitions in their relationships, marriage, family, or their work life" (p. 4). The report goes on to conclude, however, that "there is little reliable information on the extent of impairment among social workers" (p. 6).

Given the distressing absence of empirical data on social workers, it is not possible to estimate precisely the prevalence of impairment within the profession. Therefore, social workers must look primarily to what is known about impairment in professions that are allied with social work, such as psychology and psychiatry. Of course, prevalence rates for social workers cannot be inferred on the basis of data from these professions. However, despite some important differences in their mission, methods, and organizational context, practitioners in these professions offer a number of similar services and face similar forms of occupational stress and strain.

Prevalence studies conducted among psychologists, for example, suggest a significant degree of distress within that profession. In a study of 749 psychologists, Guy, Poelstra, and Stark (1989) found that 74.3 percent reported "personal distress" during the previous three years and 36.7 percent of this group believed that their distress decreased the quality of care they provided to clients. Pope, Tabachnick, and Keith-Spiegel (1987) reported that 62.2 percent of the members of Division 29 (Psychotherapy) of the American Psychological Association admitted to "working when too distressed to be effective" (p. 993). In their survey of 167 licensed psychologists Wood et al. (1985) found that nearly one-third (32.3 percent) reported experiencing depression or burnout to an extent that interfered with their work. They also found that a significant portion of their sample reported being aware of colleagues whose work was seriously affected by drug or alcohol use, sexual overtures toward clients, or depression and burnout. In addition, evidence exists that psychologists and psychiatrists commit suicide at a rate five to six times higher than the general population (Farber 1983, cited in Millon, Millon, and Antoni 1986).

In the one published prevalence study that included social workers, Deutsch (1985) found that more than half her sample of social workers, psychologists, and master's-level counselors reported significant problems with depression. Nearly four-fifths (82 percent) reported problems with relationships, approximately one-tenth (11 percent) reported substance abuse problems, and 2 percent reported suicide attempts. Bissell and Haberman (1984:65) indicate that 24 percent of a sample of 50 alcoholic social workers they surveyed reported overt suicide attempts, a rate higher than that reported by dentists, attorneys, and physicians in the Bissell and Haberman sample of alcoholics.

In a comprehensive review of a series of empirical studies focused specifically on sexual contact between therapists and clients, Pope (1988) concluded that the aggregate average of reported sexual contact is 8.3 percent by male therapists and 1.7 percent by female therapists. Pope reported that one study (Gechtman and Bouhoutsos 1985) found that 3.8 percent of male social workers admitted to sexual contact with clients.

Not all sexual abuse engaged in by social workers involves clients. A compelling example of this appeared in a prominently placed newspaper article:

> A social worker who at one time counseled abused children was sentenced yesterday to serve 20 years in prison for sexually assaulting two minors.
>
> Lawrence F. Coleman, 41, of 1540 Douglas Ave., North Providence was sentenced by Judge John F. Sheehan. The judge imposed a 30-year sentence but suspended 10 years.
>
> The victims, who are now adults, were not in any counseling program with Coleman.
>
> One of the victims addressed the court before sentencing. Her voice choked with emotion, she said that the sexual assaults had devastated her and given her low self-esteem. . . .
>
> In January Coleman was arraigned on 10 counts of first degree sexual assault before Superior Court Judge John P. Bourcier. He was freed on $100,000 surety bail. In March he pleaded guilty before Judge Sheehan, who kept bail at the same amount.
>
> Coleman earned a degree in clinical psychology from Rhode Island College in 1981 and another in social work from Boston University in 1984.
>
> He worked as a counselor at a health center in Greenville, counseling children who were victims of physical and sexual abuse. (Crombie 1989:B3)

Causes of Impairment

Several studies report a variety of forms and sources of impairment among mental health professionals. Guy, Poelstra, and Stark (1989) and Thoreson, Miller, and Krauskopf (1989) found diverse sources of stress reported in clinicians' lives, including their jobs, the illness or death of family members, marital or relationship problems, financial problems, mid-life crises, personal physical or mental illness, legal problems, and substance abuse.

Lamb et al. (1987) argued that professional education itself can produce unique forms of stress and impairment, primarily as a result of the close clinical supervision to which students are typically subjected, the disruption in their personal lives that is often caused by the demands of schoolwork and internships, and the pressures of their academic programs. These authors found that the most common sources of impairment are personality disorders, depression and other emotional problems, marital problems, and physical illness. It is interesting that academic problems and alcohol or drug abuse were rarely cited as sources of impairment.

This review of research suggests that distress among clinicians generally falls into two categories: environmental stress, which is a function of employment conditions (actual working conditions and the broader culture's lack of support of the human services mission) or professional training and personal stress, caused by problems with marriage, relationships, emotional and physical health, and finances. Of course, these two types of stress are often interrelated.

With respect to psychotherapists in particular, Wood et al. (1985) noted that professionals encounter special problems from the extension of their therapeutic role into the nonwork aspects of their lives (such as relationships with friends and family members), the absence of reciprocity in relationships with clients (therapists are "always giving"), the frequently slow and erratic nature of the therapeutic process, and personal issues that are raised as a result of their work with clients. As Kilburg, Kaslow, and VandenBos conclude,

> [the] stresses of daily life—family responsibilities, death of family members and friends, other severe losses, illnesses, financial difficulties, crises of all kinds—quite naturally place mental health professionals, like other people, under pressure. However, by virtue of their training and place in society, such professionals face unique stresses. And although they have been trained extensively in how to deal with the emotional and behavioral crises of others, few are trained in how to deal with the stresses they themselves will face. . . . Mental health professionals are expected by everyone, including themselves, to be paragons. The fact that they may be unable to fill that role makes them a prime target for disillusionment, distress, and burnout. When this reaction occurs, the individual's ability to function as a professional may become impaired. (1988:723)

A recurring theme in cases involving practitioner impairment is the problem of professional boundaries. Particularly in cases involving sexual involvement with clients, practitioners typically display confusion about what constitutes appropriate boundaries between themselves and their clients and about the need to clearly delineate the practitioner's and client's involvement in each other's lives (Landers 1992). The combination of a needy social worker and needy client can be disastrous. In these instances both parties are more likely to be confused about, or will simply ignore warning signs and risks related to, inappropriate involvement that may take the form of sexual contact, socializing, or business involvement unrelated to treatment. The phenomenon of what has come to be known as *dual relationships* has generated a wide range of ethical problems and liability risks. As Brodsky (1986) notes,

> A sexual intimacy between patient and therapist is one example of a dual relationship. Dual relationships involve more than one purpose of relating. A therapy relationship is meant to be exclusive and unidimensional. The therapist is the expert, the patient the consumer of that expertise. Once a patient accepts an individual as a therapist, that individual cannot, without undue influence, relate to that patient in any other role. Relating to the patient as an employer, business partner, lover, spouse, relative, professor, or student would contaminate the therapeutic goal. The contamination is much more intense in a psychotherapy relationship than it would be in the relationship between a client and a professional in any other field—for example, between a client and an internist, a dentist, a lawyer, or an accountant. (p. 155)

The problems of confused boundaries and dual relationships were readily apparent in a case on which I recently consulted. In this case, a thirty-seven-year-old woman with a history of childhood sexual abuse sought counseling from a clinical social worker. They worked together for a number of months. Over time, however, the social worker and the client began spending time together outside of counseling sessions. Ultimately, the client sued the social worker, alleging that the social worker's improper maintenance of boundaries was injurious. In addition, the state's attorney general's office filed an action in administrative court seeking to revoke the social worker's license. Evidence presented in the suit and in depositions filed in the case suggested that the social worker and client shared a motel room while the social worker attended a professional conference, that the social worker provided the client with a number of gifts and wrote affectionate and intimate notes to the client, they dined together in the social worker's home, they had inappropriate physical contact, the social worker disclosed personal details of her own life to the client, and together they viewed a videotape while both were on the social worker's bed in the social worker's home. In her defense the social worker argued that all the actions she took in the case were for "therapeutic purposes."

In recent years the two problems of sexual contact between social service professionals and clients and of substance abuse among social service professionals have begun to receive particular attention. These two phenomena have figured prominently in a significant number of liability and malpractice claims against social workers.

Sexual Abuse of Clients

As I indicated in chapter 1, a staggering percentage of liability claims against social workers involve allegations of sexual contact between practitioner and client. Between 1969 and 1990 nearly one in every five claims (18.5 percent) against social workers insured through the program sponsored by the NASW Insurance Trust alleged some form of sexual impropriety, and more than two-fifths (41.3 percent) of insurance payments were the result of claims concerning sexual impropriety. Clearly, this is a serious problem, one that is not unique to social work. Other therapeutic professions and disciplines (for example, psychiatry, psychology, counseling) face comparable problems.

All the available data suggest that the vast majority of cases involving sexual contact between professionals and clients involve a male practitioner and female client (Brodsky 1986; Pope 1988). Gartrell et al. (1986, cited in Meyer, Landis, and Hays 1988:23) report in their nationwide survey of psychiatrists that 6.4 percent of respondents acknowledged sexual contact with their own patients; 90 percent of the offenders were male.

A relatively small number of cases involve sexual contact between a female practitioner and male client and between practitioner and client of the same gender. However, as Brodsky (1986) suggests in her discussion of offending psychologists, typically

the following characteristics constitute a prototype of the therapist being sued: The therapist is male, middle aged, involved in unsatisfactory relationships in his own life, perhaps in the process of going through a divorce. His patient caseload is primarily female. He becomes involved with more than one patient sexually, those selected being on the average 16 years younger than he is. He confides his personal life to the patient, implying to her that he needs her, and he spends therapy sessions soliciting her help with his personal problems. The therapist is a lonely man, and even if he works in a group practice, he is somewhat isolated professionally, not sharing in close consultation with his peers. He may have a good reputation in the psychological or psychiatric community, having been in practice for many years. He tends to take cases through referral only. He is not necessarily physically attractive, but there is an aura of power or charisma about him. His lovemaking often leaves much to be desired, but he is quite convincing to the patient that it is he above all others with whom she needs to be making love. (pp. 157–58)

Brodsky (1986) also describes other sexually abusive therapists, including those who tend to be inexperienced and in love with one particular client and therapists with a personality disorder (typically antisocial personality disorder) who manipulate clients into believing that they—the therapists—should be trusted and that they have the clients' best interest at heart.

The case of *Walker v. Parzen* (Association of Trial Lawyers, June 1983) typifies the sexual abuse of a client by a therapist. According to court records, Dr. Parzen, a psychiatrist, had sex with Walker during a two-and-a-half year period, during which time he charged her $55 per session. The plaintiff eventually divorced her husband, lost her rights under California community property law, and lost custody of her two children. Dr. Parzen had also prescribed excessive medication for Walker, who claimed that she had tried to commit suicide more than a dozen times using pills obtained from Dr. Parzen or his office, according to court records. Dr. Parzen ultimately referred Walker to another physician, referring to her as a "borderline psychotic." The jury awarded damages in the amount of $4,631,666 (cited in Reaves 1986:175).

Therapists who are sued and try to defend their sexual contact with clients usually offer two arguments (Schutz 1982:34–35). The first is that the sexual contact was an essential legitimate component of therapy. The therapist typically claims that he was merely trying to be helpful to the client. The defense offered by a Dr. Cooper in *Cooper v. California Board of Medical Examiners* (1972) is illustrative:

> Dr. Cooper is a firm believer in the fact that the body has a tremendous significance and influence on our actions; and the awareness of one's body is one of the keys to personal health; mental health; and his techniques may be considered new, revolutionary, and even bizarre perhaps to some people. But none of us knows the potential of the human body in relation to the human mind, and to explore that and make a person whole is Dr. Cooper's dedicated professional goal.   (cited in Schutz 1982:34–35)

The second common defense is that the sexual relationship was conducted independently of the therapeutic relationship. In these instances the defendant-therapist usually argues that he and the client were able to separate their sexual involvement from their professional relationship. As Schutz (1982) suggests, however, this argument "has not been a very successful defense, since courts are reluctant to accept such a compartmentalized view of human relationships. A therapist attempting to prove the legitimacy of sexual relations between himself and a patient by establishing that two coterminous-in-time but utterly parallel relations existed has a difficult task" (p. 35).

Listed here is a mere sample and diverse cross section of a distressingly large number of recent court cases and disciplinary hearings involving allegations of sexual misconduct:

- A married couple were receiving counseling from a clinical social worker. The wife learned that the social worker and her husband had gotten involved in a homosexual relationship. The social worker claimed that the plaintiffs, the husband and wife, suffered no harm and that the husband consented to the physical contact. The husband alleged that his injuries included long-term depression and loss of libido. The wife alleged that her injuries included depression and debilitating fear of AIDS. The Massachusetts jury returned a verdict for both plaintiffs in the amount of $1.29 million (*Doe v. Fanning*, cited in "Marriage Counselor Sexually Abuses," 1990:6).

- A psychiatrist hospitalized a thirty-year-old housewife and had sexual contact with her in the hospital and subsequently during office visits. A psychologist involved in the case was accused of encouraging the woman to have sexual relations with the psychiatrist. The psychiatrist did not deny the sexual contact but claimed that he was in love with the plaintiff. The psychologist argued that she did not encourage their relationship. The Pennsylvania case was settled for $275,000 (*Petroski and Petroski v. Anonymous Psychiatrist, Psychologist and Hospital*, cited in "Psychologist Encourages," 1989:2).

- The patient of a psychiatrist claimed that they had sexual relations in the psychiatrist's office. The plaintiff alleged that the psychiatrist told her that they could not have a sexual relationship if she was his patient and that the psychiatrist orchestrated a phony termination process. Under the doctrine of comparative negligence the jury found the defendant 82 percent liable and the plaintiff 18 percent liable. The Colorado jury awarded the plaintiff $218,000 (*Roberts-Henry v. Jason Richter*, cited in "Psychiatric Patient Has Sexual Relationship," 1989:4).

- A fifty-five-year-old housewife claimed that she and her psychiatrist had a sexual relationship for thirteen years during office visits. The psychiatrist admitted the sexual relations but claimed that the relationship had been consensual. The plaintiff was awarded $3 million in the Oregon case (*Hinkle v. Dr. Petroske*, cited in "Psychiatrist Has Sex," 1989:6).

- A troubled wife sought counseling from a marriage therapist. The husband also attended three sessions. When the husband mentioned suicide during one session, the suit claimed that the therapist suggested that he should go ahead and kill himself. Ten months after the wife moved from the area, the therapist contacted her and convinced her to meet with him again, according to the suit. They began to have sexual relations. Both the wife and husband sued, the latter claiming loss of consortium, professional malpractice, outrageous conduct, and reckless infliction of emotional distress. The wife settled for $375,000 during trial. The California jury returned a verdict for the husband in the amount of $1.85 million in compensatory damages and $1.53 million in punitive damages. After the verdict, the parties settled for $850,000 (*Ertel v. Kersenbrock*, cited in "Marriage Therapist Has Affair," 1990:3).

- A woman sought counseling from a psychologist regarding the effects of childhood sexual abuse by her father. The woman sued the psychologist, alleging that within weeks after treatment began the psychologist had her sitting near his feet, then on his lap, and then began stroking her hair and back. According to the suit, shortly thereafter the two were involved in sexual relations. The suit claimed that as a result the woman would not be able to hold a meaningful job, was unable to maintain a normal relationship with men, attempted to commit suicide, and would require treatment for the rest of her life. The New York case was settled for $2.6 million (*Grogan v. Osborne* 1990, cited in "Patient Sexually Abused," 1990:3).

- A woman sought counseling from a counselor, a lesbian, to address issues related to a sexual problem she was having with her female roommate and occasional lover. The client believed that the counselor's own sexual orientation would help her deal with the issues. During the course of treatment the client invited the counselor to have dinner with her and three other women. The counselor and client became sexually involved while the counselor was still providing the woman with counseling services. The counselor was found grossly negligent by the California Board of Behavioral Science Examiners and her license was revoked (*In re Doyle*, cited in "Counselor Begins Sexual Relationship," 1991:1).

- A fifteen-year-old was admitted to a residential treatment center for substance abuse counseling. One month before the youngster's discharge, he and his father learned that the boy's counselor was having an affair with the boy's mother. The Texas jury awarded $3.34 million, including $3 million in punitive damages (*Wasson v. Westbranch Residential Treatment Center, Inc.*, cited in "Drug Treatment Counselor," 1992:3).

In some cases involving allegations of sexual contact, courts have ruled that a counselor was not negligent because the client did not have a "trust relationship" with the counselor. In *Sisson v. Seneca Mental Health/Mental Retardation Council, Inc.* (1991), for example, the court ruled that because an outpatient at a mental health facility had met the counselor only once in his professional capacity at the hospital, their subsequent relationship had been outside the context of therapy sessions ("No 'Trust Relationship,' " 1991:4).

Rehabilitation of mental health professionals who have been sexually involved with clients is daunting. One-time offenders who made an isolated mistake with an individual client can often be helped through therapy and education. However, the rehabilitative prospects for chronic offenders and professionals with personality disorders, such as antisocial personality disorder, are often grim. As Brodsky (1986) concludes, "The therapist whose motives were less than honorable, who had intimacies with several patients, and who, in the case of men, is chronically problematic in relationships with women outside of therapy is probably not easily rehabilitated. In some cases of personality disorder, it is questionable whether or not retraining of the therapist is possible" (p. 164).

Practitioner Substance Abuse

Most studies related to substance abuse among social service professionals focus on alcohol. Relatively little research has been conducted on other drug use among practitioners. Here is an illustrative case example:

Miss Jones was the clinical supervisor for an off-site social work follow-up counseling service of a large public hospital.

She was 61 years old, and she had recurring mild back pain resulting from a herniated disk, a problem that could be managed without surgery through diet control, exercise, and correct posture. She had worked for the agency for approximately 8 years, serving for the last 2 as supervisor of the off-site outpatient counseling and guidance service. She supervised a clinical staff of four social workers, one psychologist, and three counselors, all of whom were between 25 and 45 years old. Miss Jones had gradually become the agency's resident "alcohol expert" because she had been sent to a number of seminars and workshops on alcohol-related problems during the last 5 years.

Some months after Miss Jones had transferred to the off-site office, individual staff members began to note an apparent deterioration in her work performance. She became less available for supervision of and consultation with staff members, less systematic in the review of cases, and erratic in keeping supervision appointments, and she began to end supervision sessions abruptly after only 10 to 15 minutes. Moreover, clinical staff also was beginning to hear complaints from clients who had direct clinical contact with Miss Jones. Furthermore, Miss Jones's administrative functioning seemed to be deteriorating; she seemed unable to produce needed administrative reports, was erratic and inconsistent in administrative decision making, and was unable to systematically follow through on administrative details.

Concurrently, her co-workers noted an apparent change in personality and behavior. She seemed to have withdrawn and become aloof. She spent less time informally chatting with staff, and she stopped sharing lunch hours with her co-workers. Her absences from work increased, and it became more and more frequent that she would arrive at work late or leave work early because of "not feeling up to par." Clinical and clerical staff began to note a pattern of Miss Jones's having alcohol on her breath during the afternoon and to appear more frequently to be behaviorally "under the influence of alcohol."

Initially individual staff members commented in private to Miss Jones about one or another concern about her behavior. Her response to such comments or expressions of concern was defensive. She attributed all of her present difficulty to her "back problems," subtly suggested a lack of empathy on the part of the given staff member, and intimated that the staff member's "concern" was placing more pressure on her. . . .

After administrative staff found liquor bottles in her desk and filing cabinets, the program director placed Miss Jones on indefinite administrative leave with the option that if she sought "appropriate help" (still undefined) and adequately demonstrated a return to "normal functioning," she could return to her previous position. Miss Jones decided to seek voluntary hospitalization in a facility specializing in the treatment of stress disorders. While in the facility, she ultimately decided to seek early retirement for "health reasons." (VandenBos and Duthie 1986:224–26)

Estimates of the prevalence of alcoholism among professionals vary. Many are based on data from treatment groups or impressions from practitioners' clinical experience. Unfortunately, a precise way to measure the incidence of substance abuse among professionals does not exist. The more thorough, detailed estimates suggest that roughly 5 to 6 percent of professionals are alcoholic, with a somewhat higher incidence among men and lower incidence among women (Thoreson and Skorina 1986:85–87).

Professionals, like the general public, manifest various signs of impairment because of alcohol use. Freudenberger (1986) claims to have found a recognizable pattern among many alcoholic professionals:

I have worked with at least 60 impaired professionals, psychologists, social workers, dentists, physicians, and attorneys during the past ten years and have found certain personality characteristics to be common. For the most part, impaired professionals are between 30 and 55 years of age. This is in essential agreement with Farber and Heifitz (1981) who suggested that "suicides of physicians, when they happen, are most likely to occur in the 35–54 age group" (p. 296). Early childhood impoverishment is another common characteristic. This is in agreement with Vaillant, Brighton, and McArthur (1970), who pointed to the "lack of consistent support and concern from their parents" in his study of drug-using physicians.

Most, if not all, of the patients I worked with led consistently unhealthy lifestyles. They tended to be masochistic, to have low self-images, and to be self-destructive in their personal and professional lives. Eighteen of the 60 had been married more than one time, 10 were bachelors, and the remainder were separated or divorced. Those who were married had frequent extramarital affairs. They all worked excessively long hours and, as Pearson and Strecker (1960) suggested, "had poor organizational habits . . . seldom took vacations, lunch hours and had few outside interests" (p. 916).

Their masochism made them prone to their patients beyond their own personal limits. All tended to be perfectionists and were usually never pleased with their work. "I know I can be better, I'm not good enough, I could have done more" are frequently heard refrains. They tended to conduct their lives, both at home and in the office, in such a way that they found little, if any, relief from their chores. They had a desperate need to be needed and rationalized taking drugs as doing something for themselves. . . . They rationalized, denied, and overcompensated to an excessive degree. While expressing a sense of dedication and commitment, they denied that abusing drugs or alcohol or sexually abusing clients might eventually lead to their destruction. As a group they were risk takers with their own as well as their patients' lives. (pp. 137–38)

Regrettably, as with other forms of impairment, little is known about the prevalence of alcoholism among social workers. Although various estimates have been made of the incidence of substance abuse among social workers—generally about 5 to 15 percent (see estimates contained in NASW 1987a:4, 6)—no one really knows how widespread the problem is. As Bissell and Haberman (1984) conclude after surveying fifty alcoholic social workers, along with other professionals, "An attempt to review the literature on all aspects of impairment in social workers revealed very little. Except for a 1980 study conducted by one of us, the studies mentioned above, and a brief description of social workers included in a hospital EAP, nothing could be located on the subject of alcoholism in this group" (p. 153).

Response to Impairment

To minimize liability and malpractice risks social workers must devise ways to prevent impairment and respond to impaired colleagues. Unfortunately, little is known about the extent to which impaired social workers and other professionals voluntarily seek help for their problems. A comprehensive search of the literature produced few empirical studies of impaired practitioners' efforts to seek help. Guy, Poelstra, and Stark (1989) found that 70 percent of the "distressed" clinical psychologists they surveyed sought some form of therapeutic assistance. One-fourth (26.6 percent) entered individual psychotherapy, and 10.7 percent entered family therapy. A small portion of this group participated in self-help groups (3.4 percent) or was hospitalized (2.2 percent). Some were placed on medication (4.1 percent). Exactly 10 percent of this group temporarily terminated their professional practice.

These findings contrast with those of Wood et al. (1985), who found that only 55.2 percent of clinicians who reported problems that interfered with their work (substance abuse, sexual overtures toward clients, depression, and burnout) sought help. Two-fifths (42 percent) of all clinicians surveyed by Wood et al., including impaired and unimpaired professionals, reported having offered help to impaired colleagues at some time or having referred them to therapists. Only 7.9 percent of the sample said they had reported an impaired colleague to a local regulatory body. Approximately two-fifths (40.2 percent) were aware of instances in which they believed no action was taken to help an impaired colleague.

Several hypotheses may be drawn concerning impaired professionals' reluctance to seek help and the reluctance of their colleagues to confront them about their problems. Until recently, professionals were hesitant to acknowledge impairment within their ranks because they feared how practitioners would react to confrontation and how such confrontation might affect the future relationships of colleagues who must work together (Bernard and Jara 1986; McCrady 1989; Wood et al. 1985). VandenBos and Duthie (1986) present the problem succinctly:

> The fact that more than half of us have not confronted distressed colleagues even when we have recognized and acknowledged (at least to ourselves) the existence of their problems is, in part, a reflection of the difficulty in achieving a balance between concerned intervention and intrusiveness. As professionals, we value our own right to practice without interference, as long as we function within the boundaries of our professional expertise, meet professional standards for

the provision of services, and behave in an ethical manner. We generally consider such expectations when we consider approaching a distressed colleague. Deciding when and how our concern about the well-being of a colleague (and our ethical obligation) supersedes his or her right to personal privacy and professional autonomy is a ticklish matter. (p. 212)

Thoreson et al. (1983) also argue that impaired professionals sometimes find it difficult to seek help because of their mythical belief in their infinite power and invulnerability. The involvement of an increasing number of psychotherapists in private practice (Goleman 1985; Khinduka 1987; NASW 1983) exacerbates the problem because of the reduced opportunity for colleagues to observe their unethical or inept practice.

In a valuable study by Deutsch (1985) a diverse group of therapists, including social workers, who admitted to personal problems indicated a variety of reasons for not seeking professional help, including believing that an acceptable therapist was not available, seeking help from family members or friends, fearing exposure and the disclosure of confidential information, concern about the amount of effort required and about the cost, having a spouse who was unwilling to participate in treatment, failing to admit the seriousness of the problem, believing they should be able to work their problems out themselves, and believing that therapy would not help.

As mentioned previously, in recent years several organized efforts have been made to identify and address the problems of impaired professionals. The consensus is growing that a model strategy for addressing impairment among professionals should include several components (Schoener and Gonsiorek 1988; Sonnenstuhl 1989; VandenBos and Duthie 1986).

First, adequate means for identifying impaired practitioners are needed. Professionals must be willing to assume some responsibility for acknowledging impairment among colleagues. And as Lamb et al. (1987) noted, it certainly would help to develop reasonably objective measures of what constitutes the failure to live up to professional standards, incompetent skills, and impaired professional functioning.

Second, a social worker's initial identification and documentation of a colleague's impairment should be followed by speculation about the causes and by what Sonnenstuhl (1989) described as "constructive confrontation." Third, once a social worker decides who shall confront the impaired colleague, the social worker must decide whether to help the impaired colleague identify ways to seek help voluntarily or to refer the colleague to a supervisor or local regulatory body (such as a committee on inquiry of NASW or a local licensing or registration board).

Assuming the data are sufficient to support a rehabilitation plan, the impaired practitioner's colleague, supervisor, or local regulatory body should make specific recommendations. The possibilities include close supervision, personal psychotherapy, and treatment for substance abuse. In some cases a local registration or licensing board or an NASW committee on inquiry may need to impose some type of sanction such as censure, limitations on the professional's social work practice (for example, concerning clientele that can be served), termination of employment, suspension or expulsion from a professional association, or loss of license or registration. Whatever action is taken should be monitored and evaluated. Here is an illustration of effective intervention with an impaired professional:

> Mr. Brown was the director of a community-based county work release/rehabilitation program in a medium-sized town. He was 34 years old. Mr. Brown was noted for his friendliness, his openness with colleagues and community leaders, his dedication to making the program work for the community and those enrolled, and his well-balanced approach in solving problems and in instructing others about how best to approach the participants in the program. Due to a cut in state funding to be made available to the county, the county board of administration found it necessary to reallocate funds for the next year's budget in such a way that several programs, including the program directed by Mr. Brown, would have to be redefined or possibly even eliminated. Mr. Brown prepared extensive documentation on the success of his program and presented it to the board, making an impassioned plea for its continuation. The board began its deliberations.
>
> Although not directly involved in the decision-making process, Mr. Brown was well known to many of the board members and, as

the board's deliberations progressed, some board members formed factions representing a range of opinions about what should happen to the program and shared information on the board's day-to-day deliberations, which were marked by continual changes in opinions, with Mr. Brown. As a result, over a period of six months, Mr. Brown became progressively more frustrated, uncertain, and stressed about the eventual outcome.

Mr. Brown's co-workers began to notice him gradually withdrawing from those around him. Rather than having his lunch in the cafeteria with his colleagues, he began to eat alone in his office, declaring that he was too busy to do otherwise, and he participated less and less in the ordinary social activity of the staff. He also began to limit "business" contact with his colleagues and members of the community to meetings that were as brief as possible. Several of his co-workers as individuals expressed concern about these changes to him. Mr. Brown's explanation was that the uncertainty about the outcome of the board's deliberations was creating a great deal of pressure on him and, as a result, it was difficult for him to concentrate, and he had to focus more intensely on getting his work done.

Others also noted the changes in Mr. Brown. In particular, these changes were noted by an industrial/organizational psychologist working for a large company, which had participated in the work release program for many years, and who considered Mr. Brown to be both a colleague and a friend. His colleague asked Mr. Brown to conduct a training session for several new employees on the staff on how to work effectively with participants in the work release program. On the day following the session, she called Mr. Brown and asked to meet with him in order to share feedback on the session, and they set a meeting time. During the meeting, she expressed concern about the changes she had noted in Mr. Brown's behavior both personally and professionally and her feeling that those changes seemed to represent a pattern of behavior indicating depression. She went on to say that it was apparent that the depression was not being attended to by Mr. Brown.

As an example of what had caused her to be concerned, she pointed out that during the training session Mr. Brown, who was ordinarily a patient, flexible individual, had responded to members of the group with anger and hostility when they challenged or even questioned elements of his presentation and when they expressed disagreement with his interpretations of material. She noted that this was very inconsistent with his usual behavior. At the same time, she mentioned in passing that she had overheard comments by others—

including co-workers and community members—regarding his apparent inaccessibility, both professionally and emotionally. She suggested that Mr. Brown's attempts to control and cope with his distress were not being fully effective and that she and his co-workers wanted to offer whatever support they could. At the same time, she suggested that Mr. Brown might consider entering therapy.

Initially, Mr. Brown reacted defensively and angrily. He expressed his feeling that his colleague was intruding. However, after continued discussion, it became apparent to him that her concern was genuine and that she expressed the shared caring and frustration of herself, his co-workers, and others. The effect of her simultaneously confrontational and supporting approach was to break through Mr. Brown's defensiveness and denial. He began to identify and acknowledge other indications of depressive symptomatology. He also mentioned that his rumination about possible "political outcomes" and his withdrawal from others was further complicating the situation for him. Following this confrontation, he went into short-term therapy and his depression was quickly resolved—Mr. Brown again became his friendly, open, effective self. (VandenBos and Duthie 1986:227–29)

Unfortunately, relatively little research has been conducted on the effectiveness of efforts to rehabilitate impaired professionals (Sonnenstuhl 1989; Trice and Beyer 1984). Moreover, the few published empirical evaluations—which report mixed results for various treatment programs—focus primarily on impaired physicians (Herrington et al. 1982; Morse et al. 1984; Pearson 1982; Shore 1982). Studies typically report only whether the practitioner is still alive, still licensed, or in practice. Many investigations have serious methodological flaws or limitations. Few studies compare the outcome of efforts to treat impaired professionals with control groups or even other patient groups, and follow-up periods tend to be relatively short (Bissell and Haberman 1984). The results of the handful of "outcome" studies on the treatment of impaired professionals are as follows:

- Goby, Bradley, and Bespalec (1979, cited in Bissell and Haberman 1984:104) report on their follow-up survey of 43 alcoholic physician-patients treated over a 10-year period at Lutheran General Hospital in Illinois. One was in prison, and 7 had died (1 committed suicide, 1 died of lung cancer, 3 died drinking excessively, and 2 died from unknown causes). Nineteen of the 43 (44 percent) had been abstinent since discharge from the program; 9 reported some drinking but were abstinent for a full year or more at the time of the survey. Only 8 did not report a significant decrease in alcohol consumption. Most of the physicians reported good physical and emotional health and were working.

- Kliner, Spicer, and Barnett (1980, cited in Bissell and Haberman 1984:104) reported on results of a mail survey of 57 alcoholic physicians treated at the Hazelden Foundation in Minnesota one year after discharge. Fifty-one of the 57 reported abstinence since discharge, 5 reported serious difficulty with continued drinking, and 1 reported continued drinking but no related problems. The respondents also reported improvements in self-image, health, professional performance, and personal adjustment.

- Morse et al. (1984, cited in Bissell and Haberman 1984:104) reported on outcomes for 53 alcoholic physicians who had been treated for at least two weeks at the Mayo Clinic. One to five years after discharge, 83 percent of the physicians reported complete abstinence or having been in relapse for no more than one week—and as abstinent when surveyed—compared to 62 percent of a non-physician "general group" of patients. Eighty-nine percent of the physicians resumed their practice.

- Herrington et al. (1982) reported on a study of 40 alcoholic physicians and dentists treated in an impaired-physician program in Milwaukee, Wisconsin. The treatment included a 30-day inpatient program, Alcoholic and/or Narcotics Anonymous, and follow-up. Seven physicians dropped out of treatment early. Of the 30 physicians and 3 dentists who remained in treatment, 22 reported abstinence since discharge and 6 reported only a single relapse. The majority continued to practice.

- Pearson (1982) reported on the treatment of 250 physicians over a 36-year period. Slightly more than one third (36 percent) had a history of substance abuse, about one fifth (18 percent) were diagnosed with psychotic symptoms or affective disorders, and slightly more than one fourth (28 percent) manifested "neurotic" or situational problems. Of the 160 who received actual treatment, 42 percent were classified as *recovered* or *much improved*, 22 percent as *slightly improved*, and 36 percent as *worse* or *unimproved*.

- Shore (1982) reported on a study of 27 alcoholic or drug-addicted physicians treated in Oregon under state board supervision. All had been placed on professional probation by the Oregon Board of Medical Examiners. Data suggested that 22 of the 27 improved, with 14 reporting no relapse. Seventy-nine percent returned to practice, but during an average 3.6 years on probation 53 percent had relapses.

The Challenge for Social Work

In his oft-cited address to the National Conference of Charities and Correction, Flexner (1915) raised the question, "Is social work a profession?" At the time Flexner noted that one essential attribute of a profession is its tendency toward self-regulation. Greenwood (1957) made a similar observation in his classic essay on the professions.

Over the years social work has certainly strengthened its regulatory functions. Through NASW the profession has developed an elaborate and active network of committees on inquiry that is responsible for adjudicating complaints filed against members. In addition, social work licensing and regulation are now widespread, and state boards of regulation and licensing often act responsibly and vigorously to discipline social workers engaged in misconduct.

However, for a profession to be truly self-regulating it cannot rely entirely on the efforts of dissatistifed or abused clients to file ethics complaints or lawsuits against impaired practitioners. For a variety of reasons clients often are reluctant to get involved in the formal adjudication process. Therefore, members of the professions must be vigilant in their efforts to confront the incompetence, unprofessional conduct, and unethical activities of their colleagues. The profession must provide active yet constructive monitoring of its members; sophisticated and sensitively administered rehabilitation services; and, when necessary, adjudication procedures that adhere to accepted principles of due process. All these activities of course should also help reduce the risk of liability and malpractice claims being filed against social workers.

Unfortunately, as a profession social work has not paid sufficient attention to the problems of impaired practitioners. Unlike a number of other professions, such as medicine, law, and psychology, social work's literature contains little on the subject. Empirical research on the prevalence of impairment in the profession also is distressingly sparse. Moreover, most states do not have ambitious efforts to identify and respond to impaired social workers (see NASW 1987a for an overview of several NASW chapters' efforts to sponsor programs for such social workers).

To the profession's credit, however, in 1992 the president of NASW created the Code of Ethics Review Task Force (chaired by the author) that proposed adding new principles to the *Code of Ethics* on the subject of impairment. The approved additions, effective in 1994, are that

- The social worker should not allow his or her own personal problems, psychosocial distress, substance abuse, or mental health difficulties to interfere with professional judgment and performance or jeopardize the welfare of those to whom the social worker has a professional responsibility, including clients, students, or colleagues.
- The social worker whose personal problems, psychosocial distress, substance abuse, or mental health difficulties interfere with professional judgment and performance should seek help, and curtail or terminate professional practice until the social worker's performance no longer jeopardizes the welfare of those for whom the social worker has professional responsibility.
- The social worker who has direct knowledge of a social work colleague's impairment due to personal problems, psychosocial distress, substance abuse, or mental health difficulties should consult with that colleague and assist the colleague to take remedial action. (additions to the

NASW *Code of Ethics,* approved by the NASW Delegate Assembly, August 20, 1993, effective July 1, 1994)

One can only speculate about why social work generally has paid less attention than other professions to the problem of impaired practitioners. It is difficult to know whether the magnitude of the problem is smaller in social work than in other professions (and hence attracts less attention), whether there is greater denial of impairment in social work than in other professions, whether social workers have a higher threshold of tolerance for impairment in general, or whether social workers simply write and publish less than members of other professions. Whatever the explanation, social work, like every profession, unquestionably has its share of impaired practitioners and needs to strengthen its efforts to respond to them.

Toward this end social work must actively pursue a number of goals. First, social work must embark on a program of empirical research designed to produce valid and reliable measures of impairment, its prevalence in the profession, and its consequences. For social work to mount an ambitious effort to address impairment, it must have an adequate database on the extent of the problem. Surveys of social workers and agency administrators need to be conducted to establish a baseline against which to measure changes in levels of impairment over time.

In addition, the profession must strengthen its efforts to identify impaired practitioners and to respond to them in a meaningful way. Social workers, like many other professionals, may be reluctant to confront impaired colleagues. This reluctance is understandable. Nonetheless, it is incumbent on the profession to confront incompetence and unethical behavior and to offer humane assistance. Attention should be paid to social workers in solo private practice, as well as those who work in group settings where the opportunity to observe impairment may be greater.

NASW—at the national level and through its state chapters—must take the lead in strengthening efforts to identify and assist impaired members. Local regulatory bodies, such as licensing and regulatory boards, should also be encouraged to address this challenge. As stated in the NASW *Code of Ethics,* "The social worker should take action through appropriate channels against unethical conduct by any other member of the profession" (1990:8).

Social workers must expand education about the problem of impaired social workers. Relatively few social workers have been trained to identify and confront impairment. The profession's organizations and associations must begin to conduct workshops and in-service training on the subject to acquaint social workers with current information about the forms that impairment can take, the signs to look for, and ways to confront the problem.

Social work students, especially, need to be introduced to the subject. The emphasis of course should be on prevention through acquainting prospective practitioners with warning signs to look for in their own and colleagues' lives and with potential remedies, including therapy, time management, stress management, and career planning. Such training should be part of an aggressive effort to expand education about professional ethics in social work (Joseph 1989; Reamer 1990; Reamer and Abramson 1982).

Social workers should develop collegial assistance programs to assist impaired practitioners. Although some cases of impairment must be dealt with through formal adjudication procedures (NASW committees on inquiry or reviews by local licensing or registration boards), many cases can be handled primarily by arranging therapeutic or rehabilitative services for distressed workers. Impaired social workers should have access to competent service providers who are trained to understand professionals' special concerns and needs. For instance, state chapters of NASW can enter into agreements with local EAPs, to which impaired members can be referred (NASW 1987a).

As social workers intensify their focus on impairment in the profession, they must be careful to avoid reductionist explanations of the problems that colleagues experience. Although emphasizing psychotherapeutic and other rehabilitative efforts in instances that call for them (including chemical dependence or mental illness) is certainly appropriate, social workers must not lose sight of the environmental stresses that often lead to such disabilities. Distress experienced by social workers often is the result of unique challenges in the profession for which the resources are inadequate. Social workers who work day by day with clients who are subjected to poverty, hunger, homelessness, child abuse, crime, mental illness, and so forth are prime candidates for stress and burnout. Inadequate funding, thin political support, and public criticism of social workers' efforts often combine to produce low morale and high stress (Jayaratne and Chess 1984; Johnson and Stone 1986; Koeske and Koeske 1989). In addition to responding to the private troubles of impaired colleagues, social workers must simultaneously confront the public issues and environmental flaws that can produce impairment. Those who confront impairment among colleagues must avoid blaming the victim, just as they resist doing so with their own clients.

Social work is a grand and noble profession with a grand and noble mission. Its tradition is addressing the problems of individuals and the environmental stresses that surround them. The same tradition must be extended to impaired colleagues. This form of self-regulation is a hallmark of a profession and is especially important in one that exercises considerable influence over the lives of others.

5 | Supervision: Clients and Staff

The concept and practice of supervision have always been central in social work. Practitioners' training typically includes considerable attention to theory and skills related to supervision (Kadushin 1992; Miller 1987). Over the years the social work literature has addressed a variety of issues related to supervision, including the administrative and clinical responsibilities of the supervisor, the challenge in moving from practitioner to supervisor, and the importance of leadership qualities in supervision.

Not surprisingly, social workers who have supervisory responsibilities are sometimes named in liability claims and lawsuits. Although supervisors may not have been directly involved in the event or circumstances immediately surrounding the case, they may be found liable, at least in part.

The malpractice and liability claims related to supervision tend to be of two types. The first includes cases involving client supervision, that is, instances in which social workers are alleged to have failed in their duty to properly supervise clients. The second includes cases involving staff supervision. These cases usually allege that a social worker failed to properly supervise a staff member who was negligent or who committed some act of misfeasance, malfeasance, or nonfeasance.

Client Supervision

Howard C., B.S.W., was a social worker in a residential facility for emotionally disturbed adolescents. He had worked at the facility for three years; during that time he had worked as a child-care worker and, most recently, a unit supervisor. In his position as unit supervisor Howard C. supervised three child-care workers on his shift and also had responsibility for helping to supervise the youngsters on the unit. Most youths on the unit had been admitted with such symptoms as severe depression, self-mutilation, eating disorders, hallucinations and delusions, and attempted suicide.

On one particular Thursday morning only two child-care workers and Howard C. were on the unit. The third child-care worker had called in sick. As a result Howard C. was expected to put his administrative duties aside and assume the responsibilities of the third child-care worker. That is, Howard C. was to be physically present on the unit instead of spending much of his time in the corner office where the unit supervisors shared a desk.

Howard C. began the shift on the unit. The residents were engaged in various activities. Several were involved in counseling sessions, some were being tutored by an educational consultant, and others were working on their journal entries. The youths for whom Howard C. was primarily responsible were relaxing, watching television.

Howard C. decided to use this time to finish up some paperwork each unit supervisor was expected to complete (incident reports). He told the youths for whom he was responsible that he would be in his office. After about twenty minutes, two youths began to argue about the television station they were watching. They could not agree on what show to watch and began screaming at each other. One youth picked up a chair and hit the other over the head with it. The youth who was assaulted fell to the floor unconscious. He was rushed to the hospital with a brain concussion.

The youth suffered permanent brain damage. His parents sued Howard C. and the program, alleging that supervision of residents was inadequate and that Howard C., in particular, failed to carry out his supervisory responsibilities as called for in the program's policies.

The social service field is filled with cases in which individual practitioners and their agencies have been sued because of alleged failure to supervise clients adequately. Ordinarily, the plaintiff alleges that staff did not monitor clients' activities closely enough or that the staff-client ratio was inadequate for proper supervision. As illustrated by cases cited in this chapter, these cases often include instances in which clients attempted suicide, assaulted one another or staff, or were injured when restrained by staff, actions that plaintiffs allege could have been prevented with proper supervision (issues related to supervision of suicidal clients were also addressed in chapter 3).

In *Clites et al. v. State of Iowa et al.*, parents of a resident of a hospital for the mentally retarded filed suit alleging that staff members should be held responsible in connection with injuries their son received in an assault at the hospital. The man was bitten by his roommate at least fourteen times and suffered a broken jaw, broken foot, and various cuts and bruises. Some inflictions of injuries were not witnessed by staff or occurred under circumstances in which staff members could not protect the injured resident. The judge found that the staff should have separated the roommates four months earlier. The Iowa court awarded the plaintiffs $146,000 ("Resident at Hospital," 1989:4).

Failure to supervise a hospitalized client was also alleged in *H.H. for S.L.H. v. St. Luke's Hospital and Dr. Dutmers* after a fourteen-year-old girl was raped by another patient. She had been admitted to a psychiatric facility after attempting suicide. The plaintiffs alleged that the girl was not adequately protected while at the facility; the suit claimed that a sixteen-year-old male patient sneaked into the girl's room and attacked her. Upon her admission the staff had been concerned that the girl might attempt suicide and she was placed on a fifteen-minute watch schedule. On the night of the assault, however, the girl was not watched by staff because, staff claimed, her condition had improved. The plaintiff's attorney contended that the girl was in a facility in which she was supposed to feel safe and that she would never feel safe again. The Colorado jury awarded the plaintiffs $24,218 ("Psychiatric Patient Raped," 1989:4).

Similar issues were raised in *Kozak v. Mercy Hospital*, in which the plaintiff, a psychiatric patient, alleged that she was raped by another patient and that the Florida hospital was negligent when that patient gained access to her room. The plaintiff was awarded $35,000 ("Patient Raped," 1989:6).

In contrast, in the 1989 case of *Hothem v. Fallsview Psychiatric Hospital* the court did not find the hospital negligent in an assault on one patient by another. One patient was admitted to the hospital for treatment of organic delusional syndrome. The second patient was admitted several days later with a diagnosis of paranoid schizophrenia. The second patient accused the first patient of communicating with the devil, threatened to kill her, and then assaulted her. The court ruled, however, that the hospital did not have reason to anticipate the second patient's actions and was not negligent in its supervision of him ("Hospital Not Negligent," 1992:3).

Many cases involve allegations that staff members failed to properly supervise clients in residential facilities who attempted suicide. In *Carpenter v. Dr. Grubb & Overlake Hospital*, a forty-year-old woman who was admitted to a hospital for psychiatric treatment was allowed to make telephone calls in an interview room with an unscreened window. This occurred one day after admission. The patient claimed that she had a panic reaction and attempted to escape from the hospital through the window. She suffered fractured vertebrae, neurogenic bowel and bladder dysfunction, and head and foot injuries. The patient claimed that being left alone in a room with an unscreened window constituted negligence on the part of the staff. The defendants argued that the woman showed no suicidal ideation and that the family had failed to provide a complete psychiatric history. The Washington State case was settled for $150,000 ("Patient Jumps," 1989:2).

The circumstances in *Plachy and Plachy v. Green Oaks Hospital, Inc.* are also common. In this Texas case parents took their daughter to a hospital after she told them she was going to commit suicide. The parents told hospital staff that their daughter had tried to commit suicide previously by hanging herself while a patient at another hospital. Shortly after her parents left, the daughter walked out of her room, left the building, climbed to the top of a nearby parking garage, and jumped to her death. The plaintiffs argued that hospital staff members should be held negligent in that the actions of a patient the staff had been told was suicidal were not supervised or controlled. The case was settled for $290,000 ("Suicidal Patient," 1990:3). Other cases that present similar allegations of improper supervision and suicides committed by hospitalized patients include *McNamara v. Honeyman* (1989) and *Bramlette v. Charter-Medical-Columbia* (1990).

Some cases also involve allegations that staff at a secure residential setting did not properly supervise clients who as a result escaped and then attempted suicide. In *Marrow v. Commonwealth of Virginia, Dept. of Mental Health and Mental Retardation and Dr. Rogers*, the plaintiff, a woman diagnosed with schizophrenia, claimed she was not supervised adequately after she was committed involuntarily to an inpatient mental health facility. The woman attempted to escape four times during the last three days of her two-week hospitalization. On the fourth attempt the woman walked onto a busy highway and into the path of an oncoming car. The plaintiff suffered compound fractures of both legs and permanent nerve injury. The plaintiff was awarded $115,000 by a jury ("Mental Patient Escapes," 1990:3).

In some instances social service staff and agencies may be found liable when clients injure themselves by accident. In *Heirs of Mary Manteuffel v. Mounds Park Hospital*, a woman's family sued after their relative, a thirty-nine-year-old homemaker and mother, died; the Minnesota suit claimed that she was not adequately supervised and monitored. The woman had been admitted to a locked psychiatric ward with a diagnosis of schizo-affective disorder. During lunch the woman and nine other patients were supervised by a nurse and an orderly. The woman stuffed large amounts of food in her mouth; the nurse offered to cut the woman's food, but the woman refused. The woman ate all the food on her plate. She subsequently choked on her food and died shortly thereafter. The jury awarded $613,695 to the plaintiffs ("Psychiatric Patient Not Properly Monitored," 1990:4).

Staff Supervision

Sue S., M.S.W., was the clinical director at North County Mental Health Services, Inc., a local community mental health center. Sue S. was responsible for supervising five clinical social workers on the center's staff. One of her supervisees was Scott M., M.S.W. Scott M.'s case load was diverse, including patients recently discharged from a nearby state psychiatric hospital and clients referred by the local school district.

Scott M. was working with a ten-year-old boy who had been referred by the local grade school. The boy had been having a number of problems in school, including several instances of fire setting and self-mutilation. Scott M. had been working with the boy for about three months. Scott M. also had extensive contact with the boy's family. Scott M. and Sue S. spent considerable time during supervision discussing this clinically complex case.

One afternoon the principal of the boy's school, who had initially referred the case to the mental health center, called Scott M. and asked him how the boy and his family were doing. The principal asked whether Scott M. could summarize the boy's progress and forward it to her. The next week Scott M. prepared a case summary, which included details of the boy's disclosure that his father had sexually abused him.

During a subsequent conversation with the school principal the father learned that Scott M. had disclosed this information to the school without his consent. The father sued Scott M. and his supervisor, Sue S., alleging that they breached his right to privacy. The father specifically alleged that Sue S. failed to properly perform her supervisory duties in that she did not ensure that his consent had been obtained before disseminating Scott M.'s report to the school principal.

Large numbers of social workers supervise staff. A clinical director in a family service agency may supervise caseworkers. A unit supervisor in a residential treatment facility may supervise mental health or child-care workers. An assistant director of a public welfare agency may supervise administrative staff. In each setting supervisors must carry out a variety of tasks, which may include monitoring workers' activities, providing feedback about workers' performance, conducting personnel evaluations, and teaching.

Social work supervision has historical roots in the Charity Organization Society, when the "master" exercised control over the tasks and activities of the "apprentice." The "paid agents" of the Charity Organization Society's agencies provided what was essentially supervision of the large numbers of "visitors" who provided direct services.

Most references to supervision in the social work literature, however, have appeared since 1920. Between 1920 and 1945 *Family* and *Social Casework* published roughly thirty-five articles devoted to supervision (Kadushin 1976:14). The first half-century of social work also saw several seminal publications on the subject, including Virginia Robinson's *Supervision in Social Case Work* (1936) and *The Dynamics of Supervision Under Functional Controls* (1949), Bertha Reynolds's *Learning and Teaching in the Practice of Social Work* (1942), and Charlotte Towle's discussion of supervision in *Common Human Needs* (1945) and in *The Learner in Education for the Professions* (1954). This solid intellectual foundation helped pave the way for a steady progression of scholarly discussions of supervision. As Miller (1987) suggests, "Supervision has remained the principal method—with the individual conference as its keystone—by which knowledge and skill are transmitted from the experienced to the inexperienced, from the trained to the untrained, and in professional education, from the teacher and field instructor to the student" (p. 749).

Over time a variety of norms have emerged in social work supervision, related primarily to the content and implementation of supervision (Kadushin 1976, 1992; Miller 1987). Although variation exists, the literature provides considerable conceptual guidance related to the goals, functions, tasks, and styles of supervision.

To date, social work's literature on supervision has focused almost exclusively on pedagogical and technical aspects of supervision (Reamer 1989b), particularly issues related to professional accountability (Slavin 1982), role strain involved in shifting from practitioner to supervisor (Patti 1983), administrative and managerial tasks of the supervisor (Kadushin 1976), leadership in supervision (Austin 1981), the quasipsychotherapeutic function of supervision (Munson 1983), and the relationship between organizational dynamics and supervision (Miller 1987). Broad ethical issues related to the match of supervisors and supervisees, contracting, informing clients of supervisors' involvement, evaluation of supervisees, and providing feedback to supervisees also have been addressed (Cohen 1987; Levy 1973).

Although literature on supervision has matured considerably over the years, relatively little has been written about malpractice and liability risks associated with supervision. In fact, some risks are unique. Many supervisors, I have found, do not fully understand the ways in which they may be held liable in the actions or inactions of the staff they supervise.

Although many malpractice claims allege mistreatment of a client by a practitioner, a number of claims also implicate the practitioner's supervisor. Such claims typically cite the legal doctrine of *respondeat superior*, which means "let the master respond." The doctrine also is known as *vicarious liability*, in that supervisors may be found liable in actions or inactions in which they were involved only vicariously. According to respondeat superior and vicarious liability, supervisors are responsible for the actions or inactions of their supervisees that were conducted during the course of employment and over which the supervisor had some measure of control (Cohen 1979). As Gifis (1991) notes,

> This doctrine is invoked when there is a master-servant relationship between two parties. The "respondeat superior" doctrine stands for the proposition that when an employer, dubbed "master," is acting through the facility of an employee or agent, dubbed "servant," and tort liability is incurred during the course of this agency due to some fault of the agent, then the employer or master must accept the responsibility. Implicit in this is the common law notion that a duty rests upon every person to conduct his or her affairs so as not to injure another, whether or not in managing the affairs he or she employs agents or servants. (pp. 416–17)

Although the doctrine of respondeat superior creates liability on the part of the supervisor for the actions or inactions of supervisees, the supervisee also may be held liable. Thus, respondeat superior simply provides a client-plaintiff with an additional party to sue. If both supervisor and supervisee are negligent or responsible for the plaintiff's injuries, the finding may be one of *joint liability*. In these instances responsibility for damages may be divided between the parties on a percentage basis. For example, if a caseworker and supervisor were sued because the caseworker released confidential information to a third party without the client's consent and evidence shows that the supervisor had not addressed the issue of consent properly in supervision, the finding could be of joint liability with, say, the supervisor held 35 percent responsible and the caseworker 65 percent responsible. If the plaintiff were awarded $120,000 in damages, the supervisor would be responsible for $42,000 and the caseworker for $78,000.

Of course, the agency's insurance company might cover both sets of damages and related legal expenses, although this is not always the case. In some instances the agency's insurer may want to distance itself from both the supervisor and the supervisee, or the insurer may want to defend only the supervisor by arguing that the supervisee was grossly negligent and therefore may argue that the supervisor is not responsible for the supervisee's actions. Given that supervisor and supervisee can become adversaries in such proceedings, *all* employees should carry their own individual malpractice and liability coverage. Relying only on an agency's group policy can be risky.

Areas of potential liability for social work supervisors are numerous, including failure to provide information necessary for supervisees to obtain clients' consent; to catch supervisees' errors in all phases of client contact, such as an inappropriate disclosure of confidential information; to protect third parties, or defamation of character; to detect or stop a negligent treatment plan or treatment carried beyond its effectiveness; to determine that a specialist is needed for treatment of a particular client; to meet regularly with the supervisee; to review and approve the supervisee's decisions; and to provide adequate coverage in the supervisee's absence. In addition, supervisors can be held liable if a supervisee is involved sexually with a client or exerts undue influence on the client or if the client's record is inadequate and the supervisor does not seek to improve it (Besharov 1985:166–67; Cohen and Mariano 1982; Hogan 1979).

Supervision Case Law

One particularly complex liability claim raises various issues about a social worker's responsibility—and liability—in the actions of a counselor she had hired to work in her group private practice. Some years earlier the social worker and her colleague had started a private practice. A number of their cases involved children with eating disorders. The partners decided to hire a former nurse to provide assessments and evaluations of children. The woman was also enrolled in a masters-level degree program in counseling at a local state university.

The group practice became involved in a case in which the child was seen by one member of the practice and the mother was seen by the former nurse. In time, the former nurse began providing counseling services to the mother, although this was before the former nurse had received her counseling degree and before she was licensed as a counselor. In her deposition the former nurse acknowledged that at this point in time she had a "therapist-patient" relationship with the mother.

The lawsuit filed by the mother and her husband alleged that the former nurse was negligent in that she failed to properly handle boundaries between herself and the mother and that the mother was seriously injured as a result. The suit alleged, for example, that the former nurse employed the mother in the former nurse's side business, which was completely unrelated to counseling. In addition, the suit claimed that the former nurse and the client-mother had taken care of each other's children during their professional relationship and on one occasion had traveled out of state together.

The mother claimed in her lawsuit that the former nurse had mishandled the professional-client relationship and that this caused her great psychological damage, resulting in her hospitalization and lengthy psychiatric treatment. Her husband claimed that his relationship with his wife was severely damaged as a result of the former nurse's actions.

Also named in the suit were the social worker who had started the practice and had hired the former nurse and her partner. The claim alleged that the social worker was liable in several respects. First, the plaintiffs claimed that the social worker knew or should have known that the former nurse was providing counseling services without the requisite formal training or credentials, in the form of a graduate degree and license. Second, the plaintiffs alleged that under the doctrine of respondeat superior, or vicarious liability, the social worker's supervision of the case was not adequate. The plaintiffs argued that the social worker was aware that the client-mother was suicidal and in need of competent skilled care by a trained professional and that the social worker should have arranged for the client to be cared for by someone with considerably more expertise than the former nurse's. Similar allegations were made in a claim filed against the social worker's partner. According to the lawsuit,

> After a number of sessions with defendant [the former nurse who was "counseling" the plaintiff] with regard to the therapy for [her son], defendant in early July, 1990, recommended to plaintiff that she likewise enter therapy for her own depression arising at least in part from the problems associated with her child.
>
> Plantiff consented and began therapy with defendant on a regular basis.
>
> As time went by, plaintiff became exceedingly dependent upon defendant and became extremely involved in a variety of aspects of defendant's life all with the knowledge, consent and encouragement of defendant.
>
> Defendant provided therapy in both private and group sessions on a regular basis from July, 1990, through early 1992.
>
> During this period of professional therapy, defendant encouraged plaintiff to become increasingly dependent upon defendant.
>
> Defendant allowed and encouraged their relationship to change from a professional therapeutic relationship into a social and business relationship. . . .
>
> Defendant caused an increasingly close and personal relationship to develop between her and plaintiff which relationship dramatically interfered with plaintiff's marriage and her ability to interact with her family and friends.
>
> Defendant encouraged and induced plaintiff to participate in her . . . business during her ongoing therapeutic relationship and induced plaintiff to work for her without pay on a regular basis assisting with her independent . . . business. . . .

Defendant repeatedly professed an abiding love for plaintiff and engaged in regular social, nonprofessional outings and activities with plaintiff during the time that she was continuing therapy.

Defendant would frequently meet plaintiff at various times and locations to engage in "therapy sessions."

Their relationship continued to evolve into a more intense one in which there was far more contact between plaintiff and defendant than just therapy sessions. . . .

Defendant breached applicable psychological and counseling principles in the following nonexclusive particulars:

(A) Violating boundary standards between therapist and patient;

(B) Failing to utilize appropriate therapeutic and counseling skills.

(C) Failing to properly diagnose and treat plaintiff;

(D) Engaging in unethical duality violations;

(E) Interfering with plaintiff's relationship with her husband, children and other friends;

(F) Inducing, causing or allowing plaintiff to become exceedingly reliant and dependent upon defendant;

(G) Encouraging, soliciting and inducing plaintiff to participate in defendant's independent . . . business while defendant was plaintiff's therapist;

(H) Borrowing money from plaintiff to operate defendant's independent . . . business;

(I) Causing, inducing and allowing an excessively social and personal relationship to develop and continue while still serving as plaintiff's therapist;

(J) Otherwise breaching ethical and professional standards of conduct with regard to her relationship with plaintiff.

As a result of the aforestated medical negligence of defendant, plaintiff has suffered severe psychiatric disorders including severe depression, panic, mental anguish, inconvenience, humiliation, disruption of marital relationship, suicidal tendencies, rage, helplessness and a severe deterioration of her mental and emotional well being. . . .

Upon information and belief, plaintiff shows that [the social worker and her partner] were defendant's direct supervisors charged with responsibility for supervising, directing and overseeing the quality of counseling provided by defendant to plaintiff.

Upon information and belief, plaintiff shows that [the social worker and her partner] either knew or should have known of the aforestated medical negligence, conflict of interest and ethical breaches by defendant.

Plaintiffs further show that [the social worker and her partner] breached their independent duty to plaintiffs by failing to properly supervise, guide, direct and oversee the counseling and therapy provided by defendant to plaintiff and further in failing to respond appropriately to the multiple acts of medical negligence on the part of defendant set forth hereinabove.

Plaintiffs further show that [the group private practice, as a corporate entity], as the employer of defendant, is directly responsible to plaintiffs for all damages resulting from the aforestated medical negligence of defendant under the doctrine of *respondeat superior* or, alternatively, under the doctrine of actual or apparent authority.

The social worker's partner settled the case out of court; the lawsuit against the social worker is pending. The social worker may be vulnerable if she knew that the former nurse had not completed her training to be a counselor and was not licensed. Moreover, the suit alleges that the social worker knew of the client's severe symptoms, including suicidal ideation, that she did not become more closely involved in the client's treatment, and that no referral was made.

Other cases also raise a variety of important issues related to supervisor liability. In some instances clients have sued the practitioner, the supervisor, and the employing agency. In some of these cases only one defendant was found liable, although it is common for a judge or jury to decide on joint liability.

Court cases described thus far have addressed three sets of circumstances. Their outcomes suggest that social work supervisors may be legally responsible for (1) actions of supervisees who ordinarily are directly under their supervision, (2) actions of supervisees who ordinarily are not under the social worker's direct supervision, and (3) the delegation of responsibility by the social worker to a paraprofessional or unlicensed assistant.

For example, in *Rule v. Chessman* (1957) a surgeon who taught medical residents at a hospital was sued when a resident he had supervised and advised during surgery left a sponge in a patient's abdomen (Cohen 1979:181). The Kansas Supreme Court found the supervisor and supervisee jointly liable in the errors of the supervisee, who was under the direct supervision of the surgeon.

The findings in *Cohen v. State of New York* (1976) are also instructive. Suit was filed by the widow of Alan Cohen, who committed suicide the same day he was released from an inpatient voluntary stay at the Downstate Medical Center's psychiatric department. Cohen had been diagnosed as having paranoid schizophrenia. He had been hospitalized for four months. The suit alleged that his medical care, particularly that related to the decision to release Cohen, was not properly supervised, despite the involvement of several physicians. At issue was "whether or not a qualified psychiatrist was actively supervising the care of the decedent" (382 N.Y.S.2d 128 at 130, cited in Austin, Moline, and Williams 1990:232; also see *Tabor v. Doctors Memorial Hospital* 1990).

In some instances the agency itself may be found vicariously liable. In *Samuels v. Southern Baptist Hospital* (1992) a sixteen-year-old psychiatric patient was sexually assaulted by a nursing assistant. The hospital was found liable in the nursing assistant's actions ("Hospital Liable for Employee's Sexual Assault," 1992:6). In *Gilchrist v. The Ark, Pattison and McFadden*, a drug and alcohol rehabilitation center in Colorado was found partially liable when a female client became involved in a sexual relationship with the center's assistant director within a month after the client left the program. The woman sued, alleging that the center and its executive director were aware of the assistant director's previous involvement in another similar relationship but did not reprimand him or take steps to prevent a recurrence. The award to the plaintiff included $42,175 from the center and its executive director on the negligent supervision claim ("Official of Alcohol Center," 1990:5).

The court made a similar finding in *Doe v. Samaritan Counseling Center* (1990). According to the plaintiff, a pastoral counselor at a counseling center made sexual advances toward her during two counseling sessions and had sexual contact with her after treatment ended. The Alaska Supreme Court ruled that the agency may be held liable under the doctrine of respondeat superior for the therapist's sexual contact with the client ("Employer May Be Held Liable," 1990:1; also see *Stropes v. Heritage House Childrens Center of Shelbyville, Inc.* 1989).

An important issue in many of these cases is whether the workers' actions fall within the scope of their employment. If they do, the employer and/or supervisor may be found liable. In *Birkner v. Salt Lake County* (1989), for example, the Utah Supreme Court ruled that a mental health facility could *not* be held liable in an employee's sexual misconduct with a client. The plaintiff claimed that a social worker had a sexual relationship with her during treatment. The trial court found that the social worker was negligent. However, the state Supreme Court reversed the trial court's ruling on the issue of respondeat superior and vicarious liability, concluding that the social worker's actions did not fall within the scope of his employment. The appellate court noted that neither the plaintiff nor the social worker viewed their sexual contact as part of the therapeutic relationship, that these actions are not the type of activities a therapist is hired to perform, and the actions did not further the employer's interests ("Employer Not Vicariously Liable," 1989:1).

Liability also can be incurred when a practitioner temporarily depends to some extent on assistance provided by another agency employee or colleague, even if the assistant is not ordinarily under the direct supervision of the practitioner. In *Minogue v. Rutland Hospital* (1956) a nurse who was assisting an obstetrician was considered a "borrowed servant" of the obstetrician. The obstetrician was found liable when the nurse pressed on the rib of a woman during childbirth, thereby causing a fracture (Cohen 1979:181).

Similar findings appeared in *Yorsten v. Pennell* (1959) and *Norton v. Argonaut Insurance Company* (1962). In *Yorsten* a patient sued a surgeon claiming that an error had been made by a resident the surgeon was supervising. The resident had removed a nail from a worker's leg and prescribed penicillin. Earlier, however, a fourth-year medical student had taken the patient's history and noted that the patient was allergic to penicillin. The patient had a severe allergic reaction to the penicillin. The court ruled that the surgeon was liable for damages (Cohen 1979:181).

In *Norton* a nurse injected in a patient medication that the physician had intended to be administered orally. The physician, however, did not note in the patient's chart that the medication was to be administered orally. As a result the patient received about five times the intended dosage and died. The physician was found liable in the nurse's actions (Cohen 1979:181).

These rulings have implications for social workers who provide treatment in an agency as outside consultants and who occasionally might rely on the assistance of an agency employee not ordinarily under their direct supervision. For example, a social work consultant who oversees a behavioral treatment program in an agency and uses agency employees to help implement the behavioral regimen would be in this category.

However, in *Marvulli v. Elshire* (1973) the state court found that the supervisor, a physician, was not liable in the actions of an assistant, an anesthesiologist. The court reasoned that because the anesthesiologist had been selected in the normal course of events from among available, qualified, reputable, and competent anesthesiologists, the surgeon had no control over his performance. (The case against the anesthesiologist was settled out of court.) The ruling in *Marvulli* suggests that careful and diligent screening of assistants by social workers may prevent findings of liability. If a social worker takes on an assistant or supervisee without adequately checking that person's training, license status, and references and the supervisee is incompetent, the supervisor may be liable under what is known as the *tort of negligent entrustment* (Schutz 1982:50).

A number of cases involving supervisory liability concern the delegation of responsibility or specific duties to paraprofessionals and unlicensed supervisees. A number of popular clinical social work interventions—for example, biofeedback or group treatment—may involve the use of unlicensed assistants. As a psychiatrist commented after he had been involved in four malpractice suits alleging negligence on the part of supervisees,

> I never saw three of these plaintiffs, nor did I talk to the families. In the other case I saw the plaintiff patient only for 1/2 hour. My asso-

ciates and partners were not negligent in these cases, but the plaintiff thought so.

The point is that as a senior partner I was considered responsible for the actions of my associates, even though I had never seen the patients. This is an important point to be remembered by every senior physician.

The senior officer in every organization is legally responsible for every act of his juniors, both omission and commission. (G. W. Robinson 1962:780)

Unfortunately, the law concerning the amount of responsibility professionals can delegate legally to unlicensed assistants is vague. Clearly, however, the law does not permit mental health professionals to delegate all their responsibilities to an unlicensed person. In addition, the assistant or supervisee must be competent to perform the delegated duties (Cohen 1979).

Particular problems can arise when an unlicensed employee of a professional is functioning in a way that leads reasonable people to mistake the employee for a licensed professional. This practice is referred to as *lending out a license*, and the professional may be held liable and subject to disciplinary action. In many states an assistant to a licensed professional is considered legally an extension of the professional (Cohen 1979:237).

Another major source of risk involves situations in which psychiatrists sign a form attesting to the supervision of a social worker, when such supervision was never performed—for example, in order to qualify for reimbursement from an insurance company. In a New Jersey case a psychiatrist signed a social worker's written statement that a client was not dangerous, although the psychiatrist had never interviewed the client. The client subsequently killed his wife and children (Schutz 1982:50). Of course, a supervisee could simply fail to share with the supervisor all the case-related details required for competent supervision. In principle, however, the supervisor may be at risk.

Liability and Field Education

Special liability concerns arise with respect to field supervision of social work interns. Traditionally, social work faculty based in colleges and universities and the staff of agencies in which students carry out their field placements share some responsibility for student supervision. Unfortunately, there is little consensus about which parties are primarily liable if a student causes some form of harm during the field placement. Although it is likely that the doctrine of respondeat superior would apply in liability cases involving students, the extent to which the field supervisor and the college or university would be regarded as supervisors is not clear.

In an effort to address these issues Gelman and Wardell (1988) surveyed deans and directors of accredited social work education programs. The respondents confirmed the authors' suspicion that many issues related to supervisory liability are unresolved. Deans and directors cited a number of special liability concerns they face. Some agencies, for example, require the student or university to purchase personal liability insurance of at least $3 million before permitting a student to begin placement. Some students also are required to sign a waiver that holds the agency harmless against all claims brought by a client. Other agencies do not permit students to drive agency vehicles, insist that an agency staff member be present during all sessions with clients, and restrict students' access to agency files and records.

Preventing Supervisory Liability

Case law on the subject of supervisory liability suggests that social workers can take various preventive measures. In particular a good working relationship between the supervisor and supervisee is essential. Many problems can be avoided if they collaborate closely and constructively. As Cohen and DeBetz (1977) observe,

> Under ordinary circumstances, supervisory success stands or falls on the quality of the relationship between the participants. The most carefully prepared didactic presentation of material will fall on deaf ears if the learner is alienated from the teacher. Conversely, the least hint of theory or casual reference to the literature may suffice to motivate the inspired trainee to independently research and creatively expand on his teacher's ideas. Therefore the *responsive mutuality*, the sensitivity and respect shared by the supervisor and

the supervised, is perhaps the most potent tool in the supervisory repertoire. (p. 55)

Social work supervisors must give special attention to the frequency and scheduling of supervision. As Cohen (1979) notes, although no available case law suggests specific guidelines or an explicit standard of care, it seems reasonable to assume that setting up a pro forma supervision session once a week or once a month risks legal liability. In fact, Cohen and Mariano (1982:315) argue that current norms in the mental health professions are inadequate, especially with respect to supervision of psychotherapists in training:

> It would seem to the present authors that this standard [pro forma supervision provided once a week or once a month] upon which the profession has expressed approval by its silence, is too low. If some harm or injury befalls the patient of the student psychotherapist because the supervisor improperly failed to take into account the specific and unique needs of the patient and the supervisee, then it would seem that the doctrine of *respondeat superior* would be applicable. (p. 315)

Supervisors should not assume that such routinely scheduled sessions comprise adequate supervision in all cases, although such supervision may suffice for nearly all supervisees. Rather, supervisors must anticipate the possibility of cases with extenuating circumstances that may require more frequent and lengthier supervision than is customary. In short, provisions need to be made for extraordinary supervision. Supervisees should be monitored closely, and if a referral to another professional or agency is necessary, the referring social worker should ensure that the person or agency is licensed properly and able to respond effectively to the client's needs (see chapter 6 for further discussion of liability issues related to consultation and referral). Social workers who are part of a treatment team—for example, in a residential treatment center—also should pay close attention to the actions of their colleagues because they could be held liable in the negligence of another team member.

Special mention should be made of social workers in solo private practice because they face a special challenge with respect to supervision. Solo private practitioners do not always have easy access to regular sustained supervision. Some solo private practitioners contract for supervision with a respected colleague or mentor and/or participate in peer supervision or peer consultation groups. Once again, although the standard of care with regard to these forms of supervision has not been spelled out explicitly in case law or statute, by now norms have been established with respect to the need for some form of supervision, whether it is peer or otherwise, for solo practitioners. A private practitioner who is sued for negligence and found to be completely without any form of supervision may be vulnerable.

The form of supervision also must be considered. If a supervisor relies only on brief cursory conversations with a supervisee, the supervisor may be at risk in failing to obtain detailed information from a supervisee. Relying on sparse case summaries or case record material, for example, may not be sufficient, even if this is supplemented by a brief verbal report. As Kadushin (1976) notes in his classic discussion of supervision issues,

> The traditional, and current, heavy dependence on record material and verbal reports for information regarding workers' performance necessitates some evaluation of these sources. Studies by social workers (Armstrong, Huffman, and Spain 1959; Wilkie 1963) as well as other professionals (Covner 1943; Froehlich 1958; Muslin et al. 1967) indicate that case records present a selective and often distorted view of worker performance. Comparison of process recordings with tape recordings of the same contacts indicated that workers failed to hear and remember significant, recurrent patterns of interaction. Workers do not perceive and report important failings in their approach to the client. This omission is not necessarily intentional falsification of the record in order to make the worker look good, although that does happen. It is, rather, the result of selective perception in the service of the ego's attempt to maintain self-esteem. Forty years ago Elon Moore (1934) wrote an article entitled "How Accurate Are Case Records?" The question, which he answered negatively, is still pertinent today. Supervision based on the written record supplemented by the verbal report is supervision based on "retrospective reconstructions which are subject to serious distortions" on the part of the supervisee (Ward 1962, p. 1128). (p. 414)

Consequently, Kadushin (1976) urges supervising social workers to supplement case records with direct observation, videotapes, and perhaps supervision during an interview by using a one-way mirror and transmitter (being sure of course to obtain clients' consent). Although each method has its limitations, it is feasible in many circumstances. As Kadushin (1976:415) suggests, "Valid evaluation requires that we know what the worker actually did, not what he thinks he did or what he says he did."

Of course, one function of supervision is to provide the supervisor with information on which to base personnel or performance evaluations. The process of personnel or performance evaluation also raises several risk-management and liability issues. Staff members who receive negative evaluations—and who are disciplined, demoted, released, or simply not promoted as a result—may sue the supervisor and agency, challenging the employment action, alleging defamation of character, and so on. This is another reason for the supervisor to carefully document the nature of all supervision provided and the information upon which the supervisor based the personnel evaluation.

In addition, supervisors must understand the extent of the supervisees' right of access to their personnel records. Most social work settings now recognize staff members' right to review the contents of their personnel files, although this was not always the case. As Wilson (1978) observes,

[E]mployee access to personnel records has become the standard in personnel practice. In addition, the Federal Privacy Act's definition of an "individual" and of a "record" makes it quite clear that employees in federal programs have the same right of access to their files as do consumers of services. This includes the right to have copies made and submit corrections and additions to the record. Other governmental programs have adopted a similar policy, as have most educational systems and many private businesses. (p. 183)

What this means of course is that supervisors should be careful about the content, wording, and language used in performance evaluations (indeed, supervisors should be careful even if for some reason staff members do *not* have access to their evaluations). Presumably, all employees are concerned about how their work is evaluated, and performance evaluations are often viewed with hypersensitivity. Supervisors must be careful to avoid language and terminology that are defamatory, derisive, or otherwise inappropriate. Consider, for example, the following excerpt from a personnel file summarizing a supervisor's first employment interview with an applicant who was subsequently hired (and which was ultimately read by the employee):

> Mrs. Roberts appeared for an interview as scheduled. I had not noticed the height and weight on her application and was therefore totally unprepared for her appearance. Mrs. Roberts looks to be every bit of the 200 pounds she recorded on the application. There is a role [sic] of fat almost like a hunk across her shoulders and her stomach protrudes, giving a total effect of very poor posture. Her hair, which is cut fairly short, was in disarray and she wore no makeup. She had on a blue cotton dress which was rumpled, and altogether made as unprepossessing an appearance as any college graduate I can remember interviewing.
>
> During the course of the interview, I went to another office and telephoned Dr. Smith [a reference provided by the applicant], who was at home. At first he was not familiar with Mrs. Roberts, but when I described her, he immediately remembered her. He thinks she "has a chip on her shoulder," which is undoubtedly related to the problem that is causing her obesity, whatever that is. (Wilson 1978:185)

Although exhortations about preventive measures related to supervision of staff are appropriate, given the increasing likelihood of liability suits against social work supervisors, it is important to recognize that many social workers already are so overwhelmed with responsibility that adding the additional burden of closer and more frequent supervision may be difficult. This goes for the supervisor as well as the supervisee. Therefore, agency administrators must acknowledge the importance of enhanced supervision and provide the necessary resources and staff assistance to make it feasible.

Social work agencies should also conduct training sessions with line staff. These sessions should include a discussion and review of issues related to professional ethics and liability, along with a review of relevant federal, state, and local statutes. In particular training should cover the concepts of professional liability and malpractice, clients' right to confidentiality and the prevention of inappropriate disclosure, the limits of clients' right to confidentiality, the concept of privileged communication, improper treatment, the impaired practitioner, defamation of character, consultation with and referral to specialists, and fraud and deception. Training also should cover such topics as emergency assistance and suicide prevention, proper supervision of clients in residential and nonresidential settings, informed consent procedures, guidelines for terminating intervention, boundaries and intimacy with clients, and interaction with clients who are acting out. Agency administrators and supervisors need to be able to document that they provided staff with this training if someone files suit alleging negligence on the part of the agency as a result of the actions of a staff member.

In summary, social workers should be aware of a number of specific liability risks related to supervision (see Austin, Moline, and Williams 1990:235; Slovenko 1980, cited in Schutz 1982:48–49; Wilson 1978):

- supervisors who fail to provide information necessary for the workers to obtain an informed consent or to provide an adequate disclosure to a client;
- supervisors who fail to catch an error or made a misdiagnosis themselves in the negligent diagnosis or certification of dangerousness, suicidal intent, legal insanity, or mental illness itself;
- a treatment plan that is negligent or treatment carried out beyond its effectiveness, and the supervisor is responsible for the error or does not detect it;
- supervisors who fail to determine that a new worker needs to be assigned, treatment terminated, or specialists consulted;
- workers who are involved socially or sexually with clients or exert undue influence on the client and conceal their actions from the supervisor;
- a client's record that does not contain adequate information about the care the client has received, and the supervisor does not review the record and have it improved;
- supervision that is negligent because the supervisor does not meet regularly with the supervisee, review the presented material, or elicit the information necessary to adequately supervise the case;

- workers who are negligent in caring for clients—for example, who did not adequately supervise a suicidal client, who released a dangerous client prematurely, or who failed to provide coverage when unavailable—and supervisors who failed to review and approve these decisions;
- supervisors who fail to assess the competence of supervisees as to what clienteles and types of cases they can handle;
- supervisors who provide supervision to too many supervisees to be able to provide competent supervision;
- supervisors who fail to summarize, record, or otherwise document what occurs in supervision;
- supervisors involved in a dual relationship with a supervisee;
- supervisors who fail to give detailed written and verbal evaluations to supervisees;
- supervisors who fail to review supervisees' records for accuracy and completeness;
- supervisors who sign off on insurance or other forms for cases they have not supervised;
- supervisors who fail to provide consistent, regularly scheduled supervision to supervisees; and
- supervisors who use defamatory or otherwise inappropriate language in performance evaluations of supervisees.

Clearly, supervision is essential to effective social work practice. Since the earliest days of social work, professionals have recognized that competent supervision is necessary in order to transmit the profession's values and methods and to monitor the performance of supervisees. No competent professional questions the appropriateness of at least some form of supervision. Understandably, social work literature has focused primarily on the technical aspects of social work supervision or what some consider the art of supervision (Kadushin 1992; Miller 1987). Modern circumstances, however, require social workers to broaden their perspective and learn about a range of legal and liability risks related to supervision.

Liability issues related to social work supervision continue to emerge. Although some liability risks are patently clear—namely, those risks related to the inappropriate delegation of professional responsibility to untrained staff and the failure to provide regular supervisory sessions to supervisees—other risks, such as the assumption of liability by field work agencies and colleges and universities, still need to be clarified. Therefore, social workers must enhance their understanding of liability issues and seek clarification of ambiguous circumstances that arise in supervision. In the end the best interests of clients depend on the success of these efforts.

6 | Consultation, Referral, and Records

Already discussed in some detail is the need for social workers to seek and provide competent supervision in relation to their work with clients. This supervision may be obtained in the worker's own agency or, especially in the case of solo private practitioners, as peer consultation.

Peer consultation is only one form of consultation in social work. As seasoned practitioners know well, social workers have many other occasions when they need to obtain consultation from colleagues, both social workers and other professionals, who have special expertise that may be required in work with individuals, families, groups, communities, or organizations. This is particularly true when a social worker lacks specialized training and knowledge related to a particular phenomenon, such as substance abuse, eating disorders, or domestic violence.

Clearly, social workers are wrong to attempt to provide forms of treatment and intervention outside of their range of skill. Although social workers typically receive broad-based education and are rather versatile, for a practitioner to claim specialized skill in an area for which he or she has little knowledge and training would be unethical. If a client presents a particular problem that is beyond the social worker's skill range, she or he should seek consultation or make a referral. Failure to do so risks liability. In some instances it is appropriate for the social worker to continue working with the client, with consultation necessary for only some specific aspect of the case. In other instances, however, it may not be appropriate for the social worker to continue handling the case at all; instead, a referral should be made to another practitioner who has the specialized education and knowledge required for competent intervention.

Consultation in Social Work

The nature of consultation in social work has changed over time (Kadushin 1977; Rieman 1992; Shulman 1987). Consultation was not formally recognized as an important component in social work practice until after World War II. Not until recent years, however, has the profession had substantial literature on consultation. For example, only two entries on *consultation* appeared in the *Social Service Review* between 1927 and 1966, and the concept was not indexed in the *Social Work Yearbook* until the fifteenth edition (the *Encyclopedia of Social Work*), published in 1965 (Kadushin 1977).

The earliest forms of consultation in social work, particularly in the 1950s, involved social workers as consultees, often to psychiatrists who typically provided case consultation and education about psychiatric phenomena. Common practice was, and still is, for family service agencies to have a "psychiatric consultant" to consult in individual cases. In 1955 and 1957 special workshops on psychiatric consultation to social service agencies were conducted at the annual meetings of the American Orthopsychiatric Association (Kadushin 1977).

More recently, social workers have broadened their use of consultation to include a wide range of professionals. Practitioners in protective service agencies may consult lawyers to interpret case law related to the removal of children from a home. Social workers in a battered women's shelter may consult a specialist in the area of eating disorders. Social workers in private practice may consult other social workers who have particular expertise in post-traumatic stress disorder. Social work administrators may seek consultation in relation to program evaluation or needs assessments.

Kadushin provides a useful definition of consultation:

> Consultation is regarded as an interactional helping process—a series of sequential steps taken to achieve some objective through an interpersonal relationship. One participant in the transaction has greater expertise, greater knowledge, greater skill in the performance of some particular specialized function, and this person is designated *consultant*. The *consultee*, generally a professional, has encountered a problem in relation to his job which requires the knowledge, skill, and expertise of the consultant for its solution or amelioration. Consultation is thus distinguished from other interpersonal interactional processes involving the giving and taking of help, such as casework, counseling, psychotherapy, by virtue of the fact that its problem-solving focus is related to some difficulties encountered in performing job-related functions and by virtue of the fact that the identity of the consultee is generally restricted to someone engaged in implementing professional roles. (1977:25–26)

Consultation in social work can produce two major liability risks. The first involves situations in which a social worker should seek consultation but fails to and a client is harmed as a result. The argument in such cases is that the social worker breached the standard of care by failing to seek appropriate consultation, an act of omission.

Maryann B., M.S.W., was a caseworker at the Woodholme Family Service Agency. She specialized in couples and marriage counseling.

Maryann B. began working with a young married couple who were having some difficulty managing the behavior of their four-year-old son. Maryann B. spent considerable time helping the couple to use simple behavioral techniques, such as positive reinforcement and extinction, to manage their son's behavior. In addition, Maryann B. helped the couple explore several sources of tension and conflict in their marriage.

After several months in treatment the husband in the couple disclosed that about eight years earlier he had been diagnosed as having multiple personality disorder. He told

Maryann B. that he feared that some of his symptoms were reappearing.

Maryann B. continued working with the couple, although she did not seek consultation related to multiple personality disorders. She believed that she had sufficient knowledge and skill to be able to work with her client, although he began complaining more and more about what he believed to be symptoms of the disorder.

About ten weeks after his first complaints about the multiple personality disorder symptoms, the husband stabbed his wife. The couple had gotten into a heated argument about disciplining their son. According to the wife, during the stabbing the husband spoke in a foreign accent and claimed that his name was different from the one he ordinarily used.

The wife sued the social worker, claiming that she failed to seek appropriate consultation related to the treatment of multiple personality disorders. The suit claimed that had the social worker sought proper consultation, her husband would not have assaulted her.

Case law illustrates the liability risks when a professional does not refer a client to a specialist for consultation. In *James Permetti, Maria and Russell Dupuis and Olga Dupuis v. Kelsey-Seybold Clinic, Richardo Daichman, M.D. and Robert S. Dickinson, M.D.*, the plaintiff claimed that his wife's death was the result of a lack of referral for consultation. The woman, who was twenty-four years old, was being treated for depression by her regular physician. The physician prescribed medication for several months without referring her to a psychiatrist or psychologist for consultation and the possibility of treatment. After the depressive symptoms worsened, the physician referred the woman to a psychiatrist and psychologist in the same clinic. The woman committed suicide after two visits to the clinic psychiatrist. The woman's husband alleged that the physician who did not refer his wife to a psychiatrist for timely consultation was negligent. The plaintiffs were awarded $460,000 in the Texas case ("Physician Fails," 1992:2).

Social workers can also incur liability risks when they fail to consult an *organization* for advice. This may occur when, for instance, a social worker does not consult with, or report to, the local public child protection agency in a case in which child abuse is suspected. As I noted in chapter 3, social workers and other mandated reporters do not report suspected abuse and neglect in a distressingly large percentage of cases. Often the mandated reporters are confident they can handle the situation without the public agency's involvement, do not have confidence in the child protection agency staff, and/or do not want to jeopardize their therapeutic relationship with their clients. The legal risk, however, is that the mandated reporter could be held liable in failing to consult with a specialist—the child protection agency (in addition to being subjected to whatever statutory criminal or civil penalties may exist).

Social workers should especially seek consultation when their work with a particular client seems to be stalled or going nowhere. Clients who are frustrated with the progress, or lack of progress, they are making in treatment may be particularly prone to sue. As Schutz (1982) notes,

> When therapy reaches a prolonged impasse, the therapist ought to consider consulting another therapist and possibly transferring the patient. Apart from the clinical and ethical considerations, his failure to seek another opinion might have legal ramifications in the establishment of proximate cause in the event of a suit. While therapists are not guarantors of cure or improvement, extensive treatment without results could legally be considered to have injured the patient; in specific, the injury would be the loss of money and time, and the preclusion of other treatments that might have been more successful. To justify a prolonged holding action at a plateau, the therapist would have to show that this was maintaining a condition against a significant and likely deterioration. Consultation at this point would establish the reasonableness of one's approach and help establish criteria for when to terminate one's efforts to treat a patient. (p. 47)

Social workers need to be particularly alert to the need for medical consultation. Consider the case of a social worker who was working with a client who claimed to have chronic low self-esteem:

> For months the social worker and client focused on family-of-origin issues and issues related to the client's intimate rela-

tionships as an adult. On occasion the client would also complain that she was having a hard time remembering things, such as friends' and colleagues' names, appointments she had made, and so on. Periodically, the client would complain of incapacitating headaches.

Several months after the client began complaining of headaches, she blacked out while shopping at a local mall. The client was rushed to the hospital, where she was diagnosed with a brain tumor. Surgery removed the tumor, but the client suffered some moderate brain damage.

Shortly after surgery one of the client's doctors told her that had she been seen by a physician one or two months earlier, there was a good chance they could have treated the tumor without surgery. Once the client completely recovered from her surgery, she was angry that the social worker had not referred her to a physician for a medical exam. The client shared her frustration with her sister, who suggested the client talk to an attorney about a negligence suit.

Social workers cannot, of course, be expected to be knowledgeable about organic and other medical problems clients may have. They are, however, obligated to be alert to the need for medical consultation. As Meyer, Landis, and Hays (1988) observe in their discussion of liability risks faced by psychologists, "The standard has generally been that others in the same discipline would seek the help of a specialist in the same circumstances" (pp. 50–51). In addition, these authors state,

> Failure to refer is a type of negligence if it leads to some injury to the client. For example, a client consulting a psychologist who describes a recent blow to the head followed by recurrent headaches, personality changes, and difficulty with memory and concentration, may have sustained a neurologic injury. Alternatively he may be displaying a conversion syndrome. The psychologist would be expected to ascertain whether a neurologist or other physician was involved in the case, and either consult with that person or make an appropriate referral to help in the diagnostic process. If the psychologist proceeded on the assumption that no organic damage was present, he could be held liable for negligently failing to refer the patient to a practitioner capable of treating his problem. (p. 50)

The second liability problem related to consultation has to do with the consultation itself. In these cases, typically, the claim is that the consultation a social worker *provided* was somehow flawed or negligent and that the consultation, or advice stemming from it, caused some injury. This may occur, for example, if consultants provide training, advice, or guidance on a topic outside their areas of expertise.

> Barbara C., M.S.W., was a social worker in private practice. Her practice was devoted primarily to treatment of eating disorders.
>
> One afternoon Barbara C. received a telephone call from a social worker employed at a small local private school. The social worker told Barbara C. that a student, a fourteen-year-old girl, seemed to have an eating disorder. The student had been losing weight, not eating at lunch time, exercising excessively, and had been found in the lavatory inducing her own vomiting.
>
> The school social worker, who did not have much experience treating eating disorders, asked Barbara C. to consult on the case. Barbara C. agreed and met with the social worker and two of the student's teachers. For the next two months the school social worker and Barbara C. met weekly to discuss the case and to review the school social worker's intervention.
>
> Over time it became clear that the student was also mutilating herself. She was sticking needles in her arm and cutting her wrists. The social worker/consultant advised the school social worker to ignore the self-mutilation so as not to reinforce it. The mutilation, however, got worse and worse. About three weeks after the mutilation became apparent, the student slashed her wrists and committed suicide.
>
> The student's parents sued the school, the school's social worker, and the social work consultant, claiming that they failed to provide proper treatment to their daughter. In particular the plaintiffs argued that the social work consultant provided advice outside her area of expertise. Although the plaintiffs acknowledged that the social work consultant had considerable expertise related to eating disorders, an area in which the social work consultant had received extensive training, they challenged her ability to give advice related to self-mutilation, an area in which the social work consultant had received no formal training.

Not all liability risks related to consultation involve case consultation. Social workers can also encounter problems when they provide consultation to agencies and programs. For example, social workers who have little skill related to program evaluations should not present themselves as experts. A program that relies on the social worker's claim of skill in this area may be injured if the social worker conducts a poorly designed study or evaluation, which may ultimately hurt the program's chances for funding. Clearly, social workers should provide consultation only with respect to those subjects and skill areas for which they can demonstrate competence and expertise.

Referral in Social Work

In some cases social workers find that they do not have sufficient expertise to continue working with a particular client. While it makes sense in some instances for a social worker to continue working with a client while seeking consultation on a particular aspect of the client's treatment (for example, a social worker who is trained to intervene in a client's depression but needs consultation on the client's eating disorder), in other instances social workers may need to consider referring the entire case to a professional colleague.

In such cases social workers have an obligation to exercise due care in the process they use to refer clients to colleagues. Social workers should not make referrals to others indiscriminately. Instead, they should be diligent in their efforts to refer clients to colleagues with solid reputations, who have proper credentials, and in whom they have confidence. Otherwise, a social worker may risk a claim of *negligent referral,* that is, a referral that was not made using standard procedures. A 1992 article about a mental health professional in the *Providence Journal-Bulletin* illustrates this risk:

> A Providence psychiatrist has been disciplined for referring a patient to an unqualified counselor.
> The state Board of Medical Licensure and Discipline last month imposed, but stayed, a three-month suspension on Dr. Lee H. Gold-

stein, an osteopathic physician [and psychiatrist] at 15 Benefit St. The board also fined him $1,500.

Dr. Milton W. Hamolsky, the board's administrator, said that a stayed suspension is like probation. The board, he said, believed that Goldstein's infraction was not serious enough to prohibit him from practicing, but it did warrant a more rigorous penalty than a reprimand.

According to the disciplinary board, a patient saw Goldstein for weekly psychotherapy sessions for 15 months but terminated therapy and complained to the board when Goldstein referred her to an unlicensed counselor. The board considers it unprofessional conduct for a psychiatrist to refer a patient to someone who is not licensed or certified to provide mental health care.

Hamolsky said there was no evidence that Goldstein had a pattern of making inappropriate referrals. (p. B3)

Similar issues related to referral to an unqualified service provider appear in *Selin v. Egli*. The defendant was a counselor who had worked with a woman and her sons (the plaintiffs). During the counseling the defendant referred the plaintiffs to a "colleague" for additional counseling. The colleague was described as the defendant's "associate." The associate, however, did not have a medical or psychology degree or any other training that would qualify him as a counselor. The plaintiffs claimed that the associate's counseling was incompetent, that it caused confusion, bewilderment, anger, and frustration, and that his services were worthless and counterproductive. The Utah case was settled for an undisclosed sum ("Psychological Counselor Refers Patients," 1991:6).

Cohen (1979) also comments on the legal ramifications that can arise from a negligent referral: "If a referral is indicated, the professional has a duty to select an appropriate professional or institution for the patient. Barring any extraordinary circumstances, the professional making the referral will not incur any liability for the acts of the person or institution that he refers the patient to, provided that the person or institution is duly licensed and equipped to meet the patient's needs" (p. 239). In *Stovall v. Harms* (1974) a physician—a general practitioner—referred one of his patients to a psychiatrist. The patient was subsequently involved in an automobile accident and alleged that the accident was the result of medication prescribed by his psychiatrist. The plaintiff sued the general practitioner for the injuries sustained in the accident. The general practitioner was not found liable, however, because the plaintiff had not demonstrated that he had been negligent in selecting the psychiatrist. The psychiatrist was qualified, and the general practitioner had no control over the care provided to the patient by the psychiatrist (Cohen 1979:184).

Social Work Records

Social workers who consult with other professionals about a client or refer a client to another professional must provide careful documentation of the consultation/referral in the case record. I have been involved in a number of cases over the years in which social workers were conscientious about obtaining consultation and making referrals. Some social workers have encountered problems, however, because they failed to document the consultation and referrals in the case record. When clients alleged that these social workers neglected to obtain proper consultation or make an appropriate referral, the social workers were unable to produce evidence or sufficient documentation. Lawyers sometimes offer the axioms, "If it isn't recorded, it didn't happen," and "Work not written is work not done."

In fact, in one well-known case (*Whitree v. State of New York* 1968) an inadequate record was determined to be negligent in itself because such a record does not provide guidance for adequate care in the absence of the professional and contributes nothing useful to the client's treatment history, which could affect a client's subsequent care. Victor Whitree, forty-six, was arrested in New York City on a charge of stabbing another man. Whitree was placed on probation and subsequently ordered to Bellevue Hospital for a psychiatric examination. He was then placed in maximum security confinement for more than four years and kept in a locked cell except for exercise and visits to the bathroom. Whitree eventually sued the state of New York for wrongful confinement and for injuries he sustained as a result of his hospitalization and as a result of various attacks and beatings by patients and guards.

o commenting on the negligence it determined
Whitree's care, the court found that "the hospi-
aintained by the State for claimant was about as
cord as [they had] ever examined" and that the
conform to the standards in the community; and
uacies in this record militated against proper and
competent psychiatric and ordinary medical care." Further, the
court concluded, "To the extent that a hospital record develops
information for subsequent treatment, it contributed to the inadequate treatment this claimant received" (290 N.Y.S.2d 486 at
495, cited in Austin, Moline, and Williams 1990:30). Whitree
was awarded $300,000 in damages for the negligence and for false
imprisonment.

This problem raises the much larger issue of liability risks
related to recording and note taking. Recording is one of those
skills social workers learn early in their careers and one of the
oldest social work skills, as illustrated by the 1920 publication of
Sheffield's *The Social Case History: Its Construction and Content*. In this landmark work Sheffield described the narrative
record as "a body of personal information conserved with a view
to the three ends of social case work; namely (1) the immediate
purpose of furthering effective treatment of individual clients, (2)
the ultimate purpose of general social betterment, and (3) the
incidental purpose of establishing the caseworker herself in critical thinking" (pp. 5–6, cited in Kagle 1987:463). Other critically
important works include Hamilton's *Social Case Recording*
(1936) and *Principles of Social Case Recording* (1946).

Typically, undergraduate and graduate social work education
programs include content on recording. Proficient recording
enhances the quality of services provided to clients. Records
identify, describe, and assess clients' situations; define the purpose of service; document service goals, plans, activities, and
progress; and evaluate the effect of service (Kagle 1987, 1991;
Wilson 1980). Recording also demonstrates the social worker's
thoughtful attention to detail.

In addition, recording enhances continuity of care. Carefully
written notes help social workers recall relevant detail during
the course of intervention and can facilitate coordination of services and supervision among staff members within an agency.

Recording also helps to ensure quality care if a client's primary social worker becomes unavailable because of sickness, vacation, or departure from the agency.

Of course, competent recording is not only good practice. Recording also provides some measure of protection against negligence claims. As Kagle (1987) states, "By keeping accurate, relevant, and timely records, social workers do more than just describe, explain, and support the services they provide. They also discharge their ethical and legal responsibility to be accountable. This accountability extends beyond the individual agency (and the organizations that fund and accredit it) to the profession as a whole, the community, and, ultimately, the client" (p. 463).

Social workers should keep a number of criteria in mind with respect to recording and case notes (Austin, Moline, and Williams 1990:25–44; Schutz 1982:51–52; Wilson 1978:31–55, 83–97). In particular, the social worker should record

- informed-consent procedures and enclose signed consent forms for release of information and treatment;
- all contacts made with third parties (such as family members, acquaintances, and other professionals), whether in person or by telephone. A brief description of the contacts and any significant events surrounding them should be included;
- any consultation with other professionals, including the date the client was referred to another professional for services;
- a complete social history, assessment, and treatment plan, stating the client's problems, the reason for requesting service, objectives and relevant timetable, intervention strategy, planned number and duration of contacts, assessment and evaluation of progress, termination plan, and reasons for termination;
- a brief description of the social worker's reasoning for all decisions made during the course of intervention;
- any instructions, recommendations, and advice provided to the client, including referral to and suggestions to seek consultation from a specialist;

- a description of all contacts with clients, including type of contact (e.g., in person versus telephone; individual, family, couples, group), and dates and times of contacts. Notation should also be made of failed or canceled appointments; and any previous or current psychological, psychiatric, or medical evaluations relevant to the social worker's intervention.

Ordinarily, records should not include excessively subjective or speculative observations. Many professionals advise that any speculative material be kept in a separate set of personal notes. Several jurisdictions have acknowledged therapists' right to maintain such private notes (Schutz 1982:52; Wilson 1978:49–50), although some experts strongly recommend against the practice (Austin, Moline, and Williams, 1990:34). Some years ago the Model Law on Confidentiality of Health and Social Service Information was drafted to specifically address the issue of personal notes that do not have to be disclosed:

a. A service provider is not required to but may, to the extent he or she determines it necessary and appropriate, keep personal notes regarding a client wherein he or she may record:

    (i) sensitive information disclosed to him or her in confidence by other persons on condition that such information would never be disclosed to the client or other persons excepting, at most, other service providers; and

    (ii) sensitive information disclosed to him or her by the client which would be injurious to the client's relationships to other persons;

    (iii) the service provider's speculations, impressions, hunches and reminders. No authorization to disclose confidential information shall be effective with respect to such personal notes of a service provider except on authorization to disclose the same to another service provider occupying a professional service relationship with the client by reason whereof it would serve the client's interests

for him to have the personal notes and whereby he
is bound to observe confidentiality.

Upon receipt of such personal notes by such
other service provider, they shall be deemed to be
his personal notes except to the extent that he
transfers information from such notes to regular
health and social service records pertaining to the
client.

b. The keeping of such personal notes shall not relieve a service
provider from any obligation to record and maintain in an
official record information pertaining to such matters as diagnosis, treatment, progress and all other information required
in an individualized treatment plan. (Nye 1976, cited in Wilson 1978:51)

This language is clearly reflected in the subsequently enacted Illinois Mental Health and Developmental Disabilities Confidentiality Act of 1979, one of the most explicit codified statements on the subject of personal notes. The act addresses the
issue of personal notes by stating that the client's record "does
not include the therapist's notes, if such notes are kept in the
therapist's sole possession and are not disclosed to any other
person, except the therapist's supervisor, consulting therapist
or attorney. If at any time such notes are disclosed, they shall
be considered part of the . . . record." The act goes on to say that
the therapist's personal notes may include "information disclosed to the therapist in confidence by other persons on condition that such information would never be disclosed to the
recipient or other persons; information disclosed to the therapist by the recipient which would be injurious to the recipient's
relationship to other persons; and the therapist's speculations,
impressions, hunches, and reminders" (cited in Kagle
1991:170).

Although the support for such personal notes may provide
social workers with some comfort, they must realize that such
notes *could* be subpoenaed by a lawyer, along with formal
agency or private practice records (subpoena duces tecum).
Lawyers have in fact subpoenaed such items as appointment
books, scraps of paper, calendars, and any other documents on

which the practitioner may have written notes related to the matter at hand. Also, most states do not distinguish between professional and personal notes.

In addition, social workers should not keep process (narrative) recordings in a case record, even temporarily. The record also should not contain information regarding a client's political, religious, or other personal views unless this detail is directly relevant to the intervention. Intimate, gossipy, and other personal details that are not directly germane to intervention should be omitted, as should any information that could in any way be used against the client in a court of law.

Social workers are generally advised to retain complete written records for at least three to five years, although some agencies and practitioners retain them for longer periods (Wilson 1978:32). The American Psychological Association's *Speciality Guidelines for Delivery of Services* suggests that when no statutes address the time period for retaining notes, practitioners should retain full records for three years and either the full record or a summary of the record for twelve more years; no record should be disposed of until fifteen years after completion of service (Austin, Moline, and Williams 1990:38–39). In contrast, counseling psychology's guidelines suggest that the full record be maintained for at least fourteen years after completion of planned services or after the date of last contact with the client, whichever is later; that if a full record is not maintained, at least a summary be maintained for an additional three years; and that the record may be disposed of no sooner than seven years after the completion of planned services or after the date of last contact, whichever is later (Austin, Moline, and Williams 1990:38–39). Case records pertaining to minors ordinarily should be kept longer because the statute of limitations may not begin to run until the child reaches the age of majority.

Social workers would also be wise to prepare a will that includes plans for the transfer or disposition of cases in the event of death or incapacitation. Experts suggest providing for an executor or trustee to maintain records for a period of thirty days, at the end of which the social worker's practice and all records may be sold to a designated colleague (often for a nominal fee of $1).

Because of the potential problems involved in recording and note taking some professionals have proposed doing away with records entirely. As Wilson (1978) observes, "A serious suggestion has been made, and is being carried out in some social work settings, that there simply be no records at all. Advocates of this tactic prefer that all old files be destroyed and no new recording be done on social-work activity" (p. 48). Some argue that the absence of records would be particularly helpful when practitioners are subpoenaed to court, where in principle therapists could claim that they do not fully remember what happened in the case. Most professionals agree, however, that the elimination of records would create more problems, legal and otherwise, than it would solve. Watson (1972, cited in Wilson 1978:53) states the position well in his comments about the use of records in psychoanalysis:

> In relation to legal matters, they [records] have two purposes: (1) to refresh our memory about what we are doing for a patient in order that we may maintain our own working contact with a patient accurately.... (2) In the event the therapist is called to account legally for work with his patient, records add substantially to what lawyers call his *credibility*. Mere absence of records will not keep one from being subpoenaed. There are evidentiary dangers in saying that you do not remember things about a patient whom you have treated. . . . [A] good cross-examining lawyer would then tax the analyst's narcissism rigorously as he began to explore the implications of nonmemory about the case. That could cause the therapist considerable embarrassment when he found himself in the position of saying he treats patients but does not remember anything about them. In other words, one should not fool oneself into believing that the problem of testimony will be solved by "not having any records." Neither will it be possible to readily convince the judge that he should pay attention to your notions of relevance, when you cannot demonstrate what you did through some kind of record. In short, if you jeopardize your credibility with the judge by playing games about memory, it is very likely he will pay no attention to you when you attempt to argue that certain matters are irrelevant and also damaging to your patient, so far as privilege is concerned. Therefore, such a tactic would be basically foolish and self-defeating.

Although the vast majority of social workers agree that keeping good case notes is important, some do not do so. In chapter 5, for example, I described a case involving a social worker who was a partner in a private practice and was sued under the doctrine of *respondeat superior* in connection with mistakes alleged to have been made by a former nurse the social worker had hired. In that case the plaintiff alleged that the former nurse, who was originally hired to conduct eating disorder assessments and evaluations of children, provided incompetent counseling services to her before the former nurse had completed her formal education in a counseling program and before she was licensed as a counselor. The plaintiff also claimed that the social worker should be held liable because the former nurse provided the counseling and in relation to the monitoring and intervention in the case by the social worker, which the suit claimed was inadequate. The specific allegations included claims that the former nurse promoted the client's dependency on her, involved the client in her side business, which was completely unrelated to counseling, traveled out of state with the client, and otherwise was involved in inappropriate dual relationships with the client. The client and her husband sued, claiming that she had been manifesting serious symptoms, including depression and suicidal ideation.

One of the key issues involved in the case concerned the claim that during the intervention neither the former nurse nor the social worker maintained notes concerning the case. When the plaintiff's attorney deposed the former nurse, the following dialogue took place, beginning with the lawyer:

Q: What kinds of clients do you tend to see?
A: What do you mean?
Q: Do you specialize in certain kinds of problem areas?
A: No, not really. I see lots of different kinds of clients.
Q: Do you have case notes on all of your clients?
A: Some yes, some no.
Q: What about [the plaintiff]? Why didn't you keep notes in this case?
A: You have to understand that this is a very complicated case. There were two other clinicians involved, plus lots of other service providers outside of our own agency. This wasn't my

case primarily, so I didn't feel the need to keep detailed notes. There were so many others involved, it just didn't seem necessary. I was usually in touch with the other counselors. So I just didn't think there was a problem.

Q: Well, frankly, I am confused about this. I am trying to imagine what it must be like to keep track of so many clients. I can't imagine keeping it all in my head. What if I get a call from a client I haven't seen in some time? How am I supposed to remember all those details? It seems to me that any professional who provides services to clients—or patients—ought to keep careful notes to keep track of all the details of the case. Suppose you get sick or have to go away in an emergency? What happens if some colleague of yours needs to know what's happening in the case? Don't you think you have a responsibility here?

A: I guess we see these things differently. I've been operating this way for years. I think I have the ability to remember the important things that are going on in my clients' lives. I guess it's possible that I'd forget something, but I've never considered it a problem. In this particular case I was in pretty close touch with my colleagues involved with [the plaintiff]. Whenever I felt the need for some consultation I would contact one of my colleagues here. That happened a lot. Maybe it would have been a good idea to write all this stuff down, but I didn't. I just didn't think I needed to.

That next week the social worker (the partner in the private practice who had hired the former nurse), who was being sued under the doctrine of respondeat superior, was also deposed and here too the subject of recording and note taking was pursued by the plaintiff's attorney:

Q: Let me ask you this question, Ms. [mentions the social worker's name]. Do you ordinarily keep detailed case notes?
A: It depends, but usually not.
Q: What do you think about that?
A: What do you mean?
Q: I mean, do you think that's standard procedure in social work?
A: Look, I don't really know what standard procedure is in gen-

eral. I know what I do and what I think is acceptable. I've never kept detailed case notes on every client.

Q: You've always practiced this way?

A: Yes, since day one. I've never felt the need to handle my practice any differently.

Q: Is this what you were taught to do when you went to school to become a social worker?

A: Not really. It's never been a problem before.

Q: Well, I'm not really concerned about problems before now. I want to know whether there was a problem in this case.

A: I guess we have a different view of this.

Q: Is it ever necessary for you to keep case notes?

A: Only if there's something highly unusual.

Q: Highly unusual?

A: Like a suicidal client—something like that.

Sometimes social workers whose records are subpoenaed are tempted to alter the record in order to fill in any gaps or to correct errors. In some instances social workers have actually destroyed all or a portion of a record in order to cover up some error. This is a serious mistake. In addition to engaging in deception (see chapter 7), the social worker may be liable in altering or destroying a record. As Cohen (1979) notes, "Some professionals foolishly attempt to 'tighten up' or alter the records so that the records will show them in a better light in court. What these professionals do not know is that the plaintiff's attorney may have somehow gotten to the records and copied them long before the letter advising [the defendant] of the litigation was sent. In such a case, the 'doctored' records will then reflect quite poorly on the health professional" (p. 275). In addition, destroying case notes is a felony in some states (Austin, Moline, and Williams 1990:34). Many experts argue that any material in the records is going to be less incriminating than evidence that a practitioner altered or destroyed a record.

7 | Deception and Fraud

Recently, I conducted a workshop in a large midwestern city on ethical and liability issues in social work. During a break a participant approached to ask me a question. She explained that she was a social worker in solo private practice, much of it devoted to family counseling, in a nearby suburban community. The social worker complained that many insurance companies with which she dealt were unwilling to reimburse for family sessions. She explained that because her livelihood depended on third-party payment, she felt compelled to camouflage the family therapy and on many insurance forms indicated that she provided individual counseling to members of the families she has seen. The social worker asked whether I thought she could, as a result, "get in trouble."

Unfortunately, a variety of circumstances in social work provide opportunities for some form of deception or fraud—that is, a deliberate attempt by a social worker to give a false impression to a client, colleague, insurance provider, employer, or some other party. The potential problem is sufficiently serious to warrant its own principle (I.A.2) in the NASW *Code of Ethics* (1990):

"The social worker should not participate in, condone, or be associated with dishonesty, fraud, deceit, or misrepresentation."

Fraud is typically considered an intentional tort, as Schutz (1982) suggests in his discussion of legal liability in psychotherapy:

> Fraud is the intentional or negligent, implied, or direct perversion of truth for the purpose of inducing another, who relies on such misrepresentation, to part with something valuable belonging to him or to surrender a legal right. If one misrepresents the risks or benefits of therapy for one's own benefit and not the patient's, so as to induce him to undergo treatment and pay the fee, this is fraud. Telling a patient that sexual intercourse is therapy may be seen as a perversion of the truth so as to get the patient to part with something of value. Hence, this would be seen as fraud. (p. 12)

Social workers may engage in deception and fraud for various reasons and with various motives. Some social workers—a small percentage, fortunately—are simply dishonest and attempt to take advantage of others for reasons of greed, malice, or self-protection. Other social workers engage in deceit and fraud for what appear to be more altruistic reasons, that is, to be as helpful as they can be to their clients and agencies.

Self-Interested Deception and Fraud

The vast majority of social workers enter the profession with remarkably pure motives. For a variety of reasons they are moved to help vulnerable people. Some social workers have been influenced by an admired mentor and some by family values. Some enter social work as a result of their own personal trauma or experience as a client. Whatever the reasons, most social workers are attracted to the profession for noble purposes—to assist people who are experiencing serious problems in living that are related to poverty, mental illness, substance abuse, child or elder abuse, family conflict or violence, physical disability or illness, and so on.

Sadly, however, some social workers enter the profession with ignoble motives or develop them along the way. As discussed in chapter 4, a number of impaired social workers, particularly those who sexually abuse clients, may use their power, status, and authority as professionals to seek opportunities to meet their own needs by exploiting clients. Social workers who have addictions—whether to gambling or substances such as alcohol or other drugs—may use their professional positions to extort or steal money from impressionable or incompetent clients or use deceit and undue influence to persuade clients to enter into agreements primarily designed to benefit the social worker.

Paul S., B.S.W., was a caseworker at Elder Services of Boon County. He had been employed at the agency as a case coordinator for five years. Paul S. provided case management services for a case load of twenty-five clients. Most of his clients needed assistance with home health care, homemaker services, crisis management, grief counseling, and help with income maintenance and insurance benefits. Several clients had been declared incompetent. Most, however, were able to participate in the management of their affairs.

One of his clients was a seventy-six-year-old man, John M. John M. had been a client of the agency for three years, and Paul S. had gotten to know him quite well during that time. In fact, the two men had become so close that John M. often referred to Paul S. as the "son I always wanted."

John M. was living in a congregate housing development where he had a small private apartment and shared kitchen facilities with six other residents. Before his retirement at age seventy, he had been a highly successful furniture manufacturer. He had developed a large furniture factory, ultimately employing about three hundred people. When he sold the business John M. became a wealthy man.

Recently, John M. was diagnosed with liver cancer. Paul S. spent quite a bit of time with him, reminiscing about John M.'s life and talking about his impending death. Clearly, John M. was dying and becoming more and more confused. The psychiatric consultant said that John M. would probably need to be placed on psychotropic medication to help him with his confusion.

At about this time Paul S., the social worker, was having serious financial problems. A couple of years earlier he had taken his brother-in-law's advice and without his wife's knowledge had invested most of their savings in the options market. Within a year, however, he had lost nearly everything. Paul S. had two children in private school and was feeling guilty and desperate about the money he had lost.

During one conversation with John M., Paul S. said that he was worried about one of his daughters who, Paul S. lied, was gravely ill and disabled. Over a period of three days Paul S., who had become quite important to John M., convinced John M. to rewrite his will to include Paul S. as a beneficiary.

Not all cases of this sort, in which unscrupulous social workers use undue influence and deceit to benefit themselves, involve incompetent or close-to-incompetent clients. In many cases clients are competent but vulnerable and impressionable. A social worker providing psychotherapy to a "needy" client, who originally sought counseling for a serious self-esteem problem, may find a ripe opportunity to convince the client to include the social worker as a partner in her thriving business. The social worker may deceitfully convince the client that nothing about this relationship is inappropriate. Or, a social worker who has serious financial problems may use fraud to convince an impressionable client to invest in a legitimate-sounding limited partnership that in actuality is a Ponzi scheme (a swindle in which an initial investment provides a quick return paid out of funds from new investors).

Other forms of self-interested deceit and fraud are more straightforward. One more common form involves clinical social workers—albeit, a relatively small percentage—who submit fraudulent information on claim forms to third-party payers and insurance companies. Insurance companies may be billed for counseling sessions that did not occur. Or, social workers may collude with a psychiatrist who for a fee signs forms attesting to the client's diagnosis and treatment when the psychiatrist was virtually uninvolved in the case and had no contact with the client. In one widely publicized signing-off case a social worker in private practice spent a weekend in jail after pleading guilty in an insurance fraud case. She was also ordered to perform 720 hours of community service (NASW 1987b:1).

For example, in the discussion of *respondeat superior* and problems related to staff supervision in chapter 5, I described a case involving a social worker who was a partner in a private practice and who was accused of improper supervision of an employee, a former nurse who was providing counseling services. Another aspect of that case involved allegations that a physician was signing insurance claim forms attesting to his involvement in the social worker's cases when in fact his involvement was minimal. The formal lawsuit included the following allegations, among others:

> Plaintiffs further show that [the private practice] submitted numerous charges to plaintiffs' insurer which were signed by Dr. A [identity deleted by author].
>
> Plaintiffs further show that said insurance claim forms suggest and imply that the therapy listed thereon was provided by Dr. A.
>
> Plaintiffs show that Dr. A provided no such services to plaintiff.

As the following excerpt shows, the plaintiff's attorney pursued this issue aggressively during the deposition conducted with the social worker-defendant:

Q: I'm rather confused by what I see here on the forms. These numbers here, is that a diagnostic code for the insurance company? Is that what you have to put down to get reimbursed by the insurance company?

A: Yes, that's what the number's for. That was Dr. A's diagnosis.

Q: Dr. A gave a diagnosis in this case?

A: Yes. He's my consulting psychiatrist, and he gives the diagnoses in the cases we discuss.

Q: So he's the one that came up with this diagnostic category? Dr. A's the one who said you should put this number down?

A: Sort of. We came up with the number during our discussion.

Q: Is it safe for me to assume that Dr. A examined the client?

A: No.

Q: No what? What do you mean?

A: I mean Dr. A never saw the client.

Q: Is that typical?

A: Typical of what?

Q: For Dr. A to sign the form without examining the client?

A: Are you asking whether he does this all the time?

Q: I'm asking whether he usually does this with your clients.

A: Yes, it's routine practice with us. As far as I know this is pretty common. Are we really that different?

Q: I'm just trying to figure out how you handled these procedures. You're saying that this is what usually happened?

A: That's right.

Q: So when Dr. A signed these forms he was saying, in effect, that in his professional judgment, based on his medical and psychiatric background, that this is the right diagnosis?

A: Yes.

Q: And was he saying that this person needed psychotherapy?

A: Yes.

Q: But how could he know this if he never met the client?

A: Well, Dr. A would often attend our agency staff meetings, so he would learn what was going on in different cases. He knew a lot about what was happening with clients.

Q: Do you see a problem here, with this arrangement?

A: What do you mean?

Q: I mean I'm puzzled about this arrangement where you had a psychiatrist signing a form about what a particular client needs, his or her psychiatric and therapy needs, but this psychiatrist never actually saw the client.

A: This is pretty common.

Q: That doesn't mean it's right or acceptable, does it?

A: No.

Allegations of improper billing also arose in *Suslovich v. New York Education Dept.* (1991). In this case a psychologist's license was suspended after the clinician submitted insurance reimbursement forms for ten client sessions, although the client attended only five ("Psychologist Did Not Maintain," 1992:6).

Another serious problem concerns social workers' designation of diagnostic codes on insurance or other third-party payer claim forms. Many third-party payers rely on the American Psychiatric Association's *Diagnostic and Statistical Manual* classifications. Most claim forms require the social worker to list one or more diagnostic codes to qualify for reimbursement. Some diagnostic classifications, however, are not reimbursable, and as a result some social workers use bogus—but reimbursable—diagnostic codes on claims forms.

The extent of this form of deception and fraud among social workers has been documented in an important study by Kirk and Kutchins (1988). These authors set out to investigate the extent of deliberate misdiagnosis by clinical social workers:

> Such acts are legal and ethical transgressions involving deceit, fraud, or abuse. Charges made for services not provided, money collected for services to fictitious patients, or patients encouraged to remain in treatment longer than necessary are examples of intentional inaccuracy. These activities are more likely to be reported by journalists than by the professionals who may abhor such practices but believe that they occur too rarely to be consequential. Very little has been written about these kinds of legal and ethical misdeeds in the mental health field. (p. 226)

Kirk and Kutchins surveyed a random sample including 10 percent of the individuals listed in the National Association of Social Workers' *Register of Clinical Social Workers*. At the time of their survey the *Register* included the names of more than eight thousand experienced clinical social workers. These practitioners held master's degrees, had at least two years of experience, and were members of the Academy of Certified Social Workers or were licensed by their respective states at an equivalent level. Respondents completed a lengthy questionnaire that focused on their attitudes and opinions about psychiatric diagnosis, actual diagnostic practices that they had observed in their professional work, the frequency of and reasons for their use of the *Diagnostic and Statistical Manual*, and their professional background. Open-ended comments were also invited.

The respondents were clearly familiar with the *Diagnostic and Statistical Manual*. One-fourth of the sample reported daily use of the *DSM*, and another quarter reported using the document at least once a week. Thirty percent of the sample reported using the *DSM* several times each month.

To explore the incidence of misdiagnosis Kirk and Kutchins presented the social workers with a list of various diagnostic practices. Respondents were then asked to indicate the extent to which they have observed these practices.

Respondents indicated that in many instances clinicians use a more serious diagnosis than is warranted by the client's clinical profile. About three-fifths of the sample (59 percent) reported that Axis I diagnoses (the major mental disorders) are reported to insurance companies, although they are not warranted clinically. Nearly three-fourths of the sample (72 percent) reported being aware of cases in which more-serious-than-warranted diagnoses were used to qualify for reimbursement. About one-fourth of the sample reported that this practice occurs frequently. Eighty-six percent of the social workers reported being aware of instances of listing diagnoses for individuals although the focus of treatment was on the family (again, many third-party payers do not reimburse for family treatment). More than 80 percent indicated that third-party payer requirements often influence diagnosis. Kirk and Kutchins (1988) finally conclude that "these data suggest that deliberate misdiagnosis occurs frequently in the mental health professions. If it is as widespread as these respondents suggest, it is puzzling that it has been almost unrecognized in the literature on diagnostic errors" (p. 231).

The temptation of course is to argue that deliberate overdiagnosis is done primarily to benefit clients. That is, clients may not receive needed services unless their social workers can qualify for reimbursement. Hence, deliberate overdiagnosis is a form of beneficent lying. As Kirk and Kutchins (1988) appropriately conclude, however, in many cases the social worker's self-interest may be a driving force:

> The manifest function of underdiagnosis is to protect clients; with overdiagnosis, the accurate diagnosis is replaced by a deliberately inaccurate one in order to deceive others. In particular, misdiagnosis is used so that the therapist's services will qualify for third-party reimbursement. Here the rationale is also nonclinical, but the argument that the therapist is acting only for the client's benefit is strained. The rationale that it is being done so that the client can obtain needed service is colored by the obvious self-interest of the therapist. Agencies, both public and private, also benefit when they obtain reimbursement as a result of such diagnostic practices. (p. 232)

Social workers who market or advertise their services also need to be particularly careful to avoid deception and fraud. Although most social workers provide fair and accurate descriptions of their services and expertise, some social workers who advertise intentionally or unintentionally misrepresent their programs, effectiveness, qualifications, or skills. Examples include advertising or other publicity material that essentially promises effective treatment, falsely portrays the social worker's training, credentials, or expertise (see *Corgan v. Muehling* 1991), or promises services the social worker does not intend to provide. The need for accurate representation, and to avoid deception and fraud, is highlighted in standard 9 of the NASW's *Standards for the Practice of Clinical Social Work* (1989:11):

> Standard 9. Clinical social workers shall represent themselves to the public with accuracy.
>
> *Interpretation*
> The public needs to know how to find help from qualified clinical social workers. Both agencies and independent private practitioners should ensure that their therapeutic services are made known to the public. In this regard, it is important that telephone listings be maintained in both the classified and alphabetical sections of the telephone directory, describing the clinical social work services available.
>
> Although advertising in various media was thought to be questionable professional practice in the past, recent judicial decisions, Federal Trade Commission rulings, as well as current professional practices have made such advertising acceptable. The advertisement must be factual and should avoid false promises of cures.
>
> The content of the advertisement should include the private practitioner's or agency's name and professional credentials and the address and telephone number or other contact information. It might also include the type of services provided (e.g., individual, family, or group therapy; alcoholism counseling; divorce mediation; and so forth) and the type of problems that are dealt with (e.g., marital distress, parent-child conflicts, eating disorders).

Allegations of fraud related to marketing arose in a case I discussed in chapter 3, *Gorman v. Lifespring, Inc.*. This case involved an attorney who sued an educational/psychological training program for injuries he claimed he sustained while participating in a five-day program consisting of lectures and participation in guided fantasies and experiential psychological exercises. In addition to his claim of intentional infliction of emotional distress his suit alleged that the program engaged in fraud through its representations of the nature of the program. The jury awarded the plaintiff $297,387 after finding the program liable for negligence and fraud ("Attorney Suffers Psychotic Breakdown," 1991:1).

Social workers must also avoid deception and fraud when applying for liability insurance, employment, a license, or some other form of certification. In *Gares v. New Mexico Bd. of Psychologist Examiners* (1990), for example, the state certification board revoked a practitioner's certificate because of fraud and deception in applying for certification, and the psychologist appealed the court order affirming revocation of his license by the state Board of Psychologist Examiners; his certification application had involved a statement indicating that he had not engaged "in any activities which misrepresented his professional qualifications, affiliation, or purposes or those of the institutions with which he was associated" ("Psychologist's License," 1991:6). The clinician had been sexually involved with three female clients during the course of treatment and had represented to the clients that such sex was a component of their therapy.

Falsification of records and official documents takes other forms as well. One involves staff members who falsify records to cover their tracks, so to speak. In these cases social workers typically alter or falsify records to create the impression that they provided services or supervision that never were actually provided or that they obtained informed consent when they had not done so. In some cases social workers falsify records to camouflage a genuine mistake. In other instances, however, no mistake was made. Rather, the social worker knowingly and intentionally failed to provide the service or supervision, for instance, and simply falsified or altered the record to cover up the negligence.

Several years ago I conducted in-depth training for a group of experienced social workers employed in a public child welfare agency. Most were involved in protective services, although some had responsibility for special-needs adoptions and juveniles who had been committed to the state training school. The training focused primarily on ethical and liability issues that arise in child welfare settings. During the discussion that

addressed deception and fraud in child welfare, one social worker, a supervisor, shared the following experience:

> I sure am glad you brought up this topic. I've been stewing about this
> for months and haven't really discussed it with anyone. I think I need
> to bring it up now. Perhaps my colleagues can help me figure out
> how to handle this problem I've had with one of my caseworkers.
>
> One of my caseworkers is supposed to spend most of his time con-
> ducting follow-up home visits to families whose children have been
> returned to them from temporary foster placement. The typical situ-
> ation involves a child who has been placed in foster care because of
> alleged or substantiated abuse or neglect. Often, of course, when alle-
> gations are unfounded or a family has participated in treatment and
> received various services, the child is returned.
>
> As a condition of the child's return home the family must agree to
> announced and unannounced visits from one of our caseworkers.
> During the child's return home a caseworker may visit as many as
> five times per week.
>
> One of my caseworkers was out of work because of a death in his
> family, and because we were short-staffed I took over his case load. I
> went to visit the Green family, which included a five-month-old girl
> and her mother. The infant had been returned to her mother from
> foster care about three months earlier. The child was placed initial-
> ly because of evidence of neglect (failure to thrive).
>
> I visited the family and had the impression that things were going
> reasonably well. During the visit I asked Ms. Green whether she was
> finding my caseworker's recent visits at all helpful. Ms. Green gave
> me a puzzled look and indicated that she hadn't seen the casework-
> er in about seven weeks. I tried to keep my composure and tried not
> to show my dismay.
>
> When I got back to my car I carefully reviewed the record and dis-
> covered that the caseworker had made entries indicating that he had
> been making regular home visits to the Green family during the
> recent seven-week period.
>
> When the caseworker returned to work, I confronted him with my
> discovery. He confessed that he had not in fact made the recent home
> visits, despite the entries in the record. With considerable trepida-
> tion he confessed that he had a serious alcohol problem and had not
> been functioning well at all.
>
> What do you folks think I should do?

One can only begin to imagine, of course, the liability risks involved here. If the child were neglected or abused during the period when the agency was supposed to have been making home visits, the agency quite likely would be vulnerable. The noncustodial father, for example, might sue the agency, alleging failure to supervise properly and to protect the child (see chapter 3). The casework supervisor might also have been vulnerable under the doctrine of respondeat superior.

Sometimes social workers may believe they are being pressured to alter records to protect their employing organization as well as themselves. Consider the following case involving a social worker who was employed at a public psychiatric hospital. According to the social worker, who sued the hospital for wrongful termination, the director of social work asked her and several members of the social work staff to amend records if necessary before a site visit from a national accreditation organization. According to the suit, the director of social work had sent a memo to staff members instructing each person to review a random sample of a *colleague's* case records to ensure that they included all appropriate information, such as assessment information, treatment plans, progress notes, and discharge plans. The suit alleged that the memo reiterated instructions given by the director at an earlier staff meeting. According to the plaintiff, the director of social work instructed each staff member to review the case records and to add any missing information, although the social worker would be reviewing a case for which she or he had not been responsible. The memo included the following text:

> As you know [the accreditation organization] will be here this Thur./Fri.—so we *must* be caught up and *on target* with our work.
>
> I will be reviewing *every* active chart in the hospital, paying particular attention to *MTP's* [master treatment plans] (being individualized) and *documentation of discharge planning notes.*
>
> Please re-check your charts and make any additions/deletions changes necessary. The purpose of this is *not* a witch hunt, but for us *all* to be *ready for the survey!*
>
> In addition, for QA [quality assurance], each of you will need to do *10* charts *before* Thur.
> [mentions a social worker's name]—any 10 from 4W
> [a second social worker's name]—any 10 from 2W

[a third social worker's name]—I will get with you—if you have
time—5 charts from 3W.

I will cover 3W and 5th floor. For this month's QA, do not just
note probs [problems], but where you can—*actually make the
changes on the chart.*

This does *not* mean changing dates, etc. It means if the MTP does
not have individualized strategies, then *add them.* If a signature is
needed on the plan, go get it!!

If there are no DC [discharge] planning notes, review the chart and
add a *final* soc-services DC note.

Any questions, see me. Realize that these are things we SHOULD
ALREADY HAVE BEEN DOING. Thank you.

Thus, the social worker-plaintiff claimed that the memo constituted a directive to the staff to alter records, if necessary, to
cover up any omissions. She said that the director did not instruct
the staff to indicate that the record had been amended and claimed
that he wanted staff to participate in his attempt to deceive the
accreditation team. Her view was that making entries in records
of cases on which they had not worked was unconscionable and
that this was what the director was asking staff to do.

The social worker-plaintiff claimed that she was forced to
resign her position because of her refusal to participate in the
director's plan. She alleged that she was given an ultimatum to
either quit her job or be fired. In the lawsuit she alleged that she
lost wages, her career was interrupted, and she experienced serious mental anguish as a result of the incident and her employment termination.

The director of social work defended his actions and the statements in his memo. The director claimed that aspects of the
social worker's job performance were unacceptable and that on
one occasion the worker had violated patients' privacy rights.
What follows is an excerpt from his deposition, conducted by the
social worker's attorney (I have excerpted a significant portion of
this deposition to illustrate the fine detail that is often examined
during the course of this aspect of legal proceedings, usually
called *pretrial discovery*):

Q: Can you tell me what happened that led to her [the plaintiff's]
termination then in September?

A: On September 20th we were having a group Social Service meeting. We had invited—there were two Social Work interns—I'm not sure if it was their first day, but possibly the first day they had ever seen or been in [the hospital]—and they were invited to also attend the meeting. And we had a survey approaching, I think with [the accreditation organization], I'm not sure if it was—yeah, it was [the accreditation organization].

Q: That's the national psychiatric hospital group you referred to at the beginning?

A: You know what that is.

Q: Okay.

A: And in that meeting, what I—I told each of the employees to make —part of QA—back to QA—is an ongoing, where you check your active charts to make sure that treatment plans accurately reflect the services that are being provided. So, I encouraged all of the Social Workers to continue to do that.

Q: So, in other words, keep your charts up to snuff?

A: Well, what that would mean would be: if a patient was receiving medication. And where you see that would be in the Process Notes and the Progress Notes. If a nurse administered the meds it's documented. If a patient gets activities therapy, it's documented. If nursing encourages and gets a patient's feelings, she'll document it. And if the Master Treatment Plan is not documented those procedures and services that are being performed [sic], then we have an inaccurate record.

Q: And that was the Social Worker's responsibility?

A: Correct.

Q: To make sure that the Master Treatment Plan reflected what was actually happening?

A: Correct.

Q: Okay.

A: I instructed them on their active charts to make sure and do that. And I also told each of them to pull ten charts of discharged patients and to review the Progress Notes and compare it to the treatment plan to see if there were any procedures that had been done which were not documented on the treatment plan, which would be an inaccurate chart. And if

they were documented, the Progress Notes, to add those procedures on to the treatment plan, to document what was actually being done.

Q: Was this like the usual treatment, a QA, if they didn't do their
own or did they do other people's?

A: This was like when they were doing other people's; ten random charts.

Q: So, this was on patients they did never seen [sic]?

A: Correct.

Q: Now, was usual procedure on QA [sic]?

A: I would usually get feedback from QA on exactly those same
issues routinely, and they would routinely do that on the
active charts.

Q: So, they would routinely do it on the active charts which are
their own, or other people's?

A: Their own.

Q: Okay. And this was different in that these were not their own?

A: They would routinely give feedback on those exact issues
whether it was an active record or closed charts which were
not their own.

Q: But in this case, they're going to this medical records you've
described, picking out random charts, and they are to see
whether the Progress Notes and treatment notes matched,
and if they don't, they're to add them—

A: Not if they match.

Q: Not if they match?

A: See, if there is—to see if there's documentation of services or
procedures received in the Progress Notes that that is also
documented on the Master Treatment Plan.

Q: Okay. But these were patients who had closed charts?

A: Correct. Actually, it wasn't a closed chart, really, until they
did that, because it was inaccurate record.

Q: But, routinely, it was the job of the Social Worker who worked
with that patient to do this, not people who had never seen
them?

A: Routinely, on the active charts the Social Workers would do
that and they would routinely give me feedback on those
same issues on closed charts.

Q: Had you ever asked your Social Workers to go in and add notes after the chart—the patient had left the hospital, on closed charts before?

A: No, I had never asked them to—if there was a documented procedure in the Progress Notes and it had not been on the treatment plan, I had never asked them to make sure that it was on the treatment plan.

Q: Why was it, at this time, on the 20th of September, any different than what had been done in the past? Why did you ask them to do this?

A: I probably should have done that all along. Because what was leaving was—they would give me the feedback—I was leaving inaccurate records. I was leaving a treatment plan which didn't accurately reflect what actually happened to the patients. So in retrospect, I probably should have had them do it all of the time.

Q: Go back in and fix up closed charts?

A: No, go back in and make sure the treatment plan reflects accurately the procedures that are actually performed as documented in the Progress Notes.

Q: On open charts?

A: No, on closed charts.

Q: Okay. So, your view is you should have been doctoring closed charts all of the time?

A: No, no, that's not what I said. My view is, if a closed chart—in the Progress Notes, the patient receives antidepressant medication every day and if the Master Treatment Plan, which is supposed to be a summary of all of the services that are being provided, and the patient's responses to it, doesn't document that they are receiving antidepressant medication, it's an inaccurate chart.

Q: Right. But these are supposed to be contemporaneously records [sic], correct?

A: I'm not sure what you mean.

Q: These things are supposed to be documented at the time the patient's in the hospital, not after the chart's gone to the record room?

A: The chart—it's preferable if as—it is preferable if the chart, on an ongoing basis, accurately reflects what is being performed. That is preferable, if the plan reflects that.

Q: Had you ever worked in a facility that had this procedure or after a chart had gone back to the record room as a closed chart, that people went in and made the treatment plan accurately reflecting what had happened from the Progress Notes?

A: I'm not sure. I would have to think about that.

Q: Was this your idea or did someone suggest you do this?

A: This was my idea.

Q: No one suggested it to you?

A: Initially, it was my idea.

Q: And who did you discuss it with?

A: Well, it's after [the plaintiff] said in the group, "I won't falsify records." And after I tried to discuss it with her several times, I went back and checked with [the program director and the director of medical records], to see if I had accurately expressed to [the plaintiff] what I wanted her to do. . . .

Q: And how would they know if you had accurately expressed it to [the plaintiff]?

A: I told them how I—the words I recall that I said to [the plaintiff], and said, "How do you understand that?" They said, "To make sure that the record is accurate." And I said, "Good, that's how I intended it to be understood."

Q: And did they have any problems with Social Workers going in and doing this on closed charts?

A: They didn't mention any conflict with that procedure. They felt an accurate chart was very important.

Q: You said this was in response to [the accreditation organization's] group survey?

A: That's correct.

Q: Is this one of the things they would have been looking for?

A: Whether the chart—whether the treatment plan accurately reflected—

Q: Yes.

A: Yes.

Q: So, in a funny way, this was also a part of your evaluation that you were making sure this was done?

A: It helped bring to the front an issue that I probably should have realized before.

Q: Is that a yes or a no?

A: I'm not sure of the question.

Q: The question was: then was having these charts accurate part of your evaluation as the head of this department?

A: It was never specifically said to me, [his name] had better have accurate charts. I figured—I presumed that it was a reasonable expectation that the Social Service input on the charts was accurate.

Q: And you actually put this in a memo, didn't you, to your Social Workers?

A: I put a memo out and discussed it in that meeting.

Q: Do we have a copy of that? . . . Okay. Let me mark this as Plaintiff's Exhibit 1. . . . Okay. Let me let you look at this and see if this is an outpatient's—is this your handwriting?

A: That's correct: terrible.

Q: And this is your memo, right?

A: Correct.

Q: And you state that the reason for this is because the [accreditation organization]—. . . .

A: Correct.

Q: Okay. And you said that, "You will be reviewing every active chart," and then you identified what—MTPs are Master Treatment Plans?

A: Yes.

Q: Then you say, "Please re-check your charts and make any additions or deletions." In this, you meant the active charts?

A: Correct.

Q: In addition, you said, "For QA, each of you willing [sic] to do ten charts before Thursday . . ." Now, these are the ones in the medical records?

A: Correct.

Q: And you listed who was supposed to do what. Now, at this point, was [another social worker] working for you? Is that why her name is there?

A: That's correct.

Q: She has moved over from this funny [part-time] status to go to a full-time program—

A: Correct, full-time duty.

Q: And down at the bottom, you say. "For this month's underlying QA, we will not just note problems, but where you can underline [sic], actually make the changes on the charts"; is that correct?

A: Yes.

Q: Now these are closed charts?

A: Correct.

Q: And you then have said what you have told me, that it does not mean changing dates and so forth, but if the MTP, Master Treatment Plan, does not have individualized strategies then, quote, "underline, add them. If a signature is needed on the plan, go get it." So, this was after they were closed, you wanted them to make them indicate—

A: If there was documentation in the Progress Notes that individual strategies were being used that were not documented on the chart, to make sure that was documented on the chart.

Q: And if there are no discharge planning notes, then the chart must add a final Social Services discharge note, which you explained to me was supposed to be there already?

A: That is correct. So with the disposition, to put a final note, the patient returned to New York or wherever they went.

Q: Okay. Then you say, "We're supposed to have already done this." But my concern is this paragraph that says it doesn't— again, this doesn't mean to add a final Social Service discharge note. Now, these were by your own orders, not charts that the Social Workers had ever seen the patient from [sic]?

A: That's correct.

Q: And you wanted them to go through the record and add summaries or individual strategies—which you've described as if they were receiving medication or activity—and they were to add them?

A: If there was documentation that were receiving them [sic].

Q: Okay. How, physically, were they supposed to do that in the record? This is all handwritten?

A: Correct.

Q: And they were just to stick it in where it belonged?

A: To put in under—if it was a medical intervention that was being done and it was documented in the Progress Notes, to add it in the appropriate place on the Master Treatment Plan.

Q: Would anyone looking at this have known that it was added later?

A: I'm not sure.

Q: So, it's possible that there was nothing to say it was or wasn't added later where it was done?

A: I am not sure.

Q: You did some of them didn't you?

A: Yes.

Q: Was there any way, on the ones you did, to tell—for anyone to tell that they were added at a later time then [sic] when the chart was closed?

A: Probably not.

Q: And you said that [the plaintiff] objected to this?

A: She—the minute I described it in the meeting, she said, "I will not falsify records."

Q: What happened then, what did you do?

A: Well, first I was upset because she had misunderstood —I wasn't asking her to falsify records. So, I wanted to definitely make that clear to her.

And, second, I was again upset with the way she was handling this, in that we had two new interns in there and that if she had—saying it was an issue of falsifying records, that if she thought that was what I was asking her to do, it would have been much more appropriate, as a professional to, at the end of the meeting when they had left, to say, "[the director's name], I don't understand. I think you're asking me to falsify records."

Q: How did you handle this in the meeting?

A: What I told her was—I reiterated what I expected. I told her, "I'm not asking you to falsify records. And we can talk about this further, one-to-one, after this meeting."

Q: And did you, in fact, do so?

A: That is correct.

The social worker who filed suit in this case was not successful. The case was dismissed by the lower court, and the social worker lost her subsequent appeal to the state's supreme court, which ruled that the social work director's instructions to his staff were not inappropriate.

In general, if a practitioner finds that accurate details were inadvertently omitted, a possibility in every social worker's professional life, the information can be added, but the record should clearly indicate that the entry was made subsequently. The social worker should sign and date the change to indicate that it is an amendment. It is hard to imagine any circumstance in which it would be appropriate for social workers to fill in gaps or make other entries in records for cases on which they did not work.

A troubling form of deceit and fraud I have encountered concerns social work administrators who produce false accounts of expenditures and other allocations of agency resources. Social work administrators often need to juggle budget categories in order to enhance productivity, access to services, and effectiveness. It is one of the enduring challenges of administrative positions.

Unfortunately, social work administrators occasionally have been too creative with their budgets, sometimes for self-serving reasons, and end up being deceitful or fraudulent to cover their tracks. The following anecdote describes a set of circumstances I encountered in a community action program:

> Joanne M., M.S.W., was the executive director of a community action program that served a county of 120,000. The agency's services included a meal site for the elderly, heating and fuel assistance, emergency housing assistance, a variety of concrete services for low-income women and their children, and a teen parenting program.
>
> Joanne M. had been director of the program for six years. She was well regarded in the community and by her board of directors. Several staff members, however, were critical of Joanne M.'s administrative style and leadership qualities.
>
> The community agency program depended on an annual grant from the state public welfare department to provide casework services to women with young children who were clients of the program of Aid to Families with Dependent Children (AFDC). The funds were used to pay the salaries of three caseworkers and overhead involved in the delivery of services.
>
> During a recent four-month period the program operated with only two caseworkers. One caseworker had been on unpaid leave to take care of an ailing relative. As a result the agency saved about $4,000 in staff salaries.

Joanne M. decided to use the savings to purchase computer equipment that she could use in her own home. The funding guidelines, however, prohibited use of the funds for capital expenditures. In her annual accounting and report to the state public welfare department, Joanne M. did not report the one caseworker's four-month leave of absence. She also did not report that the state's funds were used to purchase computer equipment. The unauthorized appropriation of funds was uncovered in a random audit conducted by the auditor general's office. The deputy auditor general then informed Joanne M. that the auditor general was considering taking both civil and criminal action against her.

Although administrators can often justify reallocation of funds to meet agency needs, they must abide by funders' guidelines concerning changes made after the initial allocation. Some funders provide administrators with a margin of flexibility, for example, a 5 percent shift of funds among specified categories, such as personnel or equipment lines. Some funders, however, prohibit any allocation changes without formal authorization. Of course, no funders would permit administrators to siphon funds for their personal use. Any departure from established funding guidelines and administrative practices may expose a social work administrator to civil suits and/or criminal charges.

"Altruistic" Deception and Fraud

In some instances social workers engage in deceit and fraud primarily to help clients. For example, they may eschew damaging diagnostic labels on insurance claim forms to avoid stigmatizing clients. In addition to documenting the extent of *over*diagnosis, as described earlier, Kirk and Kutchins (1988) gathered evidence that social workers sometimes *under*diagnose, presumably to benefit clients. Some of the practices observed and reported by Kirk and Kutchins's sample suggest that professionals often misdiagnose in order to help clients, that is, to avoid labeling them. For example, most respondents (87 percent) indicated that a less serious diagnosis than clinically indicated was used frequently or occasionally to avoid labeling clients. Seventy-eight percent reported that frequently or occasionally only the least serious of several appropriate diagnoses were used on official records. Most (82 percent) admitted that frequently or occasionally the diagnosis of *adjustment disorder* is used when a more serious diagnosis might be more accurate.

Social workers might intentionally deceive to benefit clients in other ways as well. Imagine, for example, a social worker who has been providing counseling services to a client, a forty-one-year-old woman, who had been manifesting relatively modest anxiety symptoms. On occasion the client experienced panic attacks, although when the attacks occurred they tended to be rather mild. The client originally sought counseling from the social worker to help her cope with a conflict-ridden divorce.

After being in counseling with the social worker for about four months, the client one day asked the social worker to write a letter in support of her application for disability benefits. The client said that she was "sick and tired" of her job as a store manager and was finding it difficult to work during the divorce proceedings. The client told the social worker that she—the social worker—would probably need to embellish her letter in order to make a convincing case for disability. The client conceded that a candid report from the social worker would not be very helpful, in light of the client's rather mild anxiety symptoms.

The social worker wanted to be supportive of her client and decided to write a convincing, albeit largely disingenuous, letter to the client's disability insurer. Shortly thereafter the social worker was contacted by an insurance company representative who at first politely challenged the social worker's assessment of her client's disability. Toward the end of the conversation the insurance company representative told the social worker that she had substantial evidence that the client was not in fact disabled and that the insurance company was concerned that the social worker was helping the client perpetrate a fraud. The insurance company representative ended the conversation by saying that according to company policy she was obligated to refer the case to the local insurance fraud investigation unit.

Although the social worker was merely trying to be helpful, the embellished letter exposed her to considerable risk. Social workers must be careful to include in letters written on clients'

behalf only those details that they can document and substantiate. To do otherwise, even for altruistic reasons, is quite risky.

Social workers should exercise similar caution and reserve
when writing reference letters on behalf of agency staff members
who may be pursuing positions elsewhere. On occasion social
workers will inflate their evaluations of a colleague in the agency
to help that individual secure employment. Here too social
workers incur considerable risk if they knowingly attest to skills
and qualifications that the subject of the letter does not have.
The other agency could hire this individual in part because of the
social worker's recommendation. If that individual ends up
engaging in some negligent action that might have been avoided
if the individual had actually had the skills endorsed in the social
worker's recommendation letter, the author of the letter could
be at risk. While it may seem unlikely that the social worker
who wrote the reference letter would be named as a defendant in
a lawsuit, this is not a risk worth taking. To be on the safe side
social workers should include in recommendation or reference
letters only those details they know to be true or have good reason to believe are true.

One final form of deception and fraud concerns social work
administrators who fabricate research or program evaluation
results to enhance the likelihood of obtaining or retaining funding from some outside source. Social work administrators whose
agencies depend on outside funding are under substantial pressure. They have a considerable incentive to present as positive a
picture as possible about the agency's efficiency and effectiveness. Unfortunately, as the following anecdote suggests, such
pressure can prove the downfall of an otherwise competent
social work administrator:

> Roland M., M.S.W., was the executive director of the Strath-
> more Substance Abuse Treatment Center. Strathmore was a
> private nonprofit agency that was about to begin its seven-
> teenth year of service.
>
> The agency received about 60 percent of its revenue from
> the local Community Fund. The remaining funds were
> obtained from the state mental health agency's substance
> abuse division (25 percent) and client fees (15 percent).

One year earlier the Community Fund implemented new guidelines for member agencies. For the first time in its history the Community Fund was insisting on program evaluation data to demonstrate the effectiveness of services provided with its funds. Member agencies were to collaborate with Community Fund staff to determine an acceptable program-evaluation strategy. Most consisted of relatively simple outcome measures using primary and secondary data. In Strathmore's case the Community Fund wanted program staff members to collect data on lengths of stays in the residential component of the program, relapse rates, and costs per unit of service.

Roland M. was nervous about the program evaluation. Given that he depended on the Community Fund for such a large portion of his budget, he felt he could not afford unfavorable results.

At the suggestion of the Community Fund's staff, Roland M. and his board of directors retained an outside evaluator, a consultant from the local school of social work. The consultant conducted the study over a nine-month period. Some of the most significant results were disappointing and unflattering. Roland M. was especially concerned about the discouraging data on relapse rates and program drop-outs.

Unbeknown to the consultant, Roland M. modified several facts and figures appearing in the consultant's final report in order to shed a more favorable light on the agency. However, an astute Community Fund staff member noticed a couple of inconsistencies in the report and telephoned the consultant for an explanation. The consultant and the Community Fund staff shortly found that Roland M. had altered some results. As a consequence Strathmore lost its Community Fund subsidy and was threatened by the Community Fund with a lawsuit in an effort to recover a portion of the current year's allocation that was based in part on the report's results.

Relatively few social workers actively engage in deceit and fraud. Among those who do, some are motivated primarily by self-interest and greed. Their sleight of hand is designed to exploit others in order to line their own pockets or advance their own careers.

Others, however, have more altruistic intentions. These social workers may be moved by clients' plights or genuine concern about the financial stability and future of agencies they administer. Their more noble motives do not excuse whatever deceit and fraud they engage in, of course. Nonetheless, these social workers' actions contrast markedly with those of their self-centered colleagues whose deceit and fraud are driven essentially by self-interest.

And, human nature being what it is, in many instances social workers' deceitful and fraudulent activities depend on mixed motives. That is, social workers are inspired by simultaneous concern about themselves and others. This phenomenon is illustrated by social workers who submit fraudulent diagnoses to insurance companies to help clients obtain needed services *and* to enhance their own income.

Whatever the motives—whether singularly self-interested or altruistic, or mixed—social workers need to be cognizant of deceit and fraud among the ranks. They must avoid whatever temptation exists in their own work to deceive and defraud—if for no other reason than to avoid the accompanying liability risks—and they must engage in preventive efforts to discourage deception and fraud elsewhere in the profession.

8 | Termination of Service

Many malpractice and liability risks in social work pertain to the initiation and provision of services. As discussed in earlier chapters, improper assessment, intervention, supervision, consultation, and referral can result in claims filed against social workers.

Similar problems can also arise in relation to the termination of services. In my experience the most prevalent problems concern allegations that professionals failed to terminate services properly, failed to continue needed services, or were unavailable to clients who were in need of care. Improper termination of service might occur, for instance, when a social worker transfers to a new position or moves out of town without adequately preparing a client for the termination or without referring a client to a new service provider. Or, a social worker might terminate services abruptly to a client in dire need of assistance because the client is unable to pay for the care. Social workers also risk liability when they are unavailable and fail to properly instruct clients about how to handle emergencies that may arise.

The Concept of Abandonment

A substantial portion of malpractice and liability claims regarding termination of services involves allegations of abandonment. *Abandonment* is a legal concept that refers to instances when a professional is not available to a client when needed. Once a social worker begins to provide service to a client, she or he incurs a legal responsibility to sustain that service or to properly refer a client to an alternative service provider. Social workers are not of course obligated to serve every individual who requests assistance. The social worker might not have room for a new client or lacks the specialized expertise a particular client may need.

However, once a social worker begins service, it cannot be terminated abruptly. Rather, social workers are obligated to conform to the profession's standard of care regarding termination of service and referral to other providers in the event the client is still in need. As Schutz (1982) suggests with respect to termination of psychotherapy services, "Once a patient makes a contact with a therapist and the therapist agrees to see him, he is that therapist's patient. The therapist then assumes the fiduciary duty not to abandon the patient. At the very least, therefore, he must refer the patient to another therapist if he elects to terminate the relationship" (p. 50).

The NASW *Code of Ethics* (1990) contains several principles concerning proper termination of services:

Principle II.F.9. The social worker should terminate service to clients, and professional relationships with them, when such service and relationships are no longer required or no longer serve the clients' needs or interests.

Principle II.F.10. The social worker should withdraw services precipitously only under unusual circumstances, giving careful consideration to all factors in the situation and taking care to minimize possible adverse effects.

Principle II.F.11. The social worker who anticipates the termination or interruption of service to clients should notify clients promptly and seek the transfer, referral, or continuation of service in relation to the clients' needs and preferences.

As Principle II.F.9. suggests, social workers have to be careful not to extend services to clients beyond the point where they are clinically or otherwise warranted. Unfortunately, as the following case illustrates, social workers sometimes fail to terminate services when termination is in the client's best interest:

> Scott N., M.S.W., was in solo private practice. He had begun his private practice approximately six months earlier after working for seven years at a local community mental health center. Scott N. decided to begin his private practice to enhance his autonomy and to get away from what was beginning to feel like onerous bureaucracy at the community mental health center.
>
> Scott N. knew building up his client base would take a number of months and that his income would be modest during this period. He was concerned, however, about the relatively small number of referrals and inquiries he had been receiving. The stagnant local economy exacerbated the problem because fewer people could afford private social work services, and the relatively high unemployment rate in the community meant that fewer people had third-party coverage for mental health services.
>
> With two children in college Scott N. was getting more and more nervous about being able to pay his bills. One consequence was that he avoided terminating three clients who clinically were ready for termination. Scott N. intentionally prolonged their treatment in order to sustain the revenue these clients generated.
>
> These clients' services were covered by two different insurance companies, both of which had contracts with managed care firms. At specified junctures in the treatment process Scott N. had to telephone the managed care companies to seek approval for additional sessions with these clients. In his conversations with the managed care representatives Scott N. had to exaggerate their symptoms to make the case for such approval.

A social worker who fails to terminate properly and in the process attempts to deceive an insurance company obviously incurs some liability risk. Clients may be upset about the prolonged treatment, and third-party payers may sue to recover fees they paid the practitioner. Thus, social workers must be particularly careful to avoid extending services beyond what is clinically or otherwise warranted.

Premature Termination

More common, however, are instances in which clients' services are terminated prematurely. Premature termination can occur for several different reasons. First, clients may initiate the termination of services, perhaps against the advice of social workers and other professionals involved in their care. Second, services might be terminated prematurely as a result of social workers' or other professionals' initiative, as when practitioners find that a particular client is not making adequate progress or is unable to pay for services. In addition, services might be terminated inappropriately when social workers find a particular client too difficult to handle.

Client-Initiated Termination

Clients in residential and nonresidential programs sometimes decide unilaterally that they do not want to continue receiving services. Clients may leave residential programs against professional advice or may decide not to return for outpatient services.

In *Charboneau et al. v. State of South Dakota*, for example, a psychiatric patient who had a history of violence was taken on an outing and escaped, thereby terminating service. Law enforcement officials were not notified of the man's dangerousness for about twelve hours after the escape. The patient broke into a home and killed a woman and her daughter. The plaintiff alleged that allowing the patient to go on the outing and not notifying law enforcement officials that the man was dangerous constituted negligence on the part of the psychiatrists in charge of the patient. The case was settled for $950,000 ("Patient Escapes," 1990:6).

In *Boles v. Milwaukee County* (1989) a woman with a history of mental illness was brought to a hospital emergency room after her sister observed her striking herself repeatedly. Because of her self-destructive behavior the woman was placed in restraints by emergency room personnel. Within less than thirty minutes the patient told a nurse that she felt better and wanted to return home. Before a psychiatrist arrived for a consultation, the woman left the hospital, shouted at cars, struck them with her hands, and was struck and killed by a car when she ran into the street.

The woman's children sued the hospital, claiming that staff failed to properly detain her in order to make an appropriate assessment. The appellate court affirmed the lower court's verdict for the plaintiffs, concluding that the hospital's failure to detain the patient until completion of the psychiatric examination was "palpably negligent" (cited in "Hospital Liable for Failing to Detain," 1990:4).

In *Smith v. Timberlawn Psychiatric Hospital, Inc.*, however, a Texas jury did not hold a hospital liable in connection with injuries sustained by a patient who essentially terminated his own services by fleeing from the hospital. The plaintiff, a voluntary psychiatric patient at the hospital, and two other patients fled the building and were pursued by hospital employees. The plaintiff climbed a fence and ran along the shoulder of a highway, attempted to cross the lanes, tripped, and was hit by a truck. The plaintiff's leg was shattered and required extensive and repeated surgery. He argued that the hospital staff breached the standard of care in pursuing a voluntary patient and attempting to restrain him against his will ("Psychiatric Patient Injured," 1990:5).

Social Worker-Initiated Termination

In contrast, clients might be terminated from care or services prematurely as a result of social workers' initiative. In residential programs, for example, clients may be terminated prematurely because staff members find that a particular client is not making adequate progress, they want to open up a bed for a client who will generate a higher reimbursement rate because of insurance coverage, or the client's insurance benefits have been exhausted. Of course, some clients are terminated prematurely because of poor clinical judgment about their readiness for community-based living.

In *Durflinger v. Artiles* (1981) Irvin Durflinger sued a hospital and its doctors, claiming his son Bradley was discharged prematurely. Bradley had been involuntarily admitted to a state hospital in Kansas in connection with an assault on his grandparents. During his stay at the state hospital, staff members decided that Bradley should be transferred to a hospital in Salem, Oregon. However, the Kansas hospital's clinical director, who had never had contact with Bradley, sent a note to the leader of the treatment team at his hospital stating that Bradley is "physically healthy and suffers from a character disorder and who furthermore is not motivated for treatment. It rather looks to me that we should discharge this patient." Bradley was discharged and killed his mother and brother.

The defendants in the suit disagreed about the reason for the discharge. The clinical director testified that Bradley was discharged because he demonstrated no motivation for treatment; the treatment team, however, stated that Bradley was discharged because he was "doing so well."

The federal district court in Kansas held that the hospital and doctors were negligent in discharging Bradley prematurely and in not conducting an adequate assessment to determine his readiness for discharge. The plaintiffs were awarded $67,300 (Austin, Moline, and Williams 1990:215–17).

Similar issues were raised in *Costello-Hicks v. New York City Health & Hospitals Corp.* (1991). The plaintiff, a young woman, sued the city agency, alleging that a county hospital prematurely released and terminated services to a seriously disturbed woman who subsequently injured the plaintiff. The plaintiff had been waiting on a subway platform in New York City. A woman who had been released from a county hospital the previous month pushed the plaintiff in front of an oncoming train. The plaintiff sustained serious injuries, including blindness in one eye and various other head injuries; she experienced memory loss and permanent injury to her head, face, arms, legs, a hip, and abdomen.

In her lawsuit the plaintiff claimed that the county hospital had discharged her attacker prematurely. The week before her release the disturbed woman had been restrained in a straitjacket after various acts of violence against herself and others. Just before her release the woman was kept in the highest form of security, and her treating physician noted her lack of understanding and concern about her treatment program upon release. The physician stated that he doubted the woman could succeed in her treatment program. A jury awarded the plaintiff $1.5 million ("Government Liable," 1992:4).

A jury also entered a judgment against a hospital in the Texas case of a son who killed his father (*Gary Scott Jensen, et al. v. Tarrant County Hospital District d/b/a John Peter Smith Hospital*). The father had sought emergency psychiatric care and detention for his son. The son had been hospitalized four previous times and had been diagnosed with chronic schizophrenia. The son was prescribed neuroleptic medication but was released without having been administered the medication or monitored for its effectiveness. The next morning the son killed his father. The plaintiffs claimed that the hospital was negligent because it failed to detain the son and follow through with proper treatment ("Man Murdered," 1992:6).

Suit can also be brought against an agency when a discharged client subsequently injures himself. In *Campbell v. Dr. Price and Oaklawn Psychiatric Center, Inc.*, the young man who filed the suit had been admitted to an Indiana state hospital after a suicide attempt and was discharged the following day. Later the same day the plaintiff attempted suicide again by pouring flammable substances over his body and igniting the substances. He suffered extensive burns. The case was settled, with the state of Indiana's Patient Compensation Fund paying the plaintiff $300,000 and the defendant's insurance company paying $100,000 ("Man Claims Improper Discharge," 1990:6; also see *Goryeb v. Pennsylvania Dept. of Public Welfare* 1990).

Allegations of premature discharge were also made in *Robinson v. Lankenau Hospital et al.*; the plaintiff was a former patient. The woman, who had a history of self-destructive behavior, had been hospitalized for treatment of severe mental illness. She was then released to another individual's custody. The plaintiff locked her custodian out of her own house and then drank or ingested lye. In her lawsuit the plaintiff alleged that she had been released inappropriately, particularly given that the defendants had knowledge of her history of mental illness, destructive behavior, and suicidal tendencies. A Pennsylvania jury entered a $140,000 verdict against the hospital ("Patient Released," 1989:3).

Courts do not always find social service staff and agencies liable when discharged clients subsequently harm another individual or themselves. For example, the court found a hospital was not liable in *Wofford v. Eastern State Hospital* (1990). A patient's mother sued a psychiatric hospital and its doctors, alleging that the release of her son two years earlier constituted negligence. After being treated for schizophrenia, the patient was discharged. More than two years later he shot and killed his stepfather. A trial court ruled that the death was too remote and unforeseeable to find the defendants liable. After a court of appeals reversed the decision, the Oklahoma state Supreme Court upheld the trial court's finding, that the hospital was not liable. Moreover, there was no evidence that the hospital knew the patient's release posed a risk of harm to the stepfather ("Hospital Not Liable," 1991:3).

In *Beck v. Forsyth-Stokes Area Mental Health, Mental Retardation and Substance Abuse Authority* (1989), a mental health center and one of its psychiatrists were sued after a recently discharged client killed a fifty-eight-year-old man in a knife fight. The man, who had been admitted to the center in an intoxicated state, had been discharged after being examined by a staff psychiatrist. The plaintiffs alleged that releasing the client and terminating services to him constituted negligence. The defendants argued that they had no legal justification to continue involuntary commitment of the client. The North Carolina jury found in the defendants' favor. ("Mental Health Facility," 1990:2).

A California court also found a hospital and its staff were not liable in *Escobar v. Dr. Braun and General Health Services, Inc., d/b/a Brotman Medical Center;* in this case the plaintiff had injured herself. The plaintiff, a nineteen-year-old survivor of incest who had a history of suicide attempts and severe depression, was admitted voluntarily to the psychiatric unit of a local medical center. Shortly after admission, however, staff learned that the woman's insurance coverage would not cover the admission. The woman was discharged despite her adamant request to remain; she had promised to borrow the money to enable her to stay hospitalized.

Several hours after discharge the woman attempted suicide by driving her automobile off a cliff. She suffered severe injuries that required hospitalization for three and one-half months. The woman claimed that her treatment was inadequate and was inappropriately terminated in light of her suicidal symptoms. Hospital staff, however, argued that the woman's financial status was unrelated to reasons for discharge and that termination of service was consistent with the standard of care ("Woman Claims She Was Improperly Discharged," 1989:2).

Insurance coverage was also an issue in *Wilson v. Blue Cross of Southern California* (1990). The patient had been hospitalized for treatment of depression, substance abuse, and an eating disorder (anorexia). His physician recommended three to four weeks of inpatient treatment, but the patient's insurance company declined to pay for more than ten days. The hospital then discharged the man because he could not afford more inpatient care. He committed suicide three weeks later.

The patient's parents sued the insurance company, arguing that its refusal to authorize additional days of inpatient care "was a substantial factor in the patient's suicide." A trial court found in favor of the insurance company, but the appeals court remanded the case because a triable issue existed as to the company's interpretation of the insurance contract's provisions. The appeals court remanded the case to the trial court ("Insurance Company," 1991:4).

The liability risks associated with premature discharge when a patient's insurance benefits have been exhausted are clearer in *Jane and Delbert Muse, Jr. v. Charter Hospital and Charter Medical Corp.* Parents of a sixteen-year-old boy sued the hospital, claiming that their son's suicide was the result of premature discharge when the insurance coverage ran out. The boy had been admitted to the psychiatric hospital and remained there until two days after his insurance coverage was exhausted. Two weeks after discharge the boy committed suicide by taking a drug overdose.

The parents argued that they received no warning that their son was suicidal, that family therapy was not provided, and the agency to which the hospital had referred the boy for follow-up care did not receive adequate information about his condition.

The psychiatrist involved in the case settled out of court for $90,000. A North Carolina jury awarded the plaintiffs $7.09 million in the case against the hospital ($1.09 million in compensatory damages and $6 million in punitive damages), although the trial judge reduced the compensatory damage award slightly (to $1.03 million) because of lack of evidence for certain amounts ("Teenager Commits Suicide," 1992:1).

Social workers in private agency-based practice and other outpatient settings have been known to terminate clients prematurely when they find them resistant, hostile, uncooperative, or otherwise difficult to handle. In one recent case a social worker was sued by a former client who claimed that the social worker terminated her relationship with the client abruptly and precipitously. The severely disabled woman had sought counseling from a social worker who specialized in treatment of people with physical disabilities. After several months of intervention the social worker found it extremely difficult to relate to the client. She claimed that the client was excessively demanding and hostile and was consuming inordinate amounts of her professional time. The social worker said that the client telephoned her frequently and left angry messages when the social worker did not return the call promptly.

The social worker became more and more resentful of the client and during one particularly heated conversation told the client that she would no longer be able to serve her. The client mailed the social worker a certified letter asking for an explanation, but the social worker refused to accept the letter. In addition, the social worker made no attempt to provide the client with names of other practitioners whom she could contact for assistance.

Although the social worker's frustration in this case may be understandable, her virtual abandonment of her client, including her refusal to accept the client's letter, is not. As Cohen (1979) states,

> No doctor in private practice is legally compelled to accept any patient for treatment. The mental health professional may feel that

he does not have the expertise to deal with a particular problem; he may not have the number of hours needed to provide adequate services; he may not see himself as able to establish a good enough rapport with the patient; the patient may not be able to pay the doctor's fee, etc. But while there are any number of perfectly acceptable reasons for refusing to treat a patient, there is *no* reason to justify abandonment of a patient once treatment begins. Before accepting a new patient, the mental health professional would be wise to schedule an initial consultation for the purpose of a mutual evaluation of suitability. If a doctor accepts a patient but some time later believes he can no longer be of value (because, for example, he has discovered factors operating that are beyond his competence to deal with), "following through" would mean advising this patient of the state of affairs and referring him to an appropriate mental health professional. (p. 273)

The reasons for termination of care were the central issue in *Tompkins v. Dr. Kusama*. A thirteen-year-old boy was being seen as an outpatient at a state hospital. According to the plaintiffs—the boy's parents—two and one-half weeks before their son committed suicide they met with the treating physician and informed him of their son's suicide threats. The parents had been referred to the physician by a psychiatric resident who had seen the boy. The physician diagnosed the boy's condition as panic anxiety accompanied by a preoccupation with death. He saw the boy during the next two days, prescribed medication, and removed himself from the case five days after his consultation with the boy's parents.

The resident's notes, however, did not indicate that the other physician had removed himself from the case or that he had transferred the boy back to the boy's original treatment team at the state hospital. Two of the original team members were no longer available (one had left the job and another was on vacation). Further, there was some question as to whether the social worker and psychiatric resident on the treatment team had seen the boy.

After discharge the boy committed suicide, just as he had threatened, by driving a car into a concrete embankment. Four teenage passengers in the car also died. The boy's family alleged, among other claims, that the defendant's termination of his involvement in the case was improper. The defendant, the treating physician, argued that he removed himself from the case because he thought the care provided by the treatment team would be adequate. He also claimed that his withdrawal from the case was not the proximate cause of the boy's death, that the death resulted from an accident, not suicide, and that the parents were at fault in allowing the boy to have access to car keys and in their monitoring of his medication. The Missouri jury awarded the parents $750,000 but under the doctrine of comparative negligence reduced the award by 25 percent because of fault by the parents ("Parents Allege Failure," 1990:4).

Arranging Coverage

Social workers can also be liable for abandonment if they fail to provide clients with sufficient instructions for times when the social workers are unavailable as a result of vacation, illness, or emergencies. Social workers should always provide clients with clearly stated information about what they ought to do in these circumstances, including whom to call and how to handle emergencies. I always recommend that social workers provide these instructions to clients in writing, including in the case record a copy of the instructions, signed by the clients to acknowledge that they received the instructions and that the instructions were explained to them.

Social workers should be especially careful to arrange for competent coverage when they know they will not be available for a period of time. The colleagues who are to provide coverage should be given information about clients' status sufficient to enable them to provide adequate care should the need arise (after having obtained clients' consent to the release of such information, of course).

In light of modern technology social workers should also be careful about using their own telephone answering machines. To avoid abandonment claims social workers must review messages left by clients frequently. Using a remote-access answering machine can facilitate this. It is important to refer clients to a colleague if they need immediate help and the social worker is unavailable. Failure to retrieve messages and provide proper referral could result in a liability claim alleging abandonment.

Prevention Strategy

Social workers can follow a number of procedures to avoid charges of abandonment (Austin, Moline, and Williams 1990; Schutz 1982):

- Provide clients with the names, addresses, and telephone numbers of at least three appropriate referrals when it is necessary to terminate services.
- Follow up with a client who has been terminated. If the client does not go to the referral, write a letter to him or her about the risks involved should the client not follow through with the referral.
- Clients who will be terminated should be given as much advance warning as possible.
- When clients announce their decision to terminate prematurely, explain to them the risks involved and suggestions for alternative care. Include this information in a follow-up letter.
- Carefully document in the case record all decisions and actions related to termination of services.
- In cases involving discharge of clients from a residential facility, be sure that a comprehensive discharge plan has been formulated and significant others have been notified of the client's discharge (clients should be informed of this). In cases involving court-ordered clients, seek legal consultation and court approval before terminating care.
- Provide clients with clear instructions to follow and telephone numbers to use in the event of an emergency. Include a copy of the instructions in clients' case records. Clients should be asked to sign this copy, indicating that they received the instructions and that the instructions were explained to them.

9 | Concluding Observations: The Social Worker as Defendant

Legal liability is one of the unfortunate risks associated with professional practice. Fortunately, it is also a relatively rare occurrence. The vast majority of social workers will never be named as defendants in lawsuits.

As I discussed in chapter 1, however, the frequency of liability claims against social workers has been rising steadily, as has the monetary value of related out-of-court settlements and judgments. In light of this trend social workers need to anticipate the possibility, however remote, that they will be named in a lawsuit and liability claim. Although this book discusses various causes of liability and sources of risk, social workers should also be acquainted with conventional advice about how to respond if they are named as a defendant or respondent (Cohen 1979; Meyer, Landis, and Hays 1988; Saltzman and Proch 1990).

In the Event of a Lawsuit

Assuming a social worker named in a lawsuit holds a liability insurance policy—which every modern social worker should—

the insurance company will appoint an attorney to handle the case. Otherwise, the social worker needs to retain a lawyer. Should this be necessary, the social worker would do well to follow Besharov's (1985) sound advice:

> Basically, selecting a lawyer is like selecting a doctor or a therapist. Personal recommendations from friends and colleagues are the best way to identify a qualified professional. Ask around. Find social workers or others who have been sued, find out who represented them, and ask whether they were satisfied with the representation they received. Do not be shy. Ask what the result was, and ask how expensive the lawyer was. Even workers who were represented by counsel provided by insurance companies can provide helpful leads. Most lawyers who handle insurance cases also handle individual clients . . .
>
> As potential lawyers are being identified, the social worker will have to decide whether to hire a general practitioner or a specialist. Many lawyers still maintain general practices, handling a variety of commercial, tax, financial, real estate, and torts cases. In smaller communities, there may be no choice but to hire a general practitioner. In larger communities, though, there will be a wide choice of specialists. (In fact, some lawyers specialize in plaintiff's tort work, while others specialize in defense work.)
>
> A specialist is more likely to do a satisfactory job handling the case than is a generalist unfamiliar or only marginally familiar with the relevant area of the law. This is crucial in the area of criminal law. *Under no circumstances should a lawyer with no experience in criminal matters be retained to handle a criminal case.* A lawyer who has never before handled a criminal case—or who has insubstantial experience—is simply incompetent to do so. In fact, an ethical lawyer conscious of this reality should decline to represent a person charged with a crime. The stakes are too high to have the lawyer learn while doing. (pp. 199–200)

In many instances a social worker's employer (for example, the state or a private agency) will retain an attorney to handle the lawsuit. The social worker should be sure to talk with the attorney about whether the attorney is planning to represent the social worker (as opposed to the agency only). Social workers who have been sued may be wise to retain their own lawyer because the attorney retained by the employer may be obligated, first and foremost, to protect the employer's interests. This could create a conflict of interest, particularly if the employer believes the social worker, not the employer, was somehow negligent.

If a social worker is sued, reacting as calmly and thoughtfully as possible is important. This can be difficult, of course, given the traumatizing nature of lawsuits. Ultimately, a carefully planned response will be more effective than an impulsive one.

The first step is to contact the insurer to notify them of the lawsuit. The best course is to make a telephone call and to follow this with a certified letter and a copy of the letter sent by the plaintiff's attorney. Although it is often tempting to talk with the client (or whoever the plaintiff is) about the lawsuit, the social worker should refrain from doing so. In fact, discussing the case with anyone other than the attorney retained to defend the social worker is generally a mistake.

The plaintiff's attorney usually asks for copies of case record material and other relevant documents. As I discussed in chapter 7, social workers must not alter records to fill in gaps or create false impressions. Not only is this wrong but the plaintiff's attorney may have already seen unaltered copies of this material and will find the alteration. This, of course, would be disastrous.

A social worker named in a lawsuit commonly is asked to give a deposition. A *deposition* is a sworn statement, obtained in question-and-answer form, that is taken before the trial (the *discovery phase* of litigation). The plaintiff's attorney poses a series of questions, and the entire proceeding is recorded in order to prepare a transcript. The primary purpose of a deposition is to obtain the social worker's version of what happened in the case and to provide leads that may be relevant. Of course, the social worker's attorney also has the option to depose the plaintiff and other parties who may be involved in the case (for example, family members of the client, colleagues of the social worker, or expert witnesses whose specialized knowledge may be drawn on by the plaintiff or defendant). Cohen (1979:277–78) offers a series of helpful guidelines for handling a deposition (some of which also pertain to testimony in court):

1. The first rule is to be honest. You are under oath and should be telling the truth at all times. If you do not tell the truth you may be subject to criminal charges. Additionally, if it

can be demonstrated that there are falsehoods in your sworn testimony on any point (however minor), then your credibility on other points will be called into question.

2. Do not answer any question unless you are absolutely certain that you understand it fully. Do not be embarrassed to ask for as much clarification as you need or to say "I don't know."

3. If you are certain of your facts, state them as forthrightly as possible. On the other hand, if you are asked a question to which you really are not 100 percent certain of the facts it is all right to use qualifiers such as "My best recollection is . . ."; "As best as I can recall . . ."; and "I believe. . . ."

4. If you are concerned about how to answer the examiner on some sensitive aspect of the case, or you believe that your answer might prove to be embarrassing, discuss the issue fully with your attorney before the deposition. Together you can decide if the matter is relevant to the case and, if so, what position to take.

5. The examiner may ask you what patient charts, documents, textbooks, or other sources you have consulted in preparing for your deposition. If you are a witness appearing on someone else's behalf he will probably ask you about the financial arrangements that have been made concerning your appearance at the deposition and your participation in the case. Be prepared for such questions by discussing them in advance with your attorney.

6. At any time during the deposition you may ask to have a private conference with your attorney. Similarly, you may at any time ask for a break if you are becoming fatigued or uncomfortable.

7. The well-known Army rule "never volunteer" is most appropriate as regards making a deposition. Do not volunteer any information that you are not specifically asked. Short answers—"yes" or "no" when possible—are best. Do not volunteer to look anything up, obtain any records, or do anything at all unless your attorney has advised you to do so. Do not volunteer the name of someone who might know the answer to a question, and do not volunteer opinions if you are not asked for them.

8. Be cautious about deciding on which patient charts, notes,

documents, or other memoranda you wish to bring with you into the deposition room, as the examiner may ask to look at such materials. It is therefore a good idea to have your attorney approve whatever it is you wish to bring with you.

9. If the examiner has in his possession a patient's chart or some other document and he asks you questions about it, read it over carefully before replying.

10. It is usually a good idea to wait a moment or two before answering any question during the deposition (as opposed to the trial). The brief pause will provide you with additional time to get your answer the way you want it, and it will provide your attorney with the time to raise any objections he might have to the question. If your attorney instructs you not to answer the question do not answer it, even if you think it will help your case to do so.

11. Speak slowly when answering all questions, and stop talking if your attorney interrupts. You may ask for some time to think about an answer to a question if the question is particularly difficult or complicated. Remember, the written transcript of your deposition will not reflect how long it took you to answer any questions, so do not feel pressured into giving quick answers.

12. If the opposing lawyers get into an argument, stay out of it. You should, however, listen carefully to what is being said and be particularly attentive to the point that your own counsel is trying to make. Such disagreements may alert you to an aspect of the case to which you may not have given due consideration before the deposition.

13. Some examiners may try to provoke you to the point where your judgment and memory is somewhat clouded. Methods of rattling you will vary, but a common technique is to accuse you of being inconsistent in your testimony. Alternatively, the examiner may refer to some document or record that your testimony supposedly contradicts. Be prepared for such contingencies, and do not let the examiner succeed in his goal. Be courteous and professional at all times.

14. Some examiners may appear to be exceptionally concerned, friendly, and understanding. In some instances

this is a ploy designed to obtain more from you than you are willing to give. The examiner is not your buddy. During the deposition the examiner will probably be sizing you up in terms of where your weak spots are as a witness on the stand. Therefore, you should be cordial but not overly friendly or anxious to please. If you are there to impress the examiner with anything, it is your credibility and self-confidence as a witness.

15. At some point in the deposition the examiner may attempt to summarize what you have said. Listen carefully to what he says when he is supposedly paraphrasing your testimony. Do not let him put words in your mouth. If what he is saying is not what you meant to say, do not hesitate to say so. Also, be aware of the fact that you can have any portion of your testimony read back to you at your request.

After the deposition transcript has been prepared, the social worker should read a copy and correct any errors before signing it. It is wise to review the transcript before going to court to testify, should the case get that far.

While many suggestions concerning depositions also apply to actual courtroom testimony, some do not. For example, many trial attorneys believe that pausing or hesitating too much can raise doubt in a jury's mind as to the witness's credibility. Also, how the social worker appears at a trial—with regard to dress (conservative professional dress is usually recommended) and manner—count much more than they do at a deposition. Jurors often react to subtleties related to a witness's physical appearance, gestures, and mannerisms. On the witness stand the social worker must be careful not to use too much professional jargon or to appear cocky, cavalier, arrogant, condescending, insincere, crude, overly technical, or overbearing. When responding to a question that is difficult to answer, saying simply "I don't know" is fine and often desirable. Contriving an answer in order to sound knowledgeable can backfire.

Maintaining composure on the witness stand, despite an opposing attorney's best efforts to be provocative, is especially important. Social workers need to be aware that litigation is an adversarial process, and the job of opposing attorneys is to do their best to challenge and discredit the witness's testimony.* As Saltzman and Proch (1990) observe,

> Attorneys use a variety of tactics to discredit witnesses and their testimony during cross examination. They use leading questions which require a yes or no answer when no such simple answer is possible or when it would be misleading. They may be condescending, attacking, or overly friendly. They may ask repetitious questions in an attempt to make you answer inconsistently or they may badger you. They may reverse your words. And they may question you about your personal beliefs and your personal life to show possible bias or prejudice or motive to lie. For example, in a child custody case involving a gay father, you may be asked your sexual preference, if you believe in the Bible, or if you know anyone who died of AIDS.
>
> The important point to remember when faced with such tactics is that this is part of the system and not something that is happening to just you. Your best defense is to remain alert and calm. Resist being lulled into a false sense of security when an attorney seems overly friendly and resist becoming defensive or hostile when an attorney seems to be attacking you. (p. 61)

A special problem sometimes arises in cases in which a social worker who is on the witness stand attempts to characterize a former client as emotionally disturbed. This might occur if a former client sues a social worker and during the trial the social worker attempts to convey the impression that the client is unstable. Cohen (1979) refers to this as the "What's-wrong-with-that?" phenomenon:

> Many mental health professionals, to their detriment, make what might be termed "What's-wrong-with-that? (WWT)" errors in their court testimony. When a supposedly revealing statement about a patient's pathology compels the majority of the jury to ask themselves, "What's wrong with that?" a WWT error has been made. For example, suppose "Mr. Citizen," the patient, is forcibly taken from

---

* Consider the following anecdote told about F. E. Smith, first earl of Birkenhead (1872–1930), who was a British barrister. Smith once cross examined a young man claiming damages for an arm injury caused by the negligence of a bus driver. "Will you please show us how high you can lift your arm now?" asked Smith. The young man gingerly raised his arm to shoulder level, his face distorted with pain. "Thank you," said Smith. "And now, please will you show us how high you could lift it before the accident?" The young man eagerly shot his arm up above his head. He lost his case (Fadiman 1985:513).

his home by the police, handcuffed, and packed into a police car in full view of his friends and neighbors. And suppose "Dr. Smith," a psychiatrist, testifies that the patient was verbally abusive and hostile to the therapist on admission. Jury members are likely to ask themselves, "What's wrong with that? Who wouldn't be verbally abusive and hostile under such conditions?" This is especially true if Mr. Citizen appears to be composed and "normal" in the courtroom. Smith may compound his WWT error by going on to say something like, "Further, Mr. Citizen denied that he was mentally ill." Again, jury members—who are more likely to identify with a patient than a psychiatrist—are likely to ask themselves, "What's wrong with that? I would deny it under the same circumstances." To weaken his testimony still further, Smith might testify that the patient's denial of mental illness demonstrated lack of insight, which was evidence of mental illness. Although all of Smith's statements might make sense to experienced mental health professionals, they will probably not make much sense to the lay people of the jury. WWT errors can be avoided with some forethought, factual documentation, and practice in presenting professional opinion to lay audiences. (pp. 280–81)

Social workers need to be completely candid with their attorney to enable the attorney to prepare the strongest defense possible. Attorneys like nothing less than surprises in the courtroom, particularly when the opposing attorney reveals damaging information that the attorney's client failed to disclose ahead of time. It is important to be as forthright with your own attorney as possible.*

Preventing Liability: Good Practice

As I said in the preface, it is unfortunate that there is a need for this book. Everyone in the field would prefer that social workers merely go about their noble business of helping people in need. No practitioner wishes to be distracted by the annoying, burdensome, and distressing problems of professional malpractice and liability.

* The lawyer for Russel Sage, the famous U.S. financier, was delighted by the case Sage had presented to him. "It's an ironclad case," he exclaimed with confidence. "We can't possibly lose!"

"Then we won't sue," said Sage. "That was my opponent's side of the case I gave you" (Fadiman 1985:485).

As in all professions, however, these phenomena are a reality in social work. Fortunately, much of the malpractice and liability risk in social work is preventable. Throughout this discussion I have reviewed a variety of practical ways in which social workers can reduce the chances of being sued. Examples include avoiding hallway conversations when discussing clients, complying with standard informed consent procedures, understanding local privileged communication statutes, documenting services provided to clients and supervision provided to staff, and seeking consultation when issues arise that are outside your range of expertise.

These and the many other practical suggestions that appear throughout this discussion can certainly go a long way toward preventing social work malpractice and liability. By themselves, however, they constitute a rather shortsighted approach to prevention. Rather, knowledge of these specific ways to prevent malpractice and liability must be supplemented by a firm grasp of two essential components of competent social work: good practice and good ethics.

In my experience over the years with respect to malpractice and liability problems in the profession, I have been struck by the frequency with which good practice would have avoided legal problems. Certainly, in some cases good practice by itself would not prevent a liability claim. A social worker who is sued by a former client because she divulged confidential information to protect a third party from violence threatened by the former client has not necessarily engaged in "bad" practice. In fact, the social worker may very well have demonstrated good practice skills and made the right decision in deciding to breach confidentiality. That the client chose to sue the social worker for the breach may simply be unfortunate.

Similarly, a social worker who is sued for improper referral of a client to a specialist may have practiced good social work. She may have followed proper referral procedures, including giving the client the names of several well-known colleagues. However, one of the colleagues may have sexually abused the client. The referring social worker may have had no way to know that her colleague would violate a client in such a way; the perpetrator's behavior may not have been well known in the professional community. In fact, the assault may have been the first such occurrence in his career. Although the outcome was tragic and unfortunate, the referring social worker may have been in no way at fault. Clearly, social workers can be competent practitioners and still get sued.

Nonetheless, social workers who understand sound practice principles and carry them out every day substantially reduce their chances of being sued. Social workers who have a firm understanding of privacy issues, the assessment process, intervention techniques, termination and boundary issues, and the nature of supervision, consultation, and referral, for example, minimize the likelihood that they will make the sort of mistake that could trigger a lawsuit. Skillful practice is the most powerful preventive. As Besharov (1985) appropriately asserts, in the event of a lawsuit "good practice is the best defense" (p. 168).

In addition, however, solid grounding in professional ethics is essential in order to prevent malpractice and liability. Unfortunately, this is often the missing link in social workers' armamentarium.

Preventing Liability: Good Ethics

Social work values and ethics have always been a central ingredient in the profession. Ever since social work's formal inauguration in the late nineteenth century, practitioners have been concerned about the values of the profession. Historical accounts of the profession's development routinely dwell on the compelling importance of social work's values and ethical tenets. Over time, beliefs about social work's values and ethics have served as the principal organizing theme of the profession's mission and as the normative linchpin in the profession's foundation.

Although the theme of values and ethics has endured in the profession, social workers' conceptions of what these terms mean, and of their bearing on practice, have changed considerably over time. Only recently in fact have social workers devoted serious attention to ethical issues as they pertain to professional malpractice and liability.

In the late nineteenth century, for example, when social work was formally inaugurated as a profession, the concern about the morality of the client was much greater than the concern for the morality or ethics of the profession or its practitioners. Organizing relief and responding to the "curse of pauperism" (Paine 1880) were the profession's principal missions. This preoccupation often took the form of paternalistic attempts to strengthen the morality or rectitude of the poor whose "wayward" lives had gotten the best of them.

Concern about the morality of the poor waned considerably—although not entirely—during the rise of the settlement house movement in the early twentieth century, when the aims of many social workers shifted from concern about the morality, or immorality, of the poor to the need for dramatic social reform designed to ameliorate a wide range of social problems related, for example, to housing, health care, child care, sanitation, employment, poverty, and education (Reamer 1980, 1990, 1992c).

Concern about the morality of the client continued to recede somewhat during the next several decades of the profession's life, as practitioners engaged in earnest attempts to establish and polish their intervention strategies and techniques, training programs, and schools of thought. Over time, concern about clients' morality was overshadowed by debate about the profession's future, that is, the extent to which social work would stress the cultivation of expertise in psychosocial and psychiatric casework, psychotherapy, social welfare policy and administration, community organization, or social reform.

By the late 1940s and early 1950s, however, concern about the moral dimensions of social work practice intensified, although in rather different form. Unlike the earlier preoccupation with the morality of the client, this mid-twentieth-century concern focused much more on the morality or ethics of the profession and of its practitioners. This was a significant shift. Nearly a half-century after its formal inauguration the profession began to develop ethical guidelines to enhance proper conduct among practitioners—the sorts of guidelines that help to reduce malpractice and liability risks. In 1947 after several years of debate and discussion, the Delegate Conference of the American Association of Social Workers adopted a code of ethics. The profession's journals also began to publish articles on the subject with greater frequency. Thus the period surrounding the 1950s marked the onset of serious scholarly interest in the subject of professional ethics.

Not surprisingly, in the 1960s social workers shifted considerable attention toward the ethical constructs of social justice, rights, and reform. The public and political mood of this turbulent period infused social work training and practice with concern about social equality, welfare rights, human rights, discrimination, and oppression (Emmet 1962; Lewis 1972; Plant 1970; Vigilante 1974). In 1960 the National Association of Social Workers adopted its first code of ethics.

The early 1980s marked yet another significant transition in social work's concern with value and ethical issues. During the 1970s interest in the broad subject of professional ethics surged dramatically. Professions as diverse as medicine, law, business, journalism, engineering, nursing, and criminal justice began to devote sustained attention to the subject. Large numbers of undergraduate and graduate training programs added courses on ethics to their curricula, professional conferences witnessed a substantial increase in presentations on the subject, and the number of publications on professional ethics increased dramatically (Callahan and Bok 1980; Reamer and Abramson 1982).

Since the late 1970s a major focus in ethics scholarship, training, and education has been on the phenomenon of ethical dilemmas. This development has especially important bearing on social workers' efforts to reduce malpractice and liability risks in the profession. Professionals have become increasingly interested in the analysis of ethical dilemmas in which practitioners must make difficult choices among competing professional duties or obligations. Beginning especially in the early 1980s social workers have been introduced to the subjects of ethical decision making and ethical theory, particularly as they pertain to the dilemmas encountered in day-to-day practice (Levy 1976; Loewenberg and Dolgoff 1992; Reamer 1980, 1982a, 1982b, 1983a, 1983b, 1987a, 1987b, 1989a, 1990, 1992c, 1993; Reamer and Abramson 1982; Rhodes 1986). There has also been some renewed interest in reexamining the content of social work's values (Siporin 1982, 1989).

Although firm grounding in social work's enduring values can go a long way toward preventing professional malpractice and liability—after all, social workers who firmly grasp the obligation to respect a client's dignity are much less likely to exploit them sexually, financially, or otherwise—social workers must refine their understanding of and ability to analyze ethical dilemmas that arise in practice.

Many malpractice and liability risks stem from decisions social workers make in these circumstances. For example, whether a social worker should divulge confidential information to prevent harm to a third party, against a client's wishes, requires keen understanding of the nature of ethical dilemmas and various ways of addressing them. Although reasonable people may disagree with a social worker's particular decision in the case, a practitioner who can explain to a court of law how he went about examining and addressing this ethical dilemma may prevent a judgment against him. Being able to demonstrate that familiarity with literature and concepts in ethical decision making, consultation with experts on the subject, and documenting efforts in this regard may convince a jury that the social worker acted in a manner consistent with the profession's standard of care. Moreover, familiarity with the general subject of professional ethics, ethical dilemmas, and ethical decision making can, by itself, enhance the likelihood that social workers will make sound judgments that may, after all, be the most powerful preventive of malpractice and liability claims.

Ethical Dilemmas and Decision Making

In many instances social workers' ethical responsibilities are clear and uncomplicated. Ordinarily, social workers understand their duty, for example, to respect clients' right to confidentiality and to protect the general welfare of members of society. These ethical principles are set forth rather clearly in the NASW *Code of Ethics* (1990), and support for them in social work literature and practice is longstanding.

On occasion, however, such duties conflict in ways that might generate a lawsuit. A social worker whose client informs her during a counseling session that he plans to harm his estranged spouse must make a difficult choice between the client's right to confidentiality and protection of a third party. Assuming clinical intervention fails to resolve the issue and there is evidence the client plans to carry out his threat, the social worker must choose between two competing duties that social workers are ordinarily expected to fulfill.

Hence, ethical dilemmas in social work include those instances in which practitioners face conflicting duties or obligations. Three categories of dilemmas are particularly relevant to social work practice and to malpractice and liability risks. The first includes ethical dilemmas related to intervention with individuals, families, and groups. Prominent dilemmas in this area concern issues of confidentiality, client self-determination, paternalism, and truth telling (Reamer 1983b, 1987a, 1990). As discussed, with regard to confidentiality social workers need to understand the extent of clients' rights and the limits of confidentiality, particularly when clients threaten to harm themselves or a third party (Arnold 1970; Promislo 1979; Reynolds 1976; Wilson 1978). Under what circumstances should social workers breach clients' right to privacy in order to protect third parties or clients from themselves?

Similar dilemmas arise with regard to clients' right to self-determination. Ordinarily, social workers respect clients' right to self-determination and help them pursue goals that are meaningful to them (Bernstein 1960; Keith-Lucas 1963; McDermott 1975; Perlman 1965). Instances arise, however, in which social workers must consider limiting clients' right to self-determination because such actions threaten to harm them or third parties. Consider, for example, a social worker whose client is a battered woman. After a period of separation from her abusive partner, who has beaten the client on several previous occasions, the client informs the social worker of her intention to once again live with her partner. The social worker feels strongly that the client is quite likely to be abused again. Empirically based literature on the phenomenon also supports the worker's hunch. To what extent should the worker respect the client's right to self-determination and help her pursue her chosen goal, as opposed to actively attempting to dissuade her from her plans to move in again with her partner? Understanding these issues may help to prevent a lawsuit alleging improper treatment or inappropriate use of coercion.

Further, how should social workers respond to severely mentally or physically disabled clients who have decided to end their lives because of the chronic emotional or physical pain they experience? Should social workers summarily reject the possibility of "rational suicide" and discourage clients from further consideration of the possibility? Is it ever defensible for social workers to respect the decision of a distressed but competent client who has decided to commit suicide? Social workers' answers to these complex questions may have important bearing on the likelihood that they will be sued for causing or failing to prevent a client's suicide.

Debate concerning the limits of clients' right to self-determination in instances in which their actions seem self-destructive inevitably leads to discussion of the concept of *professional paternalism. Paternalism* is ordinarily defined as interference with an individual's intentions or mental state in order to protect the individual from him- or herself (Buchanan 1978; Carter 1977; Dworkin 1971; Feinberg 1971; Gert and Culver 1976, 1979; Husak 1980). Common examples of paternalism include prohibiting swimming at beaches when lifeguards are not on duty, requiring members of certain religious groups to receive life-saving blood transfusions, permitting involuntary civil commitment to a psychiatric facility, and legislating against suicide.

Social workers face several types of ethical dilemmas involving paternalism (Reamer 1983b). First are those instances in which social workers decide whether to physically interfere with clients for their own protection. Should a social worker require a resourceful but troubled homeless individual to go to a shelter against her wishes when the temperature is below freezing? How a social worker handles this predicament may affect the chances of being sued for false imprisonment.

Second are those instances in which social workers decide whether to withhold information from a client because of a belief that the client's knowledge of that information will be harmful. Is it justifiable, for example, for a hospital-based social worker to withhold from a critically ill patient the information that his child was just killed in an automobile accident? Is pater-

nalism, in the form of withholding personally relevant information, justified in order to protect the hospital patient from harm?

Third are those instances in which social workers decide
whether to deliberately give clients inaccurate information, or to
lie to clients, in order to protect clients from harm. Is it justifiable on paternalistic grounds for a social worker to lie to a child
about the reason for her father's arrest by the police in order to
preserve as much as possible the child's relationship with her
father? Is it permissible to give inaccurate information to a suicidal client in an effort to prevent suicide? Would such actions
breach the standard of care in the profession and expose a social
worker to a liability claim?

Dilemmas involving paternalism frequently raise issues concerning the phenomenon of truth telling. Although social workers are typically inclined to be truthful with clients, truth telling
may seem to be harmful at times (Bok 1978). Whether deception
can ever be justified is an important matter to debate.

The second major category of ethical dilemmas in social work
pertains to the ways in which practitioners design and administer social welfare policies and programs (Reamer 1987a, 1990).
Social workers also encounter dilemmas concerning their duty
to obey laws, agency rules, and public- or private-agency regulations. In all states, for example, social workers are required to
report suspected cases of child abuse and neglect to protective
service officials. Despite this mandate, however, social workers
sometimes do not report such cases on the grounds that they are
in a better position than public officials to intervene effectively
or they do not want to betray the client's trust. As discussed,
social workers who fail to report suspected abuse or neglect risk
being sued for failure to consult a specialist.

Complicated ethical dilemmas also arise with respect to compliance with regulations. Many social service agencies, for
instance, depend on reimbursement for their services from insurance carriers or other third-party payers. To receive reimbursement agency staff members typically need to provide insurers
with documentation of reimbursable services provided. Because
some of the agency's services may not be reimbursable under the
insurer's guidelines, social workers may struggle with their
obligation to provide truthful claims information. The viability

of the agency and its services may be at stake. Of course, a social worker who decides to submit bogus information to obtain reimbursement risks criminal charges and a lawsuit filed by the insurer.

The third broad category of ethical dilemmas involves relationships among professional colleagues. The most common, perhaps, concerns instances in which social workers encounter impaired or incompetent colleagues. These circumstances—when a social worker has evidence that a colleague is abusing alcohol, drugs, or clients, for example—involve troubling ethical issues in regard to whistle-blowing (Barry 1986; Bok 1980; Nader, Petkas, and Blackwood 1972; Peters and Branch 1972; Reamer 1984, 1990, 1992a, 1992b; Siegel 1992). Under what circumstances is whistle-blowing justifiable? What conditions should first be met? How much professional and personal risk should the whistle-blower be willing to assume? On the one hand are liability risks if a social worker fails to confront an impaired employee who subsequently injures a client. On the other hand, confronting an impaired colleague and discussing the problem with other agency staff may lead to a defamation-of-character lawsuit.

Ethical dilemmas can also arise in relationships among colleagues with respect to the use of deception. Social service providers may be competitors, and such competition may sometimes tempt administrators to engage in deceptive practices to win new grants or undermine competitors' advantage in order to ensure their own agency's fiscal health or survival. Deception may also be contemplated in order to surreptitiously gather information to document wrongdoing allegedly engaged in by colleagues.

Fortunately, social workers now have greater access to literature and instruction on ethical decision making. Especially since the mid-1970s, the growth in literature and teaching on ethical decision making has been substantial. Social workers can consult a wide range of resources that provide useful introductions to and overviews of various ethical theories and frameworks for ethical decision making and analyzing ethical dilemmas in practice (Loewenberg and Dolgoff 1992; Reamer 1989a, 1990; Rhodes 1986).

Although social workers might prefer to avoid the topic of professional malpractice and liability, practitioners need to understand the risks involved and ways to mitigate them. Given the complexity of the legal and practice issues involved, the tendency may be for social workers to become preoccupied with the technical aspects of professional malpractice and liability. These high-anxiety issues often lead social workers to dwell on the trees—the mechanics of lawsuits and the mistakes, oversights, and improprieties that may give rise to them—rather than on the forest—the need to engage in good and ethical practice. In the final analysis, however, skillful and ethical practice is the most effective way to prevent malpractice and liability in social work. This is also the hallmark of a professional.

References

Antler, S. 1987. "Professional Liability and Malpractice." In *Encyclopedia of Social Work*, 18th ed., p. 346. Silver Spring, Md.: National Association of Social Workers.

Arnold, S. 1970. "Confidential Communication and the Social Worker." *Social Work* 15:61–67.

"Attorney Suffers Psychotic Breakdown from Lifespring Training." 1991. *Mental Health Law News* 6(7):1.

Austin, K. M., M. E. Moline, and G. T. Williams. 1990. *Confronting Malpractice: Legal and Ethical Dilemmas in Psychotherapy*. Newbury Park, Calif.: Sage.

Austin, M. J. 1981. *Supervisory Management for the Human Services*. Englewood Cliffs, N.J.: Prentice-Hall.

Barry, V. 1986. *Moral Issues in Business*, 3d ed. Belmont, Calif.: Wadsworth.

Berliner, A. K. 1989. "Misconduct in Social Work Practice." *Social Work* 34:69–72.

Bernard, J., and C. Jara. 1986. "The Failure of Clinical Psychology Students to Apply Understood Ethical Principles." *Professional Psychology: Research and Practice* 17:316–21.

Bernstein, B. 1981. "Malpractice: Future Shock of the 1980s." *Social Casework* 62(3):175–81.

Bernstein, S. 1960. "Self-Determination: King or Citizen in the Realm of Values?" *Social Work* 5(1):3–8.

Besharov, D. J. 1985. *The Vulnerable Social Worker: Liability for Serving Children and Families.* Silver Spring, Md.: National Association of Social Workers.

Bissell, L., and P. W. Haberman. 1984. *Alcoholism in the Professions.* New York: Oxford University Press.

Bissell, L., L. Fewell, and R. Jones. 1980. "The Alcoholic Social Worker: A Survey." *Social Work in Health Care* 5:421–32.

Bok, S. 1978. *Lying: Moral Choice in Public and Private Life.* New York: Pantheon.

——. 1980. "Whistleblowing and Professional Responsibility." *New York University Education Quarterly* 11:2–10.

Brodsky, A. M. 1986. "The Distressed Psychologist: Sexual Intimacies and Exploitation." In R. R. Kilburg, P. E. Nathan, and R. W. Thoreson, eds., *Professionals in Distress: Issues, Syndromes, and Solutions in Psychology,* p. 153. Washington, D.C.: American Psychological Association.

Buchanan, A. 1978. "Medical Paternalism." *Philosophy and Public Affairs* 7:370–90.

Buchanan, A. E., and D. W. Brock. 1989. *Deciding for Others: The Ethics of Surrogate Decision Making.* Cambridge: Cambridge University Press.

Callahan, D., and S. Bok, eds. 1980. *Ethics Teaching in Higher Education.* New York: Plenum Press.

Carter, R. 1977. "Justifying Paternalism." *Canadian Journal of Philosophy* 7:133–45.

Cohen, B. Z. 1987. "The Ethics of Social Work Supervision Revisited." *Social Work* 32:194–96.

Cohen, R. J. 1979. *Malpractice: A Guide for Mental Health Professionals.* New York: Free Press.

Cohen, R. J., and B. DeBetz. 1977. "Responsive Supervision of the Psychiatric Resident and Clinical Psychology Intern." *American Journal of Psychoanalysis* 37:51–64.

Cohen, R. J., and W. E. Mariano. 1982. *Legal Guidebook in Mental Health.* New York: Free Press.

"Counselor Begins Sexual Relationship with Client." 1991. *Mental Health Law News* 6(4):1.

"Counselor Who Suspected Child Abuse Not Liable for Interfering with Family Rights." 1990. *Mental Health Law News* 5(5):4.

Cowles, J. 1976. *Informed Consent.* New York: Coward, McCann and Geoghegan.

Crombie, D. 1989. "Social Worker Sentenced in Assaults." *Providence Journal-Bulletin* (April 20):B3.

Deutsch, C. 1985. "A Survey of Therapists' Personal Problems and Treatment." *Professional Psychology: Research and Practice* 16:305–15.

Donnelly, J. 1978. "Confidentiality: The Myth and the Reality." In W. E.

Barton and C. J. Sanborn, eds., *Law and the Mental Health Professions*, p. 185. New York: International Universities Press.

"Drug Treatment Counselor Has Affair with Patient's Mother." 1992. *Mental Health Law News* 7(1):3.

Dworkin, G. 1971. "Paternalism." In R. A. Wasserstrom, ed., *Morality and the Law*, p. 107. Belmont, Calif.: Wadsworth.

Emmet, D. 1962. "Ethics and the Social Worker." *British Journal of Psychiatric Social Work* 6:165–72.

"Employer May Be Held Liable for Psychotherapist's Sexual Misconduct." 1990. *Mental Health Law News* 5(11):1.

"Employer Not Vicariously Liable for Therapist's Sexual Misconduct." 1989. *Mental Health Law News* 4(10):1.

Fadiman, C., ed. 1985. *The Little, Brown Book of Anecdotes*. Boston: Little, Brown.

Farber, B. A., and L. H. Heifitz. 1982. "The Satisfaction and Stresses of Psychotherapeutic Work: A Factor Analytic Study." *Professional Psychology: Research and Practice* 12(5):621–30.

Fausel, D. F. 1988. "Helping the Helper Heal: Co-dependency in Helping Professionals." *Journal of Independent Social Work* 3(2):35–45.

Feinberg, J. 1971. "Legal Paternalism." *Canadian Journal of Philosophy* 1:105–24.

"$570,841 Judgment Returned; Man Committed Suicide After Leaving Psychiatric Facility." 1991. *Mental Health Law News* 6(2):3.

Flexner, A. 1915. "Is Social Work a Profession?" In *Proceedings of the National Conference of Charities and Correction*, p. 576. Chicago: Hildman.

Francis, D. D., and J. Chin. 1987. "The Prevention of Acquired Immunodeficiency Syndrome in the United States." *Journal of the American Medical Association* 257:1357–66.

Freudenberger, H. J. 1986. "Chemical Abuse Among Psychologists: Symptoms, Causes, and Treatment Issues." In R. R. Kilburg, P. E. Nathan, and R. W. Thoreson, eds., *Professionals in Distress: Issues, Syndromes, and Solutions in Psychology*, p. 135. Washington, D.C.: American Psychological Association.

Gartrell, N., J. Herman, S. Olarte, M. Feldstein, and R. Localio. 1986. "Psychiatrist-Patient Sexual Contact: Results of a National Survey." *American Journal of Psychiatry* 143(9):1126–31.

Gechtman, L., and J. Bouhoutsos. 1985. "Sexual Intimacy Between Social Workers and Clients." Paper presented at the annual meeting of the Society for Clinical Social Workers, University City, California.

Gelman, S. R., and P. J. Wardell. 1988. "Who's Responsible? The Field Liability Dilemma." *Journal of Social Work Education* 24:70–78.

Gert, B., and C. M. Culver. 1976. "Paternalistic Behavior." *Philosophy and Public Affairs* 6:45–57.

——. 1979. "The Justification of Paternalism." *Ethics* 89:199–210.

Gifis, S. H. 1991. *Law Dictionary*, 3d ed. Hauppauge, N.Y.: Barron's.

Giordano, P. C. 1977. "The Client's Perspective in Agency Evaluation." *Social Work* 22:34–39.

Goby, M. J., N. J. Bradley, and D. A. Bespalec. 1979. "Physicians Treated for Alcoholism: A Follow-up Study." *Alcoholism: Clinical and Experimental Research* 3:121–24.

Goleman, D. 1985. "Social Workers Vault into a Leading Role in Psychotherapy." *New York Times* (April 30):C1, C9.

"Government Liable for Premature Release of Psychiatric Patient." 1992. *Mental Health Law News* 7(3):4.

Gray, L. A., and A. K. Harding. 1988. "Confidentiality Limits with Clients Who Have the AIDS Virus." *Journal of Counseling and Development* 66(5):219–23.

Green, R., and G. Cox. 1978. "Social Work and Malpractice." *Social Work* 23(2):100–5.

Greenwood, E. 1957. "Attributes of a Profession." *Social Work* 2:45–55.

Grossman, M. 1978. "Confidentiality: The Right to Privacy Versus the Right to Know." In W. E. Barton and C. J. Sanborn, eds., *Law and the Mental Health Professions*, p. 137. New York: International Universities Press.

Guy, J. D., P. L. Poelstra, and M. Stark. 1989. "Personal Distress and Therapeutic Effectiveness: National Survey of Psychologists Practicing Psychotherapy." *Professional Psychology: Research and Practice* 20:48–50.

Hamilton, G. 1936. *Social Case Recording*. New York: Columbia University Press.

——. 1946. *Principles of Social Case Recording*. New York: Columbia University Press.

Herrington, R. E., D. G. Benzer, G. R. Jacobson, and M. K. Hawkins. 1982. "Treating Substance-Use Disorders Among Physicians." *Journal of the American Medical Association* 247:2253–57.

Hogan, D. B. 1979. *The Regulation of Psychotherapists: Volume I—A Study in the Philosophy and Practice of Professional Regulation*. Cambridge, Mass.: Ballinger.

"Hospital Liable for Employee's Sexual Assault on Psychiatric Patient." 1992. *Mental Health Law News* 7(10):6.

"Hospital Liable for Failing to Detain Mentally Ill Emergency Room Patient." 1990. *Mental Health Law News* 5(1):4.

"Hospital Liable for Failure to Admit Suicidal Patient Who Killed Himself." 1991. *Mental Health Law News* 6(8):4.

"Hospital Liable for Failure to Prevent Suicide of Psychiatric Patient." 1990. *Mental Health Law News* 5(2):2.

"Hospital Not Liable for Releasing Patient Who Later Killed Stepfather." 1991. *Mental Health Law News* 6(3):3.

"Hospital Not Negligent in Supervising Patient Who Attacked Another Patient." 1992. *Mental Health Law News* 7(1):3.

Husak, D. N. 1980. "Paternalism and Autonomy." *Philosophy and Public Affairs* 10:27–46.

"Insurance Company May Be Liable for Depressed Patient's Suicide." 1991. *Mental Health Law News* 6(2):4.

Jayaratne, S., and W. A. Chess. 1984. "Job Satisfaction, Burnout, and Turnover: A National Study." *Social Work* 29:448–55.

Johnson, M., and G. L. Stone. 1986. "Social Workers and Burnout." *Journal of Social Work Research* 10:67–80.

Joseph, M. V. 1989. "Social Work Ethics: Historical and Contemporary Perspectives." *Social Thought* 15(3/4):4–17.

Kadushin, A. 1976. *Supervision in Social Work.* New York: Columbia University Press.

——. 1977. *Consultation in Social Work.* New York: Columbia University Press.

——. 1992. *Supervision in Social Work,* 3d ed. New York: Columbia University Press.

Kagle, J. D. 1987. "Recording in Direct Practice." In *Encyclopedia of Social Work,* p. 463. Silver Spring, Md.: National Association of Social Workers.

——. 1991. *Social Work Records,* 2d ed. Belmont, Calif.: Wadsworth.

Kain, C. D. 1988. "To Breach or Not to Breach: Is That the Question?" *Journal of Counseling and Development* 66(5):224–25.

Keith-Lucas, A. 1963. "A Critique of the Principle of Client Self-Determination." *Social Work* 8(3):66–71.

Khinduka, S. K. 1987. "Social Work and the Human Services." In *Encyclopedia of Social Work,* 18th ed., p. 681. Silver Spring, Md.: National Association of Social Workers.

Kilburg, R. R., F. W. Kaslow, and G. R. VandenBos. 1988. "Professionals in Distress." *Hospital and Community Psychiatry* 39:723–25.

Kilburg, R. R., P. E. Nathan, and R. W. Thoreson, eds. 1986. *Professionals in Distress: Issues, Syndromes, and Solutions in Psychology.* Washington, D.C.: American Psychological Association.

Kirk, S. A., and H. Kutchins. 1988. "Deliberate Misdiagnosis in Mental Health Practice." *Social Service Review* 62:225–37.

Kliner, D. J., J. Spicer, and P. Barnett. 1980. "Treatment Outcome of Alcoholic Physicians." *Journal of Studies on Alcohol* 41(11):1217–20.

Knutsen, E. 1977. "On the Emotional Well-Being of Psychiatrists: Overview and Rationale." *American Journal of Psychoanalysis* 37:123–29.

Koeske, G. F., and R. D. Koeske. 1989. "Work Load and Burnout: Can Social Support and Perceived Accomplishment Help?" *Social Work* 34:243–48.

Kopels, S., and J. D. Kagle. 1993. "Do Social Workers Have a Duty to Warn?" *Social Service Review* 67:101–26.

Kurzman, P. A. 1991. "Managing Risk in the Workplace." In R. L. Edwards and J. A. Yankey, eds., *Skills for Effective Human Services Management.* Silver Spring, Md.: National Association of Social Workers Press.

Lakin, M. 1988. *Ethical Issues in the Psychotherapies.* New York: Oxford University Press.

Laliotis, D. A., and J. H. Grayson. 1985. "Psychologist Heal Thyself: What Is Available for the Impaired Psychologist?" *American Psychologist* 40:84–96.

Lamb. D. H., C. Clark, P. Drumheller, K. Frizzell, and L. Surrey. 1989. "Applying *Tarasoff* to AIDS-related Psychotherapy Issues." *Professional Psychology: Research and Practice* 20(1):37–43.

Lamb, D. H., N. R. Presser, K. S. Pfost, M. C. Baum, V. R. Jackson, and P. A. Jarvis. 1987. "Confronting Professional Impairment During the Internship: Identification, Due Process, and Remediation." *Professional Psychology: Research and Practice* 18:597–603.

Landers, S. 1992. "Ethical Boundaries Easily Trespassed." *NASW News* (October):3.

Levine, R. S. 1976. "Social Worker Malpractice." *Social Casework* 56:466–68.

Levy, C. S. 1973. "The Ethics of Supervision." *Social Work* 18:14–21.

——. 1976. *Social Work Ethics.* New York: Human Sciences Press.

Lewis, H. 1972. "Morality and the Politics of Practice." *Social Casework* 53(7):404–17.

Lewis, M. B. 1986. "Duty to Warn Versus Duty to Maintain Confidentiality: Conflicting Demands on Mental Health Professionals." *Suffolk Law Review* 20(3):579–615.

Litan, R. E., and C. Winston, eds. 1988. *Liability: Perspectives and Policy.* Washington, D.C.: Brookings Institution.

Litan, R. E., P. Swire, and C. Winston. 1988. "The U.S. Liability System: Background and Trends." In R. E. Litan and C. Winston, eds., *Liability: Perspectives and Policy*, p. 1. Washington, D.C.: Brookings Institution.

Loewenberg, F., and R. Dolgoff. 1992. *Ethical Decisions for Social Work Practice*, 4th ed. Itasca, Ill.: F. E. Peacock.

McCrady, B. S. 1989. "The Distressed or Impaired Professional: From Retribution to Rehabilitation." *Journal of Drug Issues* 19:337–49.

McDermott, F. E., ed. 1975. *Self-Determination in Social Work.* London: Routledge and Kegan Paul.

"Man Claims Improper Discharge Following Suicide Attempt." 1990. *Mental Health Law News* 5(11):6.

"Man Murdered by Son Following Son's Dismissal from Hospital after Evaluation." 1992. *Mental Health Law News* 7(3):6.

"Marriage Counselor Sexually Abuses Plaintiff's Husband." 1990. *Mental Health Law News* 5(9):6.

"Marriage Therapist Has Affair with Patient." 1990. *Mental Health Law News* 5(4):3.

"Member Blows Whistle on Rx Refills." 1990. *NASW News* (June):11.

"Mental Health Center's Failure to Conduct Tests for Brain Tumor Make It Liable for Patient's Death." 1992. *Mental Health Law News* 7(5):2.

"Mental Health Facility Not Liable for Release of Patient." 1990. *Mental Health Law News* 5(4):2.

"Mental Patient Escapes and Is Struck by Car." 1990. *Mental Health Law News* 5(11):3.

Meyer, R. G., E. R. Landis, and J. R. Hays. 1988. *Law for the Psychotherapist.* New York: Norton.

Miller, I. 1987. "Supervision in Social Work." In *Encyclopedia of Social Work,* p. 748. Silver Spring, Md.: National Association of Social Workers.

Millon, T., C. Millon, and M. Antoni. 1986. "Sources of Emotional and Mental Disorder Among Psychologists: A Career Development Perspective." In R. R. Kilburg, P. E. Nathan, and R. W. Thoreson, eds., *Professionals in Distress: Issues, Syndromes, and Solutions in Psychology,* p. 119. Washington, D.C.: American Psychological Association.

Morse, R. M., M. A. Martin, W. M. Swenson, and R. G. Niven. 1984. "Prognosis of Physicians Treated for Alcoholism and Drug Dependence." *Journal of the American Medical Association* 251:743–46.

Munson, C. E. 1983. *An Introduction to Clinical Social Work Supervision.* New York: Haworth.

Nader, R., P. J. Petkas, and K. Blackwood, eds. 1972. *Whistle Blowing.* New York: Grossman.

National Association of Social Workers. 1983. "Membership Survey Shows Practice Shifts." *NASW News* (November):6.

——, Commission on Employment and Economic Support. 1987a. *Impaired Social Worker Program Resource Book.* Silver Spring, Md.: National Association of Social Workers.

——. 1987b. " 'Signing Off' Fraud Charge Warns Kentucky Clinicians." *NASW News* (June):1.

——. 1989. *Standards for the Practice of Clinical Social Work,* rev. ed. Silver Spring, Md.: National Association of Social Workers.

——. 1990. *Code of Ethics.* Washington, D.C.: National Association of Social Workers.

"No 'Trust Relationship' Between Patient and Counselor." 1991. *Mental Health Law News* 6(12):4.

"No Violation of Confidentiality in Communicating Patient's Arson Confession." 1990. *Mental Health Law News* 5(4):4.

"Note: Social Worker-Client Relationship and Privileged Communications." 1965. *Washington University Law Quarterly*: 362–95.

"Nursing Home Liable in Attempted Suicide." 1990. *Mental Health Law News* 5(1):1.

"Official of Alcohol Center Entered into Sexual Relationship with Woman One Month After She Left Program." 1990. *Mental Health Law News* 5(7):5.

Paine, R. T., Jr. 1880. "The Work of Volunteer Visitors of the Associated Charities Among the Poor." *Journal of Social Science* 12:113.

"Parents Allege Failure to Document Treatment Withdrawal from Case Contributed to Son's Suicide." 1990. *Mental Health Law News* 5(12):4.

"Patient Admitted to Hospital for Detoxification; Attempted Suicide Results in Brain Damage." 1990. *Mental Health Law News* 5(7):2.

"Patient Escapes and Commits Murder." 1990. *Mental Health Law News* 5(10):6.

"Patient Improperly Treated for Panic Disorder and Agoraphobia." 1992. *Mental Health Law News* 7(7):6.

"Patient Jumps from Hospital Window." 1989. *Mental Health Law News* 4(12):2.

"Patient Raped by Fellow Patient." 1989. *Mental Health Law News* 4(11):6.

"Patient Released from Mental Hospital Ingests Lye." 1989. *Mental Health Law News* 4(11):3.

"Patient Sexually Abused by Psychologist." 1990. *Mental Health Law News* 5(12):3.

Patti, R. J. 1983. *Social Welfare Administration: Managing Social Programs in a Developmental Context.* Englewood Cliffs, N.J.: Prentice-Hall.

Pearson, M. M. 1982. "Psychiatric Treatment of 250 Physicians." *Psychiatric Annals* 12:194–206.

Pearson, M. M., and E. A. Strecker. 1960. "Physicians as Psychiatric Patients: Private Practice Experience." *American Journal of Psychiatry* 116(10):915–19.

Perlman, H. H. 1965. "Self-determination: Reality or Illusion?" *Social Service Review* 39(4):410–21.

Pernick, M. S. 1982. "The Patient's Role in Medical Decisionmaking: A Social History of Informed Consent in Medical Therapy." In President's Commission for the Study of Ethical Problems in Medicine and Biomedical and Behavioral Research, *Making Health Care Decisions: The Ethical and Legal Implicaitons of Informed Consent in the Patient-Practitioner Relationship,* vol. 3, pp. 28–29. Washington, D.C.: U.S. Government Printing Office.

Peters, C., and T. Branch. 1972. *Blowing the Whistle: Dissent in the Public Interest.* New York: Praeger.

"Physician Fails to Properly Treat Depression or Make Timely Referral." 1992. *Mental Health Law News* 7(10):2.

Plant, R. 1970. *Social and Moral Theory in Casework.* London: Routledge and Kegan Paul.

Pope, K. S. 1986. "New Trends in Malpractice Cases and Changes in APA's Liability Insurance." *Independent Practitioner* 6(4):23–26.

——. 1988. "How Clients Are Harmed by Sexual Contact with Mental Health Professionals: The Syndrome and Its Prevalence." *Journal of Counseling and Development* 67:222–26.

Pope, K. S., B. G. Tabachnick, and P. Keith-Spiegel. 1987. "Ethics of Practice: The Beliefs and Behaviors of Psychologists as Therapists." *American Psychologist* 42:993–1006.

President's Commission for the Study of Ethical Problems in Medicine and Biomedical and Behavioral Research. 1982. *Making Health Care Decisions: The Ethical and Legal Implications of Informed Consent in the Patient-Practitioner Relationship*, vol. 3. Washington, D.C.: U.S. Government Printing Office.

Prochaska, J., and J. Norcross. 1983. "Psychotherapists' Perspectives on Treating Themselves and Their Clients for Psychic Distress." *Professional Psychology: Research and Practice* 14:642–55.

Promislo, E. 1979. "Confidentiality and Privileged Communication." *Social Work* 24:10–13.

"Psychiatric Patient Has Sexual Relationship with Psychiatrist." 1989. *Mental Health Law News* 6(11):4.

"Psychiatric Patient Injured Trying to Flee Hospital." 1990. *Mental Health Law News* 5(4):5.

"Psychiatric Patient Not Properly Monitored While Eating Chokes to Death." 1990. *Mental Health Law News* 5(11):4.

"Psychiatric Patient Raped by Fellow Patient." 1989. *Mental Health Law News* 4(3):4.

"Psychiatrist Did Not Owe Duty to Warn Patient's Sister About Risk." 1989. *Mental Health Law News* 4(10):3.

"Psychiatrist Has Sex with Patient." 1989. *Mental Health Law News* 4(11):6.

"Psychiatrist Not Negligent in Misdiagnosing and Releasing Patient Who Killed Third Party." 1992. *Mental Health Law News* 7(10):1.

"Psychiatrist's Crime Tip Did Not Violate Physician-Patient Privilege." 1990. *Mental Health Law News* 5(3):1.

"Psychiatrists Liable for Patient's Attempted Suicide." 1991. *Mental Health Law News* 6(3):1.

"Psychiatrists Not Liable for Discharging Patient Who Later Committed Suicide." 1989. *Mental Health Law News* 4(10):2.

"Psychological Counselor Refers Patients to Unqualified 'Colleague.' " 1991. *Mental Health Law News* 6(8):6.

"Psychologist Did Not Maintain Proper Records." 1992. *Mental Health Law News* 7(1):6.

"Psychologist Encourages Sexual Misconduct Between Patient and Psychiatrist." 1989. *Mental Health Law News* 4(3):2.

"Psychologist's License Properly Revoked for Deception in Application." 1991. *Mental Health Law News* 6(5):6.

"Psychologist-Patient Privilege Prevents Counselor from Testifying at Divorce Trial." 1991. *Mental Health Law News* 6(6):5.

"Psychotherapist Has No Duty to Warn Third Party of Patient's Threat of Violence." 1992. *Mental Health Law News* 7(2):3.

"Psychotherapist May Not Be Sued for Erroneous Child Abuse Diagnosis." 1992. *Mental Health Law News* 7(11):4.

Reamer, F. G. 1979. "Protecting Research Subjects and Unintended Consequences: The Effect of Guarantees of Confidentiality." *Public Opinion Quarterly* 43(4):497–506.

——. 1980. "Ethical Content in Social Work." *Social Casework* 61(9):531–40.

——. 1982a. *Ethical Dilemmas in Social Service.* New York: Columbia University Press.

——. 1982b. "Conflicts of Professional Duty in Social Work." *Social Casework* 63(10):579–85.

——. 1983a. "Ethical Dilemmas in Social Work Practice." *Social Work* 28(1):31–35.

——. 1983b. "The Concept of Paternalism in Social Work." *Social Service Review* 57(2):254–71.

——. 1984. "Enforcing Ethics in Social Work." *Health Matrix* 2(2):17–25.

——. 1987a. "Values and Ethics." In *Encyclopedia of Social Work*, 18th ed., p. 801. Silver Spring, Md.: National Association of Social Workers.

——. 1987b. "Ethics Committees in Social Work." *Social Work* 32(3):188–92.

——. 1987c. "Informed Consent in Social Work." *Social Work* 32(5):425–29.

——. 1989a. "Toward Ethical Practice: The Relevance of Ethical Theory." *Social Thought* 15(3/4):67–78.

——. 1989b. "Liability Issues in Social Work Supervision." *Social Work* 34(5):445–48.

——. 1990. *Ethical Dilemmas in Social Service*, 2d ed. New York: Columbia University Press.

——. 1991a. "AIDS: The Relevance of Ethics." In F. G. Reamer, ed., *AIDS and Ethics*, p. 1. New York: Columbia University Press.

——. 1991b. "AIDS, Social Work, and the 'Duty to Protect,' " *Social Work* 36(1):56–60.

——. 1992a. "The Impaired Social Worker." *Social Work* 37(2):165–70.

——. 1992b. "Should Social Workers Blow the Whistle on Incompetent Colleagues?" In E. Gambrill and R. Pruger, eds., *Controversial Issues in Social Work*, p. 66. Boston: Allyn and Bacon.

——. 1992c. "Social Work and the Public Good: Calling or Career?" In P. N. Reid and P. R. Popple, eds., *The Moral Purposes of Social Work*, p. 11. Chicago: Nelson-Hall.

——. 1993. *The Philosophical Foundations of Social Work.* New York: Columbia University Press.

——. in press. "Malpractice and Liability Claims Against Social Workers: First Facts." *Social Work.*

Reamer, F. G., and M. Abramson. 1982. *The Teaching of Social Work Ethics.* Hastings-on-Hudson, N.Y.: Hastings Center.

Reaves, R. R. 1986. "Legal Liability and Psychologists." In R. R. Kilburg, P. E. Nathan, and R. W. Thoreson, eds., *Professionals in Distress: Issues, Syndromes, and Solutions in Psychology*, p. 173. Washington, D.C.: American Psychological Association.

"Resident at Hospital for Mentally Retarded Receives Award for Negligent Treatment." 1989. *Mental Health Law News* 4(3):4.

Reynolds, B. C. 1942. *Learning and Teaching in the Practice of Social Work*. New York: Farrar.

Reynolds, M. M. 1976. "Threats to Confidentiality." *Social Work* 21:108–13.

Rhodes, M. 1986. *Ethical Dilemmas in Social Work Practice*. London: Routledge and Kegan Paul.

Rieman, D. W. 1992. *Strategies in Social Work Consultation*. New York: Longman.

Robinson, G. W., Jr. 1962. "Discussion." *American Journal of Psychiatry* 118:779–80.

Robinson, V. 1936. *Supervision in Social Case Work*. Chapel Hill: University of North Carolina Press.

———. 1949. *The Dynamics of Supervision Under Functional Controls*. Philadelphia: University of Pennsylvania Press.

Rothblatt, H. B., and D. H. Leroy. 1973. "Avoiding Psychiatric Malpractice." *California Western Law Review* 9:260–72.

Rozovsky, F. A. 1984. *Consent to Treatment: A Practical Guide*. Boston: Little, Brown.

Saltzman, A., and K. Proch. 1990. *Law in Social Work Practice*. Chicago: Nelson-Hall.

"Schizophrenic Patient Hangs Self." 1991. *Mental Health Law News* 6(3):6.

Schoener, G. R., and J. Gonsiorek. 1988. "Assessment and Development of Rehabilitation Plans for Counselors Who Have Sexually Exploited Their Clients." *Journal of Counseling and Development* 67:227–32.

Schutz, B. M. 1982. *Legal Liability in Psychotherapy*. San Francisco: Jossey-Bass.

Sheffield, A. E. 1920. *The Social Case History: Its Construction and Content*. New York: Russell Sage Foundation.

Shore, J. H. 1982. "The Impaired Physician: Four Years After Probation." *Journal of the American Medical Association* 248:3127–30.

Shulman, L. 1987. "Consultation." In *Encyclopedia of Social Work*, 18th ed., p. 326. Silver Spring, Md.: National Association of Social Workers.

Siegel, D. H. 1992. "Should Social Workers Blow the Whistle on Incompetent Colleagues?" In E. Gambrill and R. Pruger, eds., *Controversial Issues in Social Work*, p. 66. Boston: Allyn and Bacon.

Siporin, M. 1982. "Moral Philosophy in Social Work Today." *Social Service Review* 56(4):516–38.

———. 1989. "The Social Work Ethic." *Social Thought* 15(3/4):42–52.

Slavin, S., ed. 1982. *Applying Computers in Social Service and Mental Health Agencies*. New York: Haworth.

Slovenko, R. 1978. "Psychotherapy and Informed Consent: A Search in Judicial Regulation." In W. E. Barton and C. J. Sanborn, eds., *Law and the*

Mental Health Professions, p. 51. New York: International Universities Press.

Sonnenstuhl, W. J. 1989. "Reaching the Impaired Professional: Applying Findings from Organizational and Occupational Research." *Journal of Drug Issues* 19:533–39.

Stadler, H. A., K. Willing, M. G. Eberhage, and W. H. Ward. 1988. "Impairment: Implications for the Counseling Profession." *Journal of Counseling and Development* 66:258–60.

"State Disciplines Psychiatrist for Making Improper Referral." 1992. *Providence Journal-Bulletin* (December 1):B3.

"Suicidal Patient Not Restrained by Defendant Hospital." 1990. *Mental Health Law News* 5(2):3.

"Teenager Commits Suicide by Taking Drug Overdose After Hospital Discharge." 1992. *Mental Health Law News* 7(4):1.

Thoreson, R. W., and J. K. Skorina. 1986. "Alcohol Abuse Among Psychologists." In R. R. Kilburg, P. E. Nathan, and R. W. Thoreson, eds., *Professionals in Distress: Issues, Syndromes, and Solutions in Psychology*, p. 77. Washington, D.C.: American Psychological Association.

Thoreson, R. W., M. Miller, and C. J. Krauskopf. 1989. "The Distressed Psychologist: Prevalence and Treatment Considerations." *Professional Psychology: Research and Practice* 20:153–58.

Thoreson, R. W., P. E. Nathan, J. K. Skorina, and R. R. Kilburg. 1983. "The Alcoholic Psychologist: Issues, Problems, and Implications for the Profession." *Professional Psychology: Research and Practice* 14:670–84.

Towle, C. 1945. *Common Human Needs*. Washington, D.C.: U.S. Government Printing Office.

——. 1954. *The Learner in Education for the Professions*. Chicago: University of Chicago Press.

Trent, C. L. 1978. "Psychiatric Malpractice Insurance and Its Problems: An Overview." In W. E. Barton and C. J. Sanborn, eds., *Law and the Mental Health Professions*, p. 101. New York: International Universities Press.

Trice, H. M., and J. M. Beyer. 1984. "Work Related Outcomes of the Constructive Confrontation Strategy in a Job-Based Alcoholism Program." *Journal of Studies on Alcohol* 45:393–404.

U.S. Department of Health and Human Services. 1989. *Bibliography and Resource Guide on Alcohol and Other Drugs for Social Work Educators*. Rockville, Md.: Department of Health and Human Services.

U.S. National Center on Child Abuse and Neglect. 1981. *National Study of the Incidence and Severity of Child Abuse and Neglect*. Washington, D.C.: Department of Health and Human Services.

Vaillant, G. E., J. R. Brighton, and C. McArthur. 1970. "Physicians' Use of Mood Altering Drugs." *New England Journal of Medicine* 282:365–70.

VandeCreek, L., S. Knapp, and C. Herzog. 1988. "Privileged Communication for Social Workers." *Social Casework* 69(1):28–34.

VandenBos, G. R., and R. F. Duthie. 1986. "Confronting and Supporting

Colleagues in Distress." In R. R. Kilburg, P. E. Nathan, and R. W. Thoreson, eds., *Professionals in Distress: Issues, Syndromes, and Solutions in Psychology*, p. 211. Washington, D.C.: American Psychological Association.

Vigilante, J. 1974. "Between Values and Science: Education for the Profession or Is Proof Truth?" *Journal of Education for Social Work* 10:107–15.

Wigmore, J. H. 1961. *Evidence in Trials at Common Law*, rev. ed., vol. 8, edited J. T. McNaughton. Boston: Little, Brown.

Wilson, S. J. 1978. *Confidentiality in Social Work*. New York: Free Press.

——. 1980. *Recording: Guidelines for Social Workers*, 2d ed. New York: Free Press.

"Woman Claims Psychological Problems Following 'Seminar Training.' " 1992. *Mental Health Law News* 7(2):6.

"Woman Claims She Was Improperly Discharged from Psychiatric Ward Due to Inadequate Insurance." 1989. *Mental Health Law News* 4(11):2.

Wood, B. J., S. Klein, H. J. Cross, C. J. Lammers, and J. K. Elliott. 1985. "Impaired Practitioners: Psychologists' Opinions About Prevalence, and Proposals for Intervention." *Professional Psychology: Research and Practice* 16:843–50.

Legal Citations

Alberts v. Devine, 479 N.E.2d 113 (Mass. 1985).

Alexander v. Knight, 177 A.2d 142 (Pa. 1962).

Baker v. United States, 226 F. Supp. 129 (Iowa 1964).

Bellah v. Greenson, 146 Cal. Rptr. 535 (Cal. Ct. App. 1978).

Belmont v. California State Personnel Board, 111 Cal. Rptr. 607 (Cal. Ct. App. 1974).

Berry v. Moench, 331 P.2d 814 (Utah 1958).

Birkner v. Salt Lake County, 771 P.2d 1053 (Utah 1989).

Boles v. Milwaukee County, 443 N.W.2d 679 (Wis. Ct. App. 1989).

Boyer v. Tilzer, 831 S.W. 2d 695 (Mo. App. E.D. 1992).

Brady v. Hopper, 570 F. Supp. 1333 (D. Colo. 1983).

Bramlette v. Charter-Medical-Columbia, 393 S.E.2d 914 (S.C. 1990).

Cabrera v. Cabrera, 23 Conn. App. 330 (Conn. App. Ct. 1990).

Caesar v. Mountanos, 542 F.2d 1064 (9th Cir. 1976).

Cairl et al. v. State of Minnesota et al., 323 N.W.2d 20 (Minn. 1982).

California v. Gomez, 185 Cal. Rpt. 155 (Cal. Ct. App. 1982).

California v. Kevin F., 261 Cal. Rptr. 413 (Cal. Ct. App. 1989).

Cameron v. Montgomery County, 471 F. Supp. 761 (E.D. Pa. 1979).

Chatman v. Millis, 517 S.W.2d 504 (Ark. 1975).

Chrite v. United States, 564 F. Supp. 341 (D. Mass. 1983), Civ. No. 81-73844.

Cohen v. State of New York, 382 N.Y.S.2d 128 (N.Y. App. Div. 1976).

Corgan v. Muehling, 574 N.E.2d 602 (Ill. 1991).

Currie v. United States, 644 F. Supp. 1074 (M.D.N.C. 1986).

Cutter II v. Brownbridge, 228 Cal. Rptr. 545 (Cal. Ct. App. 1986).

Darrah v. Kite, 301 N.Y.S.2d 286 (N.Y. App. Div. 1969).

Davis v. Lhim, 124 Mich. App. 291 (1983).

DeShaney v. Winnebago County Department of Social Services, 812 F.2d 298 (7th Cir. 1987), 109 S. Ct. 998 (1989).

Dill v. Miles, 310 P.2d 896 (Kan. 1957).

Doe v. Roe, 400 N.Y.S. 2d 668 (N.Y. Sup. Ct. 1977).

Doe v. Samaritan Counseling Center, 791 P.2d 344 (Alaska 1990).

Dymek v. Nyquist, 128 Ill. App. 3d 859 (1984).

Eckerhart v. Hensley, 475 F. Supp. 908 (Mo. 1979).

Estate of Davies v. Reese et al., 248 N.W.2d 344 (Neb. 1977).

Fedell v. Wierzbieniec, 485 N.Y.S.2d 460 (N.Y. Sup. Ct. 1985).

Ferrara v. Galluchio, 152 N.E.2d 249 (N.Y. 1958).

Force v. Gregory, 63 Conn. 167, 27 A. 1116 (1893).

Gares v. New Mexico Bd. of Psychologist Examiners, 798 P.2d 190 (N.M. 1990).

Gasperini v. Manginelli, 92 N.Y.S.2d 575 (N.Y. Sup. Ct. 1949).

Geis v. Landau, 458 N.Y.S.2d 1000 (N.Y. Civ. Ct. 1983).

Goryeb v. Pennsylvania Dept. of Public Welfare, 575 A.2d 545 (Pa. 1990)

Green v. State, Southwest Louisiana Charity Hospital, 309 So. 2d 706 (La. Ct. App. 1975).

Hague v. Williams, 181 A.2d 345 (N.J. 1962).

Hammer v. Rosen, 165 N.E.2d 756 (N.Y. 1960).

Hammonds v. Aetna Casualty & Surety Co., 243 F. Supp. 793 (N.D. Ohio 1965).

Hess v. Frank, 367 N.Y.S.2d 30 (N.Y. App. Div. 1975).

Holt v. Nelson, 523 P.2d 211 (Wash. Ct. App. 1974).

Horne v. Patton, 287 So. 2d 824 (Ala. 1974).

Hothem v. Fallsview Psychiatric Hospital, 573 N.E.2d 803 (Ohio Ct. Cl. 1989).

Humphrey v. Norden, 359 N.Y.S.2d 733 (1974).

In re Lifschutz, 467 P.2d 557 (Cal. 1970).

In re Quinlan, 355 A.2d 647 (N.J. 1976).

Iverson v. Frandsen, 237 F.2d 898 (10th Cir. 1956).

Jablonski v. United States, 712 F.2d 391 (9th Cir. 1983).

Jensen v. Conrad, 747 F.2d 185 (4th Cir. 1984).

Kleber v. Stevens, 39 Misc.2d 712 (N.Y. Sup. Ct. 1963), 241 N.Y.S.2d 497 (N.Y. App. Div. 1963), 249 N.Y.S.2d 668 (N.Y. 1964).

Kogensparger v. Athens Mental Health Ctr., 578 N.E.2d 916 (Ohio Ct. Cl. 1989).

Lake v. Cameron, 364 F.2d 657 (D.C. Cir. 1966).

Leedy & Leedy v. Hartnett & Veterans Administration Hospital, 510 F. Supp. 1125 (M.D. Pa. 1981), Civ. No. 80-0201.

Lipari & the Bank of Elkhorn v. Sears, Roebuck & Co. & the United States, 497 F. Supp. 185, Civ. No. 77–0–458 (D. Neb. 1980).
Little v. Utah State Division of Family Services, 667 P.2d 49 (Utah 1983).
Lux v. Hansen, 886 F.2d 1064 (8th Cir. 1989).
McDermott v. Hughley, 561 A.2d 1038 (Md. 1989).
MacDonald v. Clinger, 446 N.Y.S.2d 801 (N.Y. App. Div. 1982).
McIntosh v. Milano, 168 N.J. Super. 466 (N.J. Super. Ct. Law Div. 1979), 403 A.2d 500 (1979).
McNamara v. Honeyman, 546 N.E.2d 139 (Mass. 1989).
Mammo v. Arizona, 675 P.2d 1347 (Ariz. Ct. App. 1983).
Marvulli v. Elshire, App. 103 Cal. Rptr. 461 (Cal. Ct. App. 1973).
Mavroudis v. Superior Court, 162 Cal. Rptr. 724 (Cal. Ct. App. 1980).
Meier v. Ross General Hospital, 445 P.2d 519 (Cal. 1968).
Merchants National Bank v. United States, 272 F. Supp. 409 (D. N.D. 1967).
Minnesota v. Andring, 342 N.W.2d 128 (Minn. 1984).
Minogue v. Rutland Hospital, 125 A.2d 796 (Vt. 1956).
Missouri v. Beatty, 770 S.W.2d 387 (Mo. Ct. App. 1989).
Naidu v. Laird, 539 A.2d 1064 (Del. 1988).
Narcarato v. Grob, 180 N.W.2d 788 (Mich. 1970).
Nelson v. Dahl, 219 N.W. 941 (Minn. 1928).
Norton v. Argonaut Insurance Company, 144 So. 2d 249 (La. 1962).
O'Connor v. Donaldson, 422 U.S. 563 (1975).
Patterson v. Jensen et al., 17 N.W.2d 423 (Wis. 1945).
Perreira v. State, 768 P.2d 1198 (Colo. 1989).
Porter v. Maunnangi, 764 S.W.2d 699 (Mo. App. 1988).
Reif v. Weinberger, 372 F. Supp. 1196 (D. D.C. 1974).
Rennie v. Klein, 462 F. Supp. 1131 (D. N.J. 1978).
Rogers v. South Carolina Dept. of Mental Health, 377 S.E.2d 125 (S.C. Ct. App. 1989).
Roth v. Tuckman, 558 N.Y.S.2d 264 (N.Y. App. Div. 1990).
Rouse v. Cameron, 373 F.2d 451 (D.C. Cir. 1966).
Rule v. Chessman, 317 P.2d 472 (Kan. 1957).
Salgo v. Leland Stanford Jr. University Board of Trustees, 317 P.2d 170 (Cal. Ct. App. 1957).
Samuels v. Southern Baptist Hospital, 594 So. 2d 571 (La. Ct. App. 1992).
Sayes v. Pilgrim Manor Nursing Home, 536 So. 2d 705 (La. Ct. App. 1988).
Schloendorff v. Society of New York Hospital, 211 N.Y. 125 (1914).
Schuster v. Altenberg, 424 N.W.2d 159 (Wis. 1988).
Seavy v. State, 250 N.Y.S.2d 877 (N.Y. App. Div. 1964), 216 N.E.2d 613 (1966).
Shaw v. Glickman, 415 A.2d 625 (Md. Ct. Spec. App. 1980).
Simonsen v. Swenson, 177 N.W. 831 (Neb. 1920).
Sisson v. Seneca Mental Health/Mental Retardation Council, Inc., 404 S.E.2d 425 (W. Va. 1991).
Smith v. Yohe, 194 A.2d 167 (Pa. 1963).

Snyder v. Mouser, 272 N.E.2d 627 (Ind. Ct. App. 1971).

Solano County Department of Social Services v. Ron B., 236 Cal. Rptr. 623 (Cal. App. 1987).

Stovall v. Harms, 522 P.2d 353 (Kan. 1974).

Stropes v. Heritage House Childrens Center of Shelbyville, Inc., 547 N.E.2d 244 (Ind. 1989).

Superintendent of Belchertown v. Saikewicz, 370 N.E.2d 417 (Mass. 1977).

Suslovich v. New York State Education Dept., 571 N.Y.S.2d 123 (N.Y. App. Div. 1991).

Tabor v. Doctors Memorial Hospital, 563 So. 2d 233 (La. 1990).

Tarasoff v. Board of Regents of the University of California, 13 Cal. 3d 177, 118 Cal. Rptr. 129, 529 P.2d 553 (Cal. 1974, also known as *Tarasoff I*); 17 Cal. 3d 425, 131 Cal. Rptr. 14, 551 P.2d 334 (Cal. 1976, also known as *Tarasoff II*).

Thompson v. County of Alameda, 614 P.2d 728 (Cal. 1980).

Underwood v. United States, 356 F.2d 92 (5th Cir. 1966).

Vassiliades v. Garfinckel's, 492 A.2d 580 (D.C. 1985).

Vaughn v. North Carolina Department of Human Resources, 252 S.E.2d 792 (N.C. 1979).

Vineyard v. Craft, 828 S.W.2d 248 (Tex. Ct. App. 1992).

Walker v. Parzen, 24 Ass'n. of Trial Lawyers of America L. Rep. 232 (June 1983).

Welk v. Florida, 542 So. 2d 1343 (Fla. Dist. Ct. App. 1989).

Whitree v. State, 290 N.Y.S.2d 486 (N.Y. Ct. Cl. 1968).

Wilson v. Blue Cross of Southern California, 271 Cal. Rptr. 876 (Cal. Ct. App. 1990).

Winfrey v. Citizens & Southern Natl. Bank, 254 S.E.2d 725 (Ga. Ct. App. 1979).

Wofford v. Eastern State Hospital, 795 P.2d 516 (Okla. 1990)

Yorsten v. Pennell, 153 A.2d 255 (Pa. 1959).

Index